WILD MOON HEALING

WILD MOON HEALING

Harness the Energy of Lunar Cycles to Awaken Your Inner Truth

A Program with Exercises and Journaling Prompts to Guide You on a Personal Journey of Self-Exploration through Which You Can Create Your Best Life

by
Donna S. Conley

ISBN Paperback: # 979-8-9863114-0-1
ISBN Hardcover: # 979-8-9863114-2-5
ISBN Electronic: # 979-8-9863114-1-8

Library of Congress Control Number: 2022909692

Book cover artwork by: Charlene Perkey www.charleneperkey.com

Publisher: Wild Moon Healers LLC / Donna Conley

1296 Cronson Blvd., # 3128
Crofton, MD 21114-9998
www.wildmoonhealers.com

Printed in the United States of America.

Disclaimer:

No material in this book is intended to be a substitute for professional health advice, diagnosis, or treatment. Always seek the advice of your physician or other qualified health-care provider with any questions you may have regarding a medical or mental health condition or treatment and before undertaking a new health-care regimen, and never disregard professional medical advice or delay in seeking it because of anything you have read in this book.

In Memory of David K. Conley, USMC – beloved brother.
This poem commemorates the thirtieth anniversary of his passing.

THE NIGHTS ARE LONG, BUT THE YEARS ARE SHORT

By Donna S. Conley, January 2018

When I am missing you and the tears begin to fall
Staring at a clock that barely moves at all
Sometimes it's as though the world stops spinning
It's hard to breathe, but I find strength to keep on grinning

Looking at your picture, I begin to smile
Memories come rushing back… It has been a while
It's like opening a time capsule put away for just this day
Holding on to every reminiscence before it fades away

I hear your voice, I turn, I can see into the past
A portal opened just for me; a picture collage amassed
A melody of celebrations from the time we had together
Come flooding back like winds of the changing weather

Amazing how a smell or sound can play upon the mind
In an instant, remembering what is left behind
It can go either way with a smile or a tear
You keep pushing, only to realize it has been another year

Remembering you is easy; it is what I am meant to do
Memories are precious, but sometimes make me blue
Skies turn grey because missing you is hard
Sometimes the nights get so long, and I just feel so tired

Wishing I had one more day to make more memories
It plays out on the stage of my mind in sweet reverie
Now a lifetime without you has gone by so very fast
Thirty years on my own, and I did not think that I could last

The nights seem so long with wounds still so fresh
I realize it is the years that are too short, but I know
that I am blessed
Blessed because the pain is dreadfully real
Meaning that my love is far too big for anyone to steal

When life becomes a little stormy and the nights
seem so long,
Looking back, I realize you have always been in my song
I am smiling now because I know that you are here
That smell or that sound is telling me you are near

So, when the nights seem so long and never-ending
Know that the years are short, and the heart is ever mending.[1]

---

1 Poem by Donna S. Conley, except the last two lines: author unknown.

TABLE OF CONTENTS

Exercises

Exercise List by Chapter

Exercises

Exercise List in Alphabetical Order

WILD MOON HEALING

INTRODUCTION

Be happy, do the things you love, and don't feel guilty about any of it. You can stop living with the purpose of making sure everyone else is OK and start living to make sure *you* are OK.

I've structured this book in three phases to provide you with a road map to help you create a life you love. The first phase, "Self-Exploration, Discovery, and Renewal," tells you what this book is about and shares tips on how to identify, prevent, and heal the symptoms of trauma in your life while using the moon's energy and identifying ways you create challenges. It will also cover some activities you can do to cultivate a healthy mind. The second phase, "Manifesting with the Moon," details how to coordinate healing activities with the lunar cycle to break through current behaviors and habits that hold you back from reaching your full potential. The closing phase, "Supporting Information," provides you with more tips to support you on your healing journey.

This book is designed so you can use each chapter as a standalone teaching tool once you have read through the book once. During your first full read, you will notice some repetition of ideas. This is because every aspect of mind, body, and soul healing with the moon affects every other aspect. For this reason, I have endeavored to make each section detailed, comprehensive, and able to stand on its own.

There are forty-seven exercises in this book to help guide you to happiness and a life you love. Some exercises build on one another, while others stand on their own. The exercises focus heavily on journaling because you always have the answers you seek within. Looking at situations from different angles or through a different lens is one of the best ways to gain insight into your behaviors. So, with each lunar cycle, the journaling prompts shift to help you see your situation from a different perspective. There is a small space for notes in phase 3. Sometimes you may only journal a few words, while other entries may be a few pages long. Since I cannot create enough space in this book for your longer entries, I encourage you to purchase a journal (a spiral notebook is fine).

The exercises are listed in the beginning of this book as they appear by chapter, as well as in an alphabetical list. Since we all recall information differently, I have provided both lists to help you locate exercises quickly and easily in the manner that suits you best.

While engaging in Wild Moon Healing, you have a triune purpose: 1) get to know yourself, 2) heal from unresolved trauma in your life, and 3) transform. With this book, you will learn, heal, and go after your goals simultaneously. You cannot accomplish anything without proper self-care. As you progress with your personal healing with the moon practices, you will notice the energetic leaks in your life and gain the confidence to fix them. Happiness and healing come when you promote wellness through preventive and restorative activities and prioritize wellness.

This book results from my personal journey in search of happiness and healing. I spent most of my life hiding from trauma. At first, I did not correlate the trauma I had experienced with the current state of my life. I had built a fortress around my heart to prevent ever feeling a pain so bad again, and I had to relearn how to breathe. From this protection mechanism, behaviors of promiscuity, drinking, smoking, and isolation were born. Life was hard. I was a functioning adult, raising my son, finishing my education, and working full-time. I was sad. I was just existing.

Five years ago, physical health issues came to the forefront of my life. Doctors tested me for everything known to man, but could find nothing wrong. I had to change my lifestyle and seek help for depression. For years, I tried to change, but kept sliding back into habitual patterns. My depression worsened, so my doctor prescribed medication and urged me to see a therapist. Doctors on my medical care team had let me down, but seeking a mental health professional was even more frustrating; therapists were not taking new patients, did not call me back, or didn't have availability that matched mine.

So, I took matters into my own hands. My first internet search was "How to be happy?" How sad is that? My research led me to Emotional Freedom Technique (EFT), AKA "tapping." The program I enrolled in offered healing support plans that included tapping, affirmations, daily journaling prompts, and other activities. I didn't know what I was doing and was unsure of the process and its benefits, but I kept going. After a year, I realized that while I was living in the same house and working at the same job, I was different. I was happy.

I continued to do research and read tons of books on psychology theory and practice, empowerment, and spirituality, and scholarly articles in my search for knowledge. During my quest for answers and healing, my journey became spiritual. Part of my journey included developing a relationship with the moon. I have always been a moon lover. The moon's beauty and mystery have always captivated me. I started manifesting with moon cycles, and now, as I continue to heal myself, I want to help others find happiness. This is my motivation behind authoring this book and my blog, *Wild Moon Healers* (https://wildmoonhealers.com/).

I hope my words reach those in need and encourage and support them on their journey. Determined to become an advocate for mental health, I will continue to develop my integrated approach of teaching people to discover who they are, what they want, and how to love and accept themselves so they can live their best lives.

Dear Wild Moon Healer, I hope you will join me on this Wild Moon Healing journey.

Authentically Me,
Donna S. Conley

ACKNOWLEDGEMENTS

Writing a book has been harder than I thought, but more rewarding than I imagined, and figuring out the process as I went along resulted in duplicated effort. I wouldn't be able to change that even if I tried, as "winging it" is the way I travel through life. I was not alone on this part of my life's journey, so I want to acknowledge the people who helped make this book a reality.

To my son, David, thank you for encouraging me and believing in me. Even in our most desperate hours, we have always made it through by the grace of God. All we need—and all we have had at times—is love and a prayer. Having your love and being your mother are my greatest gifts in this life. I love you more.

To my father, Ralph, thank you for a lifelong journey of love, support, and encouragement. I may be headstrong and independent, but you have always been my rock. I love and appreciate you more than you can know, Dad. You and Diane are two of my biggest cheerleaders, and I love you both dearly.

None of this would have been possible without my wonderful friends Robin, Linda, and Kelle. Your curiosity about the actions I took to heal myself and the words I used to describe my healing journey is the foundation of *Wild Moon Healing*. I have woven your encouragement and support into every word in this book. I appreciate you and am grateful for your friendship. Let's keep manifesting!

I express great appreciation to my high school friend Charlene, the amazingly talented artist who created my cover image. I hope wherever life takes you, you can share more of your artistry with the world, and I look forward to working with you again. Thank you for taking part in this experience with me.

To my editorial team, Joan Timberlake, Michael Ireland, Lyric Dodson, and Robin Fuller. Joan, you went out on a limb and trusted me even though we have never met. I appreciate your level of effort in editing my book and helping me achieve a well-read manuscript. Your thoroughness and attention to detail quickly turned my draft into a polished copy. I made some changes that I hope you enjoy reading. Joan, I appreciate you and the guidance you provided, and it was my abundant pleasure to work with you. Michael, my sincerest gratitude. Thank you for your expert advice and for guiding my work with honest interest and truth. You set a high standard for me to follow, which ignited my creativity even more. I truly appreciate your encouragement to have fun. You erased all the intimidation as I handed off my first manuscript. You were incredibly thorough and conducted your review with the utmost professional integrity. *Wild Moon Healing* leveled up because of your invaluable feedback. I appreciate you. Lyric, your energy introduced you before I even fully read your response to work with me. I value your passionate ability to seek, find, and correct my mistakes and wording issues. You are like a private detective nosing around every crossed *t* and dotted *i* to make sure everything is just right. I was lucky the universe brought us together. I appreciate your professionalism and thank you for all your hard work. Robin, the universe once again brought me the best of the best with you. I greatly appreciate your eagle-eyed abilities and linguistic finesse that truly brought this project to perfect completion.

Kristen Wise and Maira Pedreira, you are a power team! I value your talent, your knowledge, and most of all, your time. When we met on our discovery call, I knew you were the expanders I needed to finalize my manuscript. As you guided me through the publishing process, helping me build my brand and credibility, you also pushed my limits and helped me grow in unimaginable ways. Thank you for consistently amazing me (and pushing me to amaze myself).

To you, who decided to read this book and create your best life, you humble me and encourage me to continue helping others live their amazing lives. My wish for you is *hope*:

May every storm bring a rainbow and every tear a smile.

Wild Moon Healing is my hope that you'll find blessings in each trial.

Like the tide, life's challenges will come and go;
Look to the moon and feel energy in its glow.
When you can't sleep and your thoughts begin to swim,
In those times when your inner spark seems to dim,
I wish you could see the moon every night.
Know it is always there; it's just not always bright.

Phase 1

SELF-EXPLORATION, DISCOVERY, AND RENEWAL

1

WILD MOON HEALING

Do You Need Wild Moon Healing?

Are you sick and tired of being sick and tired? Do you find yourself unhappy with who you are, what your body looks or feels like, or any other aspect of your life? Are you unable to create lasting, positive change in your life? Does it seem like everyone and everything is in control of your life, except you?

You can take control and create immeasurable happiness in your life. By following this program, you will learn not only who you are, but why you do the things you do. You will learn to love yourself as you are right now and use this knowledge to put your well-being and happiness first. You will create your best life. By practicing self-care in month long cycles that follow the phases of the moon, you will learn your truth, overcome barriers in your life, build healthy boundaries, and live authentically. Incorporating lunar cycles into your self-care practice adds consistency to your routine, because you can check in with yourself as the moon changes. If you fall out of your self-care habits, just look up and let the moon guide you back to where you need to be.

Wild Moon Healing details how I reclaimed my happiness and control over my life. Once upon a time, I lived in fear. Experiencing three very traumatic events in my childhood—and not processing the emotions related to them—shaped the trajectory of my life. After being present at my mother's failed suicide attempt, then being beaten by a babysitter's boyfriend, I adapted to quickly disconnect when I feel threatened. I find it hard to feel safe, even in a healthy relationship. After the sudden and tragic loss of my beloved brother, because of my grief, I feared intimate relationships. I did not believe I could survive the pain of losing someone I loved again. Because of low self-esteem and a lack of proper self-care, I fell into addictive behaviors. My social anxiety intensified, leading me to drink excessively. The accompanying behavioral patterns resulted in alcohol use disorder (AUD). And because of false and limiting beliefs, I began eating mindlessly, which developed into an eating disorder. My emotional binge eating fed my pain, leading to depression and obesity.

I became a mother at a young age and thus didn't learn who I was or what I wanted. With no identity or destination, my life became a routine—doing everything everyone expected of me as a mother and provider. I stopped doing things I enjoyed because I had to become an "adult."

I was going through the motions, living life like it was a linear process: I was born, I had a childhood, I became a mother, I grew up fast, I got a job, I went to school, and I turned my job into a career that I planned to remain in until I could not work… and then I would die. But life is not linear. I was living with grief and pain from past traumas, which created blinders to all other lateral aspects of living.

My life has been filled with missteps, suffering, and lessons learned. Life is never perfect, but that is what's wonderful about it. A negative life experience can take you off your path, but life can take you on an amazing journey too.

My journey has helped me discover some of my truths. Strong grief reflects the love that fills my heart. I didn't know that while missing my brother, I could simultaneously honor and release the emotion of grief associated with my loss to create space and allow happiness into my life. I know now that the post-traumatic pain I experienced was telling me, "You matter, Donna." I didn't know how to love myself. I wouldn't have experienced hurt and acted out against my body if I had believed, deep down, that I was worthy of being treated with honor and respect. I just didn't know how to get past the pain and disappointment that created untrue beliefs. So, as a result, I neglected myself. I let my lifelong expectations of others negatively affect me. I didn't know it was OK to take care of myself first. Now I do.

I have filled this book with exercises and journaling prompts to help you discover *you* and regain control of your life. Begin treating yourself the way you deserve to be treated—with respect—so others will know how to treat you right. You can gain this insight by diving deep into your issues and answering hard questions with honest reflection. Each phase of the lunar cycle offers opportunities for self-exploration through journaling, but from different perspectives. Throughout each phase of the moon, you'll discover more about yourself, your motives, and your desires. You can take charge of your life and take care of yourself by analyzing your behaviors, thoughts, and emotions. The only way to make sure you are the only thing controlling your life is by learning all you can about yourself.

Contained on these pages are the information and tools you'll need to create a lifelong habit of self-care and self-love. You'll find supporting activities to help you improve your wellness, so you can prevent needless suffering. As you incorporate these restorative activities into your life, they will help you achieve seemingly unrelated goals. Nothing about examining your behaviors and emotions is easy, but you are worth the effort.

A journal—just a spiral notebook will do—and a pen are all you need to document your thoughts as you work through the pages of this book. Put in the work. Record all your responses in your journal. Become your favorite person. Flip the page and begin the journey toward regaining your inner magic.

Introduction to Moon Work

Wild Moon Healing, or "Moon work," can be whatever you need it to be: a wellness practice, a healing therapy, a self-discovery journey, a spiritual pursuit, a psychological process, a spiritual awakening, a time management tool, or a habit-breaking model. No one's journey is the same, so whatever Moon work is for you is correct.

Wild Moon Healing is about how you move through life. It provides a paradigm to help you make life decisions. Moon work involves living on purpose, so you can gain the courage to leave an unhealthy relationship, overcome an addiction, or take inspired action toward your dreams. Through Moon work, you can learn to love yourself, so when you look in the mirror, you smile because your favorite person is looking back at you.

Life's experiences create changes in your body, mind, and spirit. Right now, you are every age you have ever been, with each of your life experiences building on one another to create who you are. All experiences affect your self-esteem differently. One experience may encourage you; another may break you down. These influences on your self-esteem affect everything you think, say, and do. You are always one decision away from changing your life experience, so choose differently time and time again. There is no limit to the number of times you can start over in pursuit of becoming the person you want to be.

The most wonderful journey you can ever go on is the one within. It is the only path to self-love. Becoming your own favorite person increases your self-esteem. Your perception of who you believe you are determines how you move through life. Having a healthy awareness of self is an internalized process that allows you the freedom to see your choices clearly. However, if your perception is based on a false sense of who you are, then the ego will control your behavior.

The ego is the thinking, surface-level, conscious mind that uses external stimuli or information as an excuse to engage in life from a place of fear. The ego mind is smart, but emotional. It does not want you to have a negative experience; it wants to protect you from harm. But in doing so, it limits all available options. Individuals with high self-esteem see all their available choices and respond accordingly with every life experience. It's those in need of Moon work who have an egoic reaction to an experience because they see no other option available to them.

Are You Reactive or Responsive?

Reactionary behavior is an emotional response to stimuli in your environment. An experience that is negative or triggering tells the ego that it failed to protect you. When the ego knows it is not in control, it responds dramatically. Therefore, because someone must be at fault for your negative experience, you react to the actions and behaviors of another person. Reactive energy shifts blame to the person, place, or thing you deem responsible, giving them power over you and allowing those external forces to determine your actions and the trajectory of your life. Responsive behavior is mindful, intentional, and inspired. You choose your actions. You are aware of your power to dictate how every moment in your life will play out.

You can live defensively, with reactionary responses to life happening to you, or you can live from love and peace, taking mindful, purposeful actions to create your life. The ego mind is a pessimist when it is fearful, so it makes your pride tell your heart that "[It] is impossible." When it is hurt, your ego mind never forgets, so it instructs your experience to tell your heart that "[It] is risky." The ego mind thrives on separating you from the now, so when it feels defeated, it guides your intelligence to tell your heart that "[It] is pointless." The ego mind is irresponsible, so when the outcome looks bleak, it makes your defenses yell at your heart that "[It] is unattainable." All you need is faith the size of a mustard seed to inspire your heart to whisper just one time, "Go ahead, you can do it," to fuel your inner spark and open your thinking mind in creative ways.

Life's complex landscape provides you with multiple paths to choose from, even if you cannot see them all. Moon work helps you build trust in yourself, strengthening an internal knowing that attracts the options and resources that are energetically available to you. People will come to you in perfect timing. You will notice different paths and trust your internal knowing to choose the correct one for you. It is more complex than just wanting your life to change for the positive, having the ability to exert willpower and change your behavior, or using your strengths to overcome weaknesses. First, you must love your entire self and believe you are worthy of love and wonderful things.

Before you can live your truth on the outside for the world to see, you need to heal mentally and physically from the inside out. Answers you seek will come from untangling the energetic connections of past experiences, and this can be difficult. Moon work quiets the ego as you journey toward accepting yourself, achieving self-love, discovering and believing in your worth, and creating your best life that's full of meaning and purpose. By turning down the volume of the ego mind, you can discover and learn all the uniqueness you bring to this world. When you embrace who you truly are, you have changed. Everyone can change, and everyone has the right to change. However, choosing differently can be difficult because you must look within. We all have history, and since the ego fears change, you may notice your history repeating itself. For example, perhaps you leave one difficult situation only to find yourself in the same situation with a different person or group of people. That means there's a lesson you still must learn so you can end the cycle. Decide right now to learn the lesson; that will help lead you to a brighter tomorrow.

When you attune to the energy of the lunar cycles, process your past, and focus on changing, you can create the life you deserve. As the moon changes in the night sky, you can align your activities with its phases and create lasting change. "But," you might ask, "where do I start?" When the sky is dark under a new moon, create an intention to change your life in meaningful ways. During the waxing phase of the moon—when the moon grows larger in the night sky—you can energetically attract growth into your life. Tackle your goal with all that you have! As the moon fully illuminates the sky, allow its energy to shed light on what might hold you back. Give this energy permission to help you see the parts of you that are afraid or hurt, so you can heal those parts of yourself. And as the moon shrinks under the waning phase, use its energy to look inward. Understand, accept, and be vulnerable.

Creating lasting change does not involve just one thing; lasting change requires you to make a series of minor changes over time. It's a cycle. Look up, meet the moon where you both are, and let it guide you to a life of self-love and self-acceptance.

Your level of satisfaction with life correlates with your level of self-esteem and self-acceptance. Wanting to experience positive change without believing you are worthy of receiving it can make you feel helpless. Taking inspired action without self-love can make you feel defeated because, on a subconscious level, you do not believe you are worthy. Knowing your strengths and weaknesses without accepting yourself can make you feel ashamed. Negative emotions such as shame create imbalance in your personal energy field, so before you can create a balanced life, you must forgive yourself and surrender the things in your life that hold you back.

You achieve balance through love and acceptance of self. If you give love but cannot receive love back, it is because you feel invalidated. When you cannot let another person in or even see your true self because of emotional barriers, it is because you are not living your truth. These obstacles in your life keep you from relishing the minor victories along your journey, and you need to praise yourself. Even if you achieve your goal, if you do not deal with the barriers that create imbalance in your life, you may still feel empty inside.

Imbalance creates emptiness and decreases self-esteem. When you accomplish things without self-love and acceptance, your life will lack meaning and purpose, causing you to settle into complacency instead of achieving abundance. Raising your vibration increases self-esteem. People with high self-esteem respect their personal boundaries. Identify what you value to help you decide whether you are acting in your best interest or not. Values are concepts—family, tradition, adventure—but these are not "action" words. Wild Moon Healing requires action, which make your values meaningful.

The first step of Moon work is to accept who you are right now. When you accept yourself, you take responsibility for everything you have done, said, or thought that helped create your present life experience. Realize that everything you have done (or have not done) has created the current state of your life and relationships. Then, through forgiveness, you can surrender what no longer serves you. Forgive yourself for the false, limiting beliefs that held you back, and identify the ways you expend your energy.

Mindlessly using your personal energy creates a deficit (an energetic leak) that does not help you in your life. Your values may lose their meaning, and you may lose your personal boundaries. When you live authentically, you do not compromise your core values. This means that you are your boundaries (as expressed through your thoughts, words, and actions). You know what you value in life, so create change and take steps to fix your behavior and reinforce your values. Practice prevention and restorative activities (see chapter 2, 6, and 7 for these activities), and surrender (see chapter 11). Quiet your ego mind, take control, and create what happens next in your life.

The purpose of following lunar cycles is to create a consistent schedule to keep you on the path toward your best life. You do not have to believe in the moon's energy or the connectedness of everything to heal. All human beings will experience at least one low point in their lives, but the people who become stuck there may experience addiction or depression that can lead to (or has led to) a bona fide medical condition. But you do not have to stay in a place of lack or suffering. With an open mind and a willingness to do the work, everyone can benefit from Wild Moon Healing.

What Is "Wild Moon Healing"?

Wild Moon Healing is the personal journey of self-exploration through which you create your life based on how you want to feel. It is not about the law of attraction, manifesting material wealth, or manifesting other people's desires. Rather, Wild Moon Healing is about recovering from the life experiences that have hurt us. It is an inward, truth-seeking journey to gain clarity about your life's purpose, and if you choose, to harness the energy of lunar cycles to gain momentum on your healing path. The moon puts us in a reflective state of mind, and its phases offer us a schedule to follow so we can heal and live an authentic life. A consistent practice of Wild Moon Healing is an investment in discovering what you believe, value, and enjoy. As you discover your strength and character, you change the way you view yourself, and you transform. Part of this transformation involves gaining clarity about what is right in your life.

People live their lives based on the beliefs and value systems others have taught them in adolescence, and they either do what their family or society expects of them, or they rebel against those expectations. When we explore ourselves, we develop our own beliefs and values. Living inauthentically because of a value system that is not your own can lead to loneliness or destructive behavior. Without your own belief system, you may feel off, or you may lose your sense of belonging. When you commit to this journey, you'll discover what is important to you, how you feel about things, and how your emotions manifest in your physical body. As you heal, you'll notice synchronicities and attract the opportunities, resources, and people necessary for your journey. It will be as if the universe is orchestrating your success!

The exercise below can help you discover what is important to you, so you can gain clarity on where to begin your journey.

Exercise – 5-5-5 Method

The 5-5-5 Method will take you on a walk down memory lane, helping you identify a wonderful memory from your life and its importance to you. The purpose of this exercise is to help you identify your values and what things add value to your life; recognize the positive feelings associated with the experience and the things that evoke positive, meaningful feelings; and pinpoint what made that experience special.

Grab your journal and find a quiet, comfortable space to sit. Take a few deep breaths to still your mind using the 5-5-5 Method below. This technique is very calming and simple to remember.

Inhale slowly through your nose for five seconds: 1-2-3-4-5. Hold that breath for 5 seconds. Exhale slowly through your nose (or your mouth if that is more comfortable for you) for 5 seconds: 1-2-3-4-5. Repeat the process for at least 1 full minute.

Take a deep breath in and think about something in your life that made (or makes) you feel happy, excited, or inspired. Hold on to that feeling as you hold your breath. Let it permeate your body, mind, and soul. Then, exhale.

Take another deep breath in. Visualize—with as much sensory detail as possible from your memory—everything that experience brings to mind. Exhale. Visualize anyone that is celebrating with you. Take one more deep breath in through your nose. Allow your memory to unfold in your mind. Exhale. When you feel ready, come back into an awareness of your breath and your space. Begin journaling about why that experience was so memorable to you and how you can recreate those feelings in your life today.

> Example: Your first thought was a word: vacation. Let's explore how thinking about a vacation can supply insight into what is important to you. Let's say you remembered your favorite vacation. What made it your favorite vacation? The people you were with? The places you went? The way you felt? The sense of adventure? Was it memorable because of simpler times? Don't discount anything that comes to mind; all your responses supply insight into what is important to you. Does thinking about that wonderful vacation make you crave a new adventure in your life? Does it make you think about the family you've lost touch with? Let's say you're clinging to an idea of what a family "should" look like (which doesn't exist in your current life). When you let go of this ideal, that is when you will find what you're looking for. Your thoughts create a physiological response in your body. Whatever your memory is, notice the emotions that are

surfacing. How do you feel? What happens in your body when you think about these things?

Having trouble? Is nothing coming to mind except your current struggle? Here's a few things to do using the "vacation" example:

- Look through old pictures.
- Focus on your senses. Maybe just thinking of ocean waves will help you get back to that favorite vacation with your family.
- Feel through your senses. In this exercise, you are mentally at the beach. Feel the sand between your toes, smell the salt in the ocean, etc.
- Call family or old friends. Ask questions, like "Do you remember when we went to…?" They'll remind you of the things you've forgotten.

Seek Awareness

The manifestation process helps people regain their personal power by removing limitations or barriers, such as calming an emotional response to a trigger. Wild Moon Healing unveils possibilities that encourage inspired action, so you can progress toward an attainable goal. In keeping with the example from the 5-5-5 Method/Positive Reminiscence exercise—where a memory of your favorite vacation made you think about the family structure that's lacking in your personal life—notice the unlimited ways you can experience "family." Why limit yourself to one idea of family, such as marriage and having biological children? Instead, focus on how you want to *feel* when you are part of a family. That feeling encompasses the energy you are missing in your life.

Energy connects everything. By doing the Positive Reminiscence exercise, you've begun identifying the energy you want to manifest in your life. When you tap into your feelings and align with that energy, you are standing on the threshold of transformation. The answers you seek are in the recesses of your mind, waiting for you to unravel them. You must let go of the idea of a "perfect ending." The perfect ending is an illusion, and the pursuit of perfection always results in struggle.

Consider, for example, the failure rates of New Year's resolutions. People create an intention or goal that involves fixing, improving, or changing themselves to achieve some happy alternative to their current life experience. First comes the decision: this year, you are going to lose weight, quit smoking, find that dream job, read a specific number of books, or stick to your budget. Then, at the stroke of midnight, you attempt to change your behavior. What happens? Failure. Your ego told you it was too hard, which made you feel anxious or deprived. Remember, the ego mind is smart, but emotional. The ego creates excuses. The ego creates struggle.

You gotta love people who give unsolicited advice, like "Try harder," "Just cut sugar out of your diet," "You are praying wrong," or "You don't want it bad enough." These folks mean well, but these types of comments often make you feel worse about yourself. Intentions like New Year's resolutions provide a great opportunity to discover if you, in fact, are the one giving yourself unhelpful comments like the ones previously mentioned. Sometimes we think this is what others will say to us, but it's really just our own words. In these moments, try to discover more about yourself. Ask yourself, "Why do I feel like I need to change my life?" or "Why haven't I found my dream job?" Do you believe that job exists? Do you feel worthy of having that job? Are you afraid of failure? Does the thought of success make you anxious because you think others will expect more of you? This type of internal dialogue helps you maintain focus on what you want and quiets the ego's excuses.

In evaluating why you want to create change, consider who you are changing for. Understanding your motivation can provide useful insight into your behavior. For example, are you going after a dream job to make your parents proud, or so you can fund your spouse's hobbies? Do you want to lose weight or change your appearance to make others like you? You cannot accomplish your goals when you give away your personal power. You may get that dream job, but if you are pursuing your parents' dream instead of yours, the negative, empty emotions will not go away. When your focus is to live up to others' expectations, you bind yourself into a social contract with the purpose of making someone else happy.

Energetically, this situation creates barriers that limit your potential because you are conflicted. You want to please others, but not at the risk of your own happiness. Our mind sets these limitations for us by defining our "perfect ending" as making other people as happy as possible. When you take care of or satisfy the needs of others without considering your own wants, you are not going after your dreams. This is a self-imposed restriction on what you can achieve, and on a subconscious level, it can result in negative behaviors and thoughts. You can become resentful of those you helped instead of focusing on your own needs and desires. If your focus is not on your personal happiness, a joyful life will elude you.

We can also limit ourselves based on what we perceive we must or should do, which means we base our actions on outside sources. There will always be something in our physical reality that directs the ego mind to self-judgment because "You are not [this]," "You need to be m[that]," or "You have to have more of [this]." Your ego mind will tell you to change and take action so society will accept you, or so you can one-up everyone else and maintain appearances with the Joneses. The "should factor" is where you tell yourself you should do this or that for a fear-based reason. Fear-based behavior is always submissive and unpleasant, as it precedes a perceived danger, threat, or conflict.

Considering what you should do is also part of your moral compass, but you should not make life decisions from a place of fear. Fear makes you tell yourself you can't. When you believe there is something you cannot do or something that is impossible, you never even start. If, for example, your child came to you and explained that he or she was going to run for class president, would you tell them not to bother because they are not that popular and the cooler kids who are running will win? I hope not. You'd do everything you could to support them as they chased their dream. We are great cheerleaders for others because it's easy to point out others' greatness. But sometimes, we lose that spark inside of us that made us believe we would grow up to be a ninja and save the world. We lose the inclination to dream big and follow those dreams because we believe they are stupid, silly, or unattainable.

You cannot create positive change when external forces are the driving force behind your life decisions. Doing things you feel you should do from a place of fear (or never even attempting to change because you believe it's impossible) does not serve you. You simply build a glass house around you, and people can see right through you. They can feel the vibe you project. If you do not believe in yourself or if you are not living authentically, you are living a lie. This fear-based programming or adherence to societal standards means your authentic self is not in the driver's seat of your life.

Your worth does not exist within the constraints of a relationship, a job, or anything outside of yourself. Your worthiness exists within you, but you can misplace it by living according to the expectations and opinions of others. For example, imagine that your lover breaks up with you, and you persist in seeking closure to find meaning in your experience. Understanding someone else's reasoning for their behavior is not your place. Your experience together has come to an end, and there is nothing the other person owes you to fulfill your expectations of them. When you create expectations and make choices based on "have to," "should," or "can't," you relinquish your personal power. In this situation, you are not participating in life; you are reacting to stimuli in your environment.

☪

Wild Moon Healing frees the delicate ego from "have to," "should," and "perfectionist" mindsets that make us machines to societal morals. Stop allowing society to define your values. Moon work conditions your mind to help you love yourself as you are, regain your personal power, and make the correct choices. The self-exploration and self-discovery processes of Wild Moon Healing allow you to make decisions from a place of love and growth rather than fear or judgment.

Personal responsibility is needed to create a healthy relationship with *yourself.* Responsibility means holding yourself accountable. When we energetically hide ourselves, fearing rejection or judgment, we diminish our power. It becomes easy to blame others for personal decisions we've made that did not work out. "It wasn't me. It's their fault." We live in an "it's not me, it's you" society, but we must become willing to accept the outcome of our lives as a result of our personal choices, behaviors, and actions, regardless of outside influences. Everyone has karma, meaning we are all responsible for our lives. If you do not take personal responsibility for your life, external forces will determine the trajectory of your future.

When external forces control the path of your life, they diminish your personal power and conceal the necessary opportunities to create change. Lacking prospects, you stay where you are, seeking comfort in familiar, low-risk, low-reward options, and you most likely will not address the self-imposed limitations that hinder your growth. You'll stay away from uncertainty and anything that might cause you pain, but unbeknownst to you, your "safety zones" are not stable; life is always changing.

You can be in a safe, secure environment and still have terrible things happen that are outside of your control. You are not responsible for the fears or negative emotions that result from such experiences, but you are responsible for your actions, behaviors, and even your thoughts regarding them. For example, consider a spouse who lost their partner in a tragic accident. Unable to shake the grief, the spouse uses alcohol to find temporary respite. Drinking provides the illusion that their broken heart has been mended. One night, another family experiences a tragic loss because that grieving spouse attempted to drive home after drinking too much. When you lose a loved one, grief is a normal emotional reaction, but if you stay there, unable to surrender to it, it can create more challenges for you.

In life, we have free will. Everyone is free to choose whatever they want at any moment. However, if your external experiences and opinions of others determine your actions, you are not exhibiting free will. You are still accountable for your actions, but your actions would not be coming from a healthy place. Experiences—including the belief systems your parents or guardians instilled in you—govern the choices you make in the present. Is anger, fear, addiction, or worry in control of your life? Only by accepting every aspect of your life can you free yourself, leave your comfort zone, heal from the negative ways you expend your energy, detach from limiting beliefs, and choose what is right for you.

Experiencing energetic barriers and unmanifested intentions stems from a lack of personal responsibility and a loss of free will. Do you believe in yourself enough to choose healthier actions and behaviors to improve your life? Are you complaining and pointing fingers because you believe others are responsible for the state of your life? Do you maintain the status quo because you believe you are not strong enough to stand on your own and do new things? Maybe you believe you cannot do better, so you stay in an unhealthy relationship. Perhaps you fear loneliness, so you keep going with the crowd. These energetic barriers rob you of free will. Moon work helps you regain control and ask yourself questions regarding your actions, behaviors, and thought patterns. Eventually, you will experience breakthroughs or "ah-ha" moments. Something inside you will click. You'll feel lighter because you'll have peeled away a protective layer and cleared an energetic block. Your energy will strengthen. You'll shift. Life will shift.

The divine feminine energy of the moon should remind you that you were made wonderfully and are whole just as life has molded you. Everything you want, desire, and need is within you, and you are worthy of love. Moon work helps you accept your internal energy and use it to speak, act, and behave in a manner befitting your authentic self. You cannot commit to anything you are not passionate about, and Wild Moon Healing will help you develop a passion for *you*.

We forge the chains we wear in life, but passion forges bonds. A bond is easy to imagine in an intimate relationship, but you can just as easily pledge an oath to yourself, commit to changing, and break through the chains that hold you back.

Intention is everything, so sync to the moon's cycles. Intend to create a consistent practice of self-care and healing. The reflective lunar energy allows us to use each phase of the moon to reveal our subconscious experience to the ego mind. False and limiting beliefs and feelings of negative self-worth exist in your subconscious, and bringing these beliefs and feelings to the conscious mind provides you with an opportunity to heal the trauma caused by negativity and unpleasant life experiences.

It is that simple, but the journey can be hard. No one can do the work for you. Wild Moon Healing helps you regain self-esteem. Becoming proactive about your mental health improves your overall wellness, because what consumes your mind consumes your life. Jump back into the driver's seat of your life.

Whatever led you to this book, it is a sign from the universe telling you that now is the time to look inside yourself for answers. You will never find your answers outside of yourself—especially not in alcohol, drugs, gossip, perfectionism, or food. The greatest journey you can ever go on is the journey of self-exploration and self-discovery. So, commit to yourself and invest in this journey. The most important thing is to show up and be open to the possibilities.

Journaling

You can manifest with the moon by simply asking yourself exploratory questions, but when you put pen to paper, you engage with a special energy that you cannot achieve with visualizations alone, or even by typing on an electronic device. The pen is mightier than Word (Microsoft pun). For example, a court stenographer types what everyone in a courtroom says verbatim. They do not process the data; they hear words, type those words, and move on. Using an electronic device or software to type your thoughts does not require a lot of cognitive coordination. When you are typing, you are using your left brain and not connecting to or processing your thoughts.

Articulating thoughts into words coordinates your left and right brain activities, which leads to richer content. When you put pen to paper, you are thinking and doing at the same time. Think about the last time you journaled or took notes on a topic. Did you circle, highlight, or underline anything? Did you draw a bold box around a phrase or a dark line under a specific word? This is your right brain entering the process, identifying what you think is important, because you are interacting with the data as you write. For example, a detailed swirl of an *S* in a specific word could express a delicate feeling. Or the way you wrote and rewrote the letter *T* in a specific word could mean you are frustrated with whatever thought you were journaling about.

Putting pen to paper is an intimate, important way to reveal more about your thoughts. Journaling lets you uncover, process, and understand your thoughts and feelings. You can capture your thoughts as notes, bullet points, or lists, or you can draw pictures. Over time, you will connect your emotions, behavioral patterns, and experiences. Overall, the reflective nature of journaling makes it a powerful self-growth activity.

Our thinking minds complicate simple things by judging, overthinking, procrastinating, and failing to plan. Our right brain identifies things that are important to us, but… The "but" introduces the complication, in the form of options or irrelevant data. We focus on the complexity of the situation instead of seeking simple solutions. If you know what brings value to your life, why not eliminate what is not of importance? That would be too simple. Human beings are complex in nature, and our emotions are multifaceted; therefore, we tend to worry.

The more you worry, the more anxious you feel, and the more complicated everything will seem. We play the mental "what if" game, creating our own discomfort about low-probability/high-consequence catastrophes. We plan for the "right" time, which invites upheaval into straightforward plans, because what is really happening is that we are planning to create the perfect moment. The obscurity of *perfect* in our unevolved minds creates even more anxiety. We are a species with the boundless potential to invent, innovate, and create. All the advancements of modern time exist because someone somewhere transcended all perceived limitations of that time and tapped into their infinite capacity to create. We all have that ability, yet despite our amazing resourcefulness, we are hardwired to worry. We can simplify our lives by understanding our thoughts, identifying our "what ifs," and recognizing our *perfect* time. Journaling on the challenges we create by overthinking helps us focus on what is important to us and why.

We also complicate our lives when we are unwilling to go on an inner journey because fear, anger, resentment, or a host of other negative feelings dominate our state of mind. We cannot reason with our emotions, hence the term "stuffing our emotions." The brain can't process them, so we bury them. They aren't really buried, though; they are wreaking havoc on our bodies. When we can't freely express our emotions through either words, tears, or screams, we must keep using things like food, alcohol, or porn to keep our emotions from surfacing. Journaling helps us become aware of our emotions without self-condemnation. Judgment and understanding cannot coexist with compassion and acceptance.

Your thoughts alone cannot identify importance, just as your words alone cannot convey understanding. When you are in need of Wild Moon Healing, your thoughts and self-speak can be dangerous and spiral into a vicious cycle that holds you back from your full potential. You can combat the negativity in your mind with positive journaling. A study showed that expressing gratitude in written form has lasting positive effects on the brain, which could lead to improved mental health.[2] You also need self-compassion and empathy to use journaling as a coordination tool for improved cognitive function.

The Effects of Trauma

The nervous system is our body's command center. It controls our movements and mental function. The brain processes the vast amounts of knowledge we accumulate over time, and through cognitive function, we understand, manipulate, reason, and choose the words, actions, and beliefs that arise because of our experiences and environment. Vascular, congenital, and degenerative conditions can damage our nervous systems, as can

[2] Joshua Brown and Joel Wong. "How Gratitude Changes You and Your Brain."

physical, mental, and emotional trauma. Wild Moon Healing is a psychological intervention for our cognitive functions.

Trauma is the mind's response to an event or experience that affects your ability to cope. Continuing to suffer past the time the actual trauma has occurred diminishes your perception of the gifts you have to offer, cripples your ability to feel a full range of emotions, and deprives you of the joy of new experiences. To heal from any type of trauma, inner work is necessary.

Trauma changes the way the nervous system, brain, and emotional energy respond to your environment. Those emotional and mental traumas not only make you feel less confident about yourself, they impose physical limitations on your life. Having an inferiority complex creates negative emotions and behavioral patterns that create risk factors, such as putting on weight or isolating yourself. Trauma will be addressed in more detail in a later section, but for now, understand that if left untreated, these risk factors can lead to the sufferer not only enduring feelings of hopelessness, but also sinking into addictions to food, alcohol, sex, porn, drugs, or even perfectionism. Addictions can lead to bona fide health issues, such as obesity, type 2 diabetes, heart disease, high blood pressure, cirrhosis, depression, and anxiety, among other things.

These health issues can beleaguer an individual who, because of feelings of inadequacy, gave their power away to food, alcohol, drugs, or other people's opinions. If there is anything in your life you struggle to control, know that it is controlling you. You cannot control or manage addictions. When a person with an unhealthy relationship with food is triggered into an eating response, they cannot control it. You cannot manage an unhealthy relationship with food by purchasing unhealthy, low-vibrational foods and telling yourself, "Next time I need a sweet treat, I will eat just one piece." If you have an alcohol addiction, you cannot purchase a nice bottle of wine to save for a special occasion. A chain smoker cannot keep a pack of cigarettes in the car "just for emergencies" because there is no emergency that smoking a cigarette will fix. If you think you are controlling something, you are lying to yourself. It is impossible to limit an addiction. If you try, you will fail. Why? Because you gave your power away to the addiction that controls your life. Thinking you can manage something that controls you is a false narrative that keeps you where you are in life.

False and limiting beliefs and feelings of negative self-worth are ego-driven and exist in your subconscious mind, which influences your autonomic nervous system. This is your nervous system's baseline, where your behavior originates. If you want to change your bad habits, like overspending, overeating, drinking too much, overworking, people pleasing, or overconsuming television, the answer lies in your autonomic nervous system. The energetic response from your autonomic nervous system determines your thoughts and emotional response, whether it's sympathetic or parasympathetic. A parasympathetic response from the nervous system means the body is in a state of homeostasis, or it has adopted a self-regulating process to maintain balance. Our sympathetic nervous system controls our fight-or-flight responses, where we remain mobilized and reactive to defend ourselves against a perceived threat—all of which creates feelings of being stuck in life.

When the nervous system's energy becomes stuck, it is because the ego mind wants to make sure an experience that once caused you harm or pain never does it again. You live in defense mode. The ego must establish lies to maintain its fortress and keep mental and emotional trauma from surfacing. For example, say a tragic accident takes the life of your true love. The ego will "lie," creating a false belief that limits you from seeking love again. The purpose behind the lie is to protect you from additional pain, but it also hardens you and keeps you from living fully. If you forgive yourself for hiding from love, accept your circumstances, and release your pain, you open yourself up to the possibility of experiencing that same pain again, but you also become energetically available to feel great love again. The only way to forgive yourself is to first accept responsibility for keeping yourself trapped.

Just as the subconscious mind affects the autonomic nervous system, the conscious mind influences the central nervous system. To heal with the moon, you must bring thoughts and patterns that create poor life habits into your thinking mind with conscious awareness. Energetic wounds created from mental and emotional trauma need to surface from your damaged autonomic nervous system so you can heal them. People with a healthy nervous system experience a self-regulated cycle of stress and calm throughout the day. People with unhealed trauma may have an overstimulated nervous system and experience a state of constant anger or anxiety. If someone's nervous system is understimulated, they can experience depression or disconnection. In extreme cases, a person can drastically fluctuate between anger and sadness.

If you are on a severe end of the spectrum between anxiety and depression, you experience severe mood swings, or you are in a dark place, seek help (see "Appendix B – Lifelines" for places that can help). If addiction is your go-to coping mechanism, Moon work will help, but you should first seek help from a medical professional to get you to a safe place.

2

MOON WORK FOR A HEALTHY MIND

People can see your emotions in your eyes if they take the time to look. The good, bad, and ugly—it's all there. The reason you hide your feelings well from yourself is because you rarely gaze into your own eyes and are honest with yourself. Moon work is a mirror to your soul. It will show you your deepest insecurities, fears, and shadows, and help you overcome them. When you do the work, it will reflect to you the true image of your character. If you hunger for personal growth, reflecting on these hard-to-see dimensions of yourself will help you cultivate authentic self-awareness, develop richer relationships, and create space for healing.

You can't heal what you don't know. The only way to get to know someone is to talk with them, spend time with them, and go out and do new things with them. We rarely do this with ourselves, but it is necessary. Self-exploration and discovery are the "getting to know you" processes that allow you to like yourself. Learning how the words, opinions, and actions of others affect you is a crucial part of having a healthy mind.

Healthy Boundaries

The way others treat you will always affect you in some way. Whenever a relationship of any type exists, our expectations of others grow, so it's important to understand the difference between an expectation and a healthy boundary. When there is a discrepancy between wanting something (expectation) and reality (outcome), disappointment and suffering results. It may appear that the source of suffering is wanting something, but wanting is not the enemy. When you practice Wild Moon Healing, you're encouraged to dream your biggest dreams, then chase them. *Wanting* is the motivation. Suffering and disappointment arise when you don't surrender your expectations and allow the outcome to be what it is. As you will learn later in this book, you must release attachment to the outcome.

Disappointment in the outcome of your situation results from a lack of communication and inaction toward your goal. Failure to act derives from three scenarios:

- Entitlement: a belief that the outcome is owed to you and no effort is required
- Fantasy: dreaming that things will perfectly (and magically) work themselves out
- Fear: worry that results in indecision, procrastination, and missed opportunities

Healthy boundaries communicate to others what behaviors are acceptable to you. If you are living in one of the above scenarios, feelings of disappointment may form a false, limiting belief about your personal worth when someone lets you down or after someone mistreats you.

Expectations form from a lack of clear communication, which has many causes:

- You do not know yourself well enough to speak your truth based on your personal values and beliefs.
- You are not living in the present moment and are not seeing circumstances for how they are right now. You know what you desire, and you wish it to be true, but it isn't.
- You experience unhealthy thought patterns about your self-worth based on past experiences, so you believe this relationship will help make things better for you. "If only he/she would … then I would be happy."
- You do not expect that you can "do better," so you stay in a relationship that "lets you down."

Expectations are dreams unless you communicate them. When you communicate your values and expectations in relationships, you create boundaries. There are consequences to setting boundaries because no one is obligated to accept them. Because of this, fear can set in, you lower your boundaries, and your expectations become dreams again. With no personal limitations, people can trample on you and your dreams. (Energetic leaks in the form of unclear relationship boundaries will be discussed in chapter 5.) You leave yourself wide open for continued disappointment when you do not know yourself well enough or you don't believe your personal power is sufficient to hold your boundaries.

By doing Moon work, you can stand in your truth, meaning your boundaries will keep you true to who you are and what you believe in. You will still experience disappointment, but it will be easier to accept and let someone or something go when you know the person or thing is holding you back from where you are going or does not value you. When you live with expectations rather than boundaries, you find yourself susceptible to many things, including depression.

Depression

Depression is situational. It is not a place you want to be, and you do not want to stay there. Millions of people suffer from depression, but barely a third seek treatment. Depression has all the numbing effects of addiction, but with addiction, there is something to quit or overcome. With depression, there is nothing to quit except life itself. If you have suicidal thoughts or tendencies, please see your doctor, call or text 988, or call the National Suicide Prevention Lifeline, day or night, at 1-800-273-TALK (8255) in the US or 116 123 in the UK (see "Appendix B" for more lifeline information). It is open for twenty-four seven service. Go to a substance abuse support group, where people with diverse backgrounds support each other without judgment.

Depression is a normal condition that exists for a purpose; if you are depressed, your body is telling you your feelings are excessive. Your body is always talking to you, supplying information about what it needs. As I write this, I am on a prescription medication to treat depression. There is no shame in that. There is no shame in asking for help. In the next section, I will share a parable that encourages you to cry out and scream for help. Doing so is empowering.

People diagnosed with depression did not give their personal power away to alcohol, food, shopping, drugs, sex, or social media, yet it is gone all the same. When you are depressed, you might know you have a problem, but you do not know what issue is causing it. There appears to be no false, limiting belief to reprogram or energetic leak to fix; it just showed up. Describing depression with words is difficult because you are numb. Any depressed person would tell you they feel a heaviness and a persistent feeling of sadness or loss of interest that affects their day-to-day activities. Even so, their depression remains a mystery to them.

The unknown creates so many questions. How do you diagnose and treat such an unseen, heavy burden? Can you heal from it, or do you have to learn to live with it? Can you make sense of or understand something nonsensical? Someone can express physical depression through tears that fall for no reason, and they are often powerless to stop them.

Gender and Depression

Men and women experience and express depression differently. No one would describe a man as "an emotional wreck," but they may describe him as "an asshat." That is because emotional responses in women are often expressed as mood swings of guilt, worthlessness, or hopelessness, while men may appear irritable or restless. Environmental stress affects men because society expects them to be... well... men. Societal standards create "have to" and "should" checklists for men, and as a result, some men build themselves a mental prison around the stigma of shame. Some cognitive symptoms of depression in men are memory problems, racing thoughts, and difficulty concentrating. The societal message to a man who exhibits symptoms of (or has been diagnosed with) depression is to "man up."

Society expects men to be strong in every sense of the word, so when their mental process becomes blurred because of depression, they tend to isolate themselves. Cognitively speaking, women internalize depression more from a self-criticism standpoint. Men internalize their roles as providers, "rocks," breadwinners, and all the things "real men" are supposed to be (because society expects them to play those roles). Women juggle many roles—career woman, mother, wife, daughter, comforter, confidante, consoler, friend—and these aspects of female life are taken for granted more times than not. Society expects successful men to not be sensitive, weak, or vulnerable, but then it belittles successful women who do not express these traits. A study by Mental Health of America[3] that classified gender-related statistics on depression stated that women experience depression more often than men, and this is *possibly* related to hormones, menstruation, pregnancy, childbirth, and menopause. However, the study still acknowledged that women's many responsibilities could be the cause of the stress that leads to depression.

I hypothesize that men mostly suffer from depression alone, hurting in secret without questioning why they do not feel good or ever seeking professional help. That is why twice as many women have been clinically diagnosed with depression. They are more attuned with their emotions, while the male ego makes it hard for men to accept responsibility for their emotions, especially if it involves admitting weakness. The stigma of depression brands it as a sign of weakness for both men and women.

Psychology of Depression

Depression is not a weakness or abnormality, but it affects the way you feel, think, and act. Because depression presents itself in different forms, people are quick to judge it as weakness, laziness, or the inability to "suck it up." Just as trauma does not affect all people in the same way, depression does not affect all people in the same way. There is no one-size-fits-all treatment for depression, and it may take trial and error to create a treatment plan that works for you. You can heal from depression the way you can heal from any emotional trauma rooted in the subconscious mind. Wild Moon Healing can help you explore your emotions and change your feelings,

[3] Mental Health of America, "Depression," https://www.mhanational.org/conditions/depression.

thought patterns, and behaviors. Some aspects of the human condition will take more time to heal than others. You may need medication or a psychologist to help work through your emotions. There is no shame in that.

Depression can result from an array of external and internal factors, including clutter, trauma, false and limiting beliefs, and energetic leaks. A cluttered external environment can provide clues to your mental health. Whether it be your home or digital clutter, it can be suffocating to have too much stuff surrounding you. Things can muck up your environment, destroying all sense of the peace you desire. Our external environment includes traumatic experiences. Depression can cause trauma, and trauma can cause depression. Trauma can result from abuse or neglect by a person in your life—or you can traumatize yourself. There are countless situations and triggers that can lead to a change in your mood, and if it's not managed early on, this can lead to depression.

Lifestyle factors or medical issues, such as a genetic factor or a chemical imbalance, can also influence your mood. A serious health diagnosis can trigger depression. Energetic leaks from overworking, excess stress, caregiving at the expense of your own health, a lack of fulfillment or purpose, perfectionism, a lack of social support, or chronic fatigue can all trigger depression.

Psychologists use the term *dysfunction* to describe depression, but also to categorize angry outbursts, anxiety, substance abuse, suicidal thoughts, self-harm, and other damaging behaviors. If medical professionals classify your already negative feelings about yourself and life as "dysfunctional," such a diagnosis can trigger an even deeper depression. The term *emotional dysfunction* means that society does not accept the way depression makes you feel. Describing the inability of a person to control or regulate an emotional response within a societally accepted range as "dysfunction" creates a stigma (see "Chapter 6 – Stop the Stigma" for more information).

When a person feels they are not "normal," a piece of them dies a little on a subconscious level. They hide parts of their true selves. If we keep telling people that society does not accept their emotions and that what they are experiencing is abnormal, people will continue to not talk about depression and their feelings. Mental health issues will worsen. When society says the uniqueness of your experience and the way you react to the world is dysfunctional, the subsequent shame or humiliation creates false, limiting beliefs.

False and limiting beliefs create behavioral and thought patterns that are untrue. Such beliefs as "I'm not normal," "I'm a freak," "I'm broken," or "I need to man up" cause you to push parts of yourself into the dark recesses of your mind. These dark places create your shadow self. Our shadows are nothing to fear; they are a part of the true self we have denied.

Receiving a diagnosis of depression, an eating disorder, or an addiction does not mean you are abnormal, have a defect, or are a bad person. There is a reason for your thoughts, feelings, and behaviors, and if you are willing, you can discover and heal from them.

According to the National Institute of Health, depression is one of the most common mental disorders in the United States.[4] Pay attention to risk factors in your life, such as a personal or family history of depression, major life changes, trauma, stress, and certain physical illnesses and medications. If you experience any of the following symptoms, reach out to your doctor, talk to a trustworthy person, and do Moon work!

- Persistent sad, anxious, or "empty" moods
- Tearfulness or crying
- Feelings of hopelessness or pessimism
- Irritability

[4] National Institute of Mental Health, "Depression," https://www.nimh.nih.gov/health/topics/depression#:~:text=Depression%20is%20one%20of%20the%20most%20common%20mental,at%20any%20age%2C%20but%20often%20begins%20in%20adulthood.

- Feelings of guilt, worthlessness, or helplessness
- Loss of interest or pleasure in hobbies and activities
- Decreased energy or fatigue
- Slowed movements or speech
- Restlessness or trouble sitting still
- Difficulty concentrating, remembering things, or making decisions
- Difficulty sleeping, early morning awakening, or oversleeping
- Appetite and/or weight changes
- Aches or pains, headaches, cramps, or digestive problems without a clear physical cause and/or those that do not ease with treatment
- Thoughts of death or suicide or suicide attempts (in the United States, call or text 988 or 1-800-273-TALK (8255), and in the United Kingdom, call 116 123)

Talk It Out

If you are having trouble deciphering your thoughts and feelings, talking to someone you trust can be beneficial. Sometimes your beliefs and prejudices can make it hard to change your perspective and shift your energy. Speaking with a close friend or family member, seeing a professional therapist, or attending a substance abuse (or addiction) support group can help you process feelings and experiences. Effective feedback invokes calmness and rationality, provides tangible information, and stimulates critical thinking in the same way writing in a journal does. Constructive advice from others should be concrete, specific, useful, and actionable. But remember, for feedback to have a positive effect, the recipient (you) must accept it. Seeing and accepting different viewpoints from others requires empathy. So, talk to someone who will listen to you without interrupting, and then, when it's your turn, with an open mind and heart, listen to them and welcome their feedback.

Mindfulness

One of the best ways to restore the mind is to be mindful of all that you do. Mindfulness is a multifaceted, intense awareness of every aspect of your life and how you feel mentally and physically. You must be mindful of all that you do to live your best life.

Being mindful helps you take control of your thoughts and actions by choosing what is best for you. It takes a lot of work to gain control so you can stop letting your life run you. Mindfulness is an effective activity that helps you notice and accept your thoughts and actions in the present moment. Having awareness of your behaviors is not self-judgment.

The primary aim of Wild Moon Healing is for you to increase your self-esteem by becoming your favorite person and learning to love yourself unconditionally. To achieve that, you need self-awareness. When you are mindful and present, you exhibit self-control and mental clarity. Being mindful and present is like having an open conversation with your body and mind in real time, so you can choose what is correct for you at that moment, instead of what was correct for you when you experienced a traumatic life event.

A combination of physical and emotional awareness can heal you from unhealthy behavioral patterns. When you are mindful, you live with intention, and you enjoy whatever you do. Notice that I did not state, "whatever you are *trying* to do." Take note, this is especially important: Simply trying is like rocking in a rocking chair. You are busy doing something that is unproductive and will cause no change. Trying is:

- deciding to have no interest in [something] without first attempting it
- an excuse to fail before you even begin

- not believing in yourself enough
- a lack of effort
- a mindless activity

Stop trying and start doing. That's how you ditch attitudes like "I'm not good enough," "I don't like it," or "I'm no good at it." You cannot know if you enjoy an activity, career path, or destination until you do it, research it, or go there. The mindset of deciding something is a certain way before you have the facts is also where prejudice is born.

You cannot get to know yourself or anyone else if you just try. Trying is a mindless activity. Behaving mindlessly is an energetic leak. Doing things that use up our energy but create no change is an energetic leak. But this behavior is also a symptom of other energetic leaks (see chapters 4 and 5) and a sign of how your false and limiting belief system affects you. Are you detaching from life when you take part in mindless activity? When we tell ourselves terrible things, like that we are unworthy or not good enough, mindless activity can seemingly stop these thoughts. But these thoughts never stop. The program runs on a subconscious level, making mindlessness a habit. Mindless activities are mechanical and mind-numbing.

Consider the activities you engage in every day. Sedentary activities, such as playing video games or watching TV, may seem relaxing because you are not thinking of anything and can lose yourself and forget your troubles. Over time, however, mindless, stationary activities can increase your stress. For example, watching TV can lead to you eating low-vibrational foods, like chips and candy, which can have a negative effect on your entire self. Physically, mindless eating results in increased caloric intake, which leads to weight gain and obesity. Mentally, weight gain lowers self-esteem and increases your risk of depression. There are many mindless activities that can lead to physical and mental stress, including mindless drinking, which can cause AUD and cirrhosis of the liver. There are also activities one would never consider mindless, but the stationary nature of the activity makes the mind drift to another level of consciousness. For example, have you ever been driving and suddenly remembered where you were? You wonder if you ran any red lights, because you do not recall the last five miles! Your daily commute becomes so monotonous that your mind wanders, and you drive without awareness.

If you develop a habitual pattern of mindless activity, you impose physical limitations on your life. This leads to untreated risk factors that cause depression. Your passive participation in life results in your body releasing hormones to deal with inaction, thus creating more challenges. Physical inactivity decreases the amount of serotonin and dopamine in the body, which are the hormones that regulate mood. Having less feel-good hormones in your body keeps you in a perpetual state of physical inactivity.

One of the most common afflictions associated with physical inactivity is uncontrolled inflammation in the body. Inflammation is the immune system's response to an irritant in the body. The ego works in a similar fashion as it responds unconsciously to situations in our lives that make us feel uncomfortable. Being inactive or engaging in mindless activity results in less movement, causing inflammation to stick around to protect you (as the ego attempts to do when we experience stuck emotions from trauma). Physical activity has an anti-inflammatory response, healing the discomfort felt in the body (just as Moon work heals mental wounds). The less you move, the more your body tries to protect you, which increases inflammation levels and creates a debilitating atmosphere in your body.

The gut is the ultimate inflammatory control center; I know because I have Crohn's disease. Eating low-vibrational foods can cause blockages in your intestines, which your body also perceives as an injury. This creates a chronic state of inflammation that, in theory, can lead to diseases such as depression, arthritis, and even cancer.

All that being said, not all inactivity is bad for you. There are sedentary activities that are healthy, such as reading a book or meditating. Your mind is active while doing these activities. Whether you read for pleasure or to learn, your mind can take you on an adventure as you comprehend and analyze the words on the page. However, being sedentary increases all causes of dis-ease in the body, leading to premature aging. So, incorporate mindful movement into your daily life, and deal with your energetic leaks. Don't worry; you don't have to deal with them all at once.

Exercise – Engage in Mindful Activity

Stress can make you believe that everything has to happen right now, but you cannot fix all your problems at once. So, get up and go for a bike ride, take a walk, or have sex. Find a way to immerse yourself in a physical activity that calms your mind. Our daily lives have become sedentary, so find creative ways to add physical activity to a sedentary activity, such as:

- While watching TV, play with a Hula-Hoop, jump with a ropeless jump rope, or walk on a rebounder.
- Place a compact elliptical machine under your desk so you can move your legs more; stand up and stretch throughout your workday; or replace your desk with a standing workstation.
- Car exercises (please remember that your priority while driving is to drive!)
    - Do Kegel exercises (tighten your pelvic floor, hold, release, repeat).

    - Clench your buttocks (clench, hold, release, repeat).
    - Shoulder raises/breathing exercise: take a deep breath, then lift your shoulders while tightening your neck and shoulder muscles as much as possible. When you exhale, release your shoulders as if you are sliding them into your back pocket.
- Download a movement therapy app to remind you to move throughout your day and guide you through easy-to-follow movements and exercises.

Physical activity is good for the body, mind, and soul. How can you add physical activity to your daily sedentary routines?

☪

Dis-Ease in the Body

Your body is full of wisdom, and it is always sharing this wisdom with you, especially if you are not good to yourself. Dis-ease starts in your nervous system. It carries your thoughts and emotions to the brain through your organs, such as the heart, intestines, and stomach. If you are overworking yourself (because you feel you must make everything happen right now) or are living a mindless, sedentary life, you may feel uneasy or even develop a full-blown disease.

Dis-ease can derive from the strangest places. When the ego is saying you cannot or should not do something because of fear, it causes a physiological response. Therefore, negative emotions cause negative physical consequences. For example, some people may experience chronic headaches, stomachaches, constipation, or shortness of breath. This type of unease may start off slowly, where your body whispers to you because it detects an energetic leak. At first, you may not feel like yourself. You might think you are tired or are coming down with a cold. Whatever your physical experience, you just don't feel like yourself.

Think about this: if you don't feel like yourself, then who are you? Are you someone else's opinions? Are you nothing more than the drink in your hand? Are you your mother, father, kids, partner, or friends? Do you have no identity of your own? All of this is an illusion created by your false and limiting beliefs. For example, your fear of turning into your mother could guide you to make decisions that oppose what you believe she would choose, regardless of whether or not it is correct for you. You can never be your mother, because you are unique. Getting to know yourself will help you make choices based on what *you* want, and it will bring calm to your body and mind.

Your beliefs shape your reality, both environmentally and physically in your body. Whatever you focus on becomes your reality. Whatever you feel becomes real. English philosopher and writer James Allen wrote, "As a man thinks, so he is; as a man continues to think, so he remains."[5] Your thoughts attach meaning to your experience, so what you feel becomes real because you believe it to be so. A psychosomatic illness originates from or becomes agitated by emotional stress, expressing a connection between the mind and body. Doctors can prescribe medication to control your symptoms, but without identifying the stressor (i.e., the energetic leak), a pill alone cannot cure your illness. There are times when the damage we create in our own bodies is irreversible because we ignored the signs for so long.

---

[5] Allen, As a Man Thinketh.

Exercise – Listen to Your Body

Through Wild Moon Healing, the theory is that you will control your feelings, thus creating a healthier you. Consistently creating stillness in your life is necessary for learning how to listen to your body and discern its messages. Slow down. Listen to your body before it is too late. Eliminate negative energy and toxicity from your body.

Here are few things that can help you create stillness:

- Epsom salt baths are great for removing toxicity from your body. Add aromatherapy to your bath with essential oils, candles, herbs, or flowers. Certain plants and herbs can also add a holistic medicinal component.
- Yoga is a fantastic way to add movement to your life while calming your mind. Through yoga, you can listen to your body by noticing the quality of your breath. Is it shallow or fast? Are you holding your breath during difficult positions? Here a few tips on how to listen to your body:
    - *Feel what you feel.* When you move into a yoga pose, your body will tell you when it has reached its maximum range of motion. You cannot deny it.
    - *Accept what you feel.* Don't judge yourself or make an excuse. Any limitation you experience is what it is.
    - *Trust your body.* You gain nothing by lying to yourself. If you push yourself, there will be consequences. Your body knows what it needs.
- Breathwork is an active meditation guided by a practitioner that draws on breath to facilitate emotional release. We mainly live in our conscious

egoic mind, while shoving emotions and traumatic events down out of our thinking mind, causing stuck emotions. Breathwork gets you out of your head and into your body, where you hold things possibly long forgotten. Here are a few tips as you use breath to connect to a deeper part of yourself:

  - Create an intention before engaging.
  - Don't fight your emotions.
  - Hold stones, crystals, or stress balls to help with intense feelings.
  - Be open and nonjudgmental with yourself.

- Sound healing uses the vibration created from sound to create calm. Certain frequencies have a profound effect on the vibration at which your personal energy resonates. Healing vibrations can come from music, singing bowls, a gong bath, or chanting. Play with sound to see what resonates with you.

  Meditation:

- Meditation uses mental techniques to train your attention and awareness and create mental and emotional calm. Practicing meditation teaches you to focus your attention and awareness in a mindful, intentional way.
  - Meditation cultivates the observation of thoughts, where you realize thoughts are separate from you. Therefore, you can detach from them mindfully by deliberately releasing the feelings that stem from your thoughts and cleanse your mind.
  - Meditation elevates you to a higher state of consciousness and calms the mind with the release of serotonin, a mood stabilizer.
  - Meditation quiets your ego mind so you can focus on your body, creating a heightened sense of awareness of dis-ease in your body.

- The easiest way to start a meditation practice is by following a prerecorded meditation in which someone guides your thoughts throughout the process.
    - If you meditate in nature, you will experience a profound effect on your mood because you will also be grounding yourself and exchanging energy with the earth.
    - Body scanning is a wonderful meditative tool to help you listen to your body. The goal is to notice and acknowledge any feelings or sensations in your body. If all you have is five minutes, this is a perfect place to start. You can do this in silence or with meditative music or nature sounds in the background.

Start with your head and move your awareness down, focusing on different body parts and organs, until you reach your toes. As your attention moves from one place to another, you will notice slight sensations. Do not analyze them; just feel them and let them be. Go where your mind takes you. If you notice your thoughts drifting to mundane activities, like your grocery list, return your thoughts to your body. Stay present, and keep returning to your breath. This takes practice.

Practice Gratitude

Practicing gratitude is a profound restorative technique that restructures your thoughts from a state of want to a state of recognition and appreciation for everything you already have.

Gratitude keeps building upon itself, meaning the more you look for things to appreciate, the more wonderful blessings you will find. Being aware of everything you appreciate and finding enjoyment in it will help raise your energetic vibration. As your energy frequency increases, your mental and physical health will also improve.

Exercise – Gratitude Journal

A fantastic way to change your emotional state is to practice gratitude by starting a gratitude journal. When you write down things you are grateful for, you give more of your energy to the things you appreciate most in life. A thankful heart raises your vibrational flow by removing negativity and creating space for you to receive beautiful things in your life.

Write down everything that is going well for you, such as moments you feel special or relaxed and the people or events that made you smile. Even if it seems insignificant, acknowledging the enjoyment of it will cause you to manifest more good things in your life. Gratitude does not make things appear magically; it brings awareness to all the blessings that are already in your life. We often get so busy with life that we take things for granted and need to shift our perspective. Shifting perspective requires relinquishing control of your negative thoughts and quieting your busy mind so you can push beyond your boundaries. The perspective of a grateful mind is always present and mindful.

To add further insight to your gratitude journal, do not just list things. State *why* you are grateful, using the following structure. List at least five things in your journal in this format: *I am grateful for… because…*

You can also use your gratitude journal to work on self-love. What do you appreciate about you? Write affirming statements in first, second, and third person to ground your energy. Then, read them aloud to strengthen your throat chakra and help you speak your truth. Use this format to write your statements:

I, (insert your name), am loved.
(Your name), you are loved.
(Your name) is loved.
OR
I, (your name), greatly appreciate my sense of humor.
(Your name), you have a great sense of humor.
(Your name) is funny.

☪

Be Kind to Yourself

When engaging in healing and growth, you must suspend self-judgment and treat yourself with patience and kindness. Over time, you will see Moon work as more effective and less painful, so always remember to be kind to yourself. Supporting activity does not create stress, but even with noble intentions, we can still self-sabotage. For example, attempting to fix everything you do not want to think about, feel, or address all at once can create stress and overwhelm and result in failure. Be patient. Build trust with yourself that what comes up during your Moon work and meditation is the correct (and only) thing you should focus on during the current lunar cycle. The process of self-exploration, discovery, and healing can be frustrating. Try to celebrate you, your accomplishments, and all the small moments along the way.

Exercise – Celebrate Yourself

The best way to show yourself kindness is to praise all things you!

Make a list of your achievements and things that make you proud. List things that are working for you that excite you. Celebrate those things about yourself. Honor your body by taking an Epsom salt bath or a dip in the ocean to cleanse your energy field. Treat your face to a charcoal mask while cooking dinner so you can feel the accomplishment of preparing a healthy meal while refreshing your face. Create a restorative bedtime routine to ensure you get a good night's sleep. Be creative.

You will figure out ways to be kind to yourself that do not interfere with your obligations. The purpose of celebrating yourself is not to do something that gets you closer to your goal, but rather to *enjoy you* and all the wonderful things you bring into this world.

☪

A Parable – Trust the Journey

Based on my life experiences, this parable is an analogy for what Moon work and healing looks like to me. There is a parable in the Bible about a blind beggar named Bartimaeus who receives his sight.[6] Bartimaeus was his own man and showed courage, while strong, able-bodied men intimidated him and tried to shut him up as he cried out for help. Although frightened, he had to shed excess weight ("…casting away his garment…"[7]) to discover how his way of thinking and behavioral patterns were holding him back. He had to detach from those limiting beliefs to progress toward what he believed was possible (his sight… seeing his truth).

Because Bartimaeus was a beggar, throwing his garment aside was a vulnerable move. His garment was his home, his security blanket, his only worldly possession. This teaches us that the material things we become attached to are often the things that hold us back in life. Casting away his garment made him vulnerable, and he was able to reveal his true, complete self for all the world to see. He could no longer hide what he perceived made him unworthy. He developed his own beliefs and values, and casting away his garment was his first step in revealing what he stood for and what path he followed.

Bartimaeus learned to not only ask for help, but to cry out for it. He learned about his authentic self and what he believed enabled him to pursue his path with grand passion. Imagine all the times Bartimaeus tripped, stubbed a toe, bumped into people, or fell as others watched, judged, yelled, or laughed at him (or in today's terms, recorded him on video) rather than helping him navigate his path. Instead of allowing these barriers to imprison him (his garment that protected him also imprisoned him), his unwavering faith led him down his chosen path. He believed the dream he had for his life was possible.

To me, Bartimaeus's story depicts the human experience, encompassing every good, bad, and meaningful event in your life that creates who you are. Every time we make a perceived mistake or a life event creates pain or a barrier for us, we build

[6] Mark 10:46–52, KJV.

[7] Mark 10:50, KJV.

a protection mechanism in our minds, and negative habits and behaviors are born. The ego's sole purpose is to prevent the recurrence of similar uncomfortable experiences in the future. Metaphorically speaking, Bartimaeus remained blind to his path (or purpose) when he was cloaked in the garment (his barrier) that hid his true self. Likewise, when we become blind to our authentic self and lose faith in our abilities, the ego cloaks us with the false belief that our experiences, while hidden, can no longer hurt us. When we are blind to our truth, what is hidden takes us down a different, inauthentic path that conceals our pain and purpose.

Just as faith in Jesus made the blind man see, you must trust your journey and believe that all your experiences along the way will make you whole instead of break you. Otherwise, you will continue to believe your false, limiting beliefs as absolute truths based on your subjective life experiences. Had Bartimaeus not released his fear, he would never have seen his truth.

Wild Moon Healing is also about surrendering to your emotions so you can discover your true self. When you are authentic, you can uncover the path that is correct for you. Underneath all your trauma, who are you? You are *you*. You are not your trauma, addiction, pain, or parents. You are not the car you drive or the house you live in. You are you—a beautiful, unique, amazing human being—so you should feel safe standing in your truth.

Our nervous system supplies us with protection in traumatic moments to safeguard us. But if we do not release those emotions, we keep that wall of protection up. In the parable, the powerful men who tried to stop Bartimaeus were his egoic lies and societal standards. Do you see? False, limiting beliefs create a life of stagnation, causing you to move through life mechanically. Fear-based reactions seem instinctual because you think you are supposed to do this or that or behave in a certain way. Guarding against the pain life brings reinforces your mental fortification. Each time you think of a painful experience, you feel the emotion of that experience, and you dig your heels in to ground yourself. But that is false protection. Each layer obstructs your energy flow and leads to an unfulfilling life.

We do not know how long Bartimaeus was cloaked in the false and limiting beliefs that created his challenges and kept him blind from all the amazing things life offers. The point is that he saw his truth, overcame his barriers, and lived true to what he believed in. The moral of the story is that no matter how long you have struggled against your experiences, lived in lack, or believed yourself to be unworthy of a good life or future, you can manifest the life you want by accepting your life experiences as a part of who you are and detaching from the fearful, negative emotions that hold you back. Just as Bartimaeus became vulnerable when he cast away his garment, you must peel away your defensive layers, including your limiting beliefs and energetic blocks, to see the experiences of your past for what they were. Opening yourself up for others to see and know can be terrifying, but healing occurs in our vulnerable moments. Through vulnerability, your energy will shift and open you up to a place of empowerment, where you can heal, experience growth, and form a healthy relationship with your entire self.

3

MOON PHASES

There is tremendous power in harnessing the energy and rhythm of the moon and its phases. So, use the moon's energy to create balance in your life physically, emotionally, mentally, and spiritually and to manifest the things that will help you live your best life. It is as if the phases of the moon exist to create an intelligent, straightforward road map for manifestation. A new moon can help you discover what you want. The energy from a waxing moon helps you explore how you react to people, places, and things. The energy of a full moon helps you explore your shadows. The energy during the waning moon helps you cultivate forgiveness. Tuning into the phases of the moon provides you with a structured approach to help you take consistent action toward achieving your goals.

Depending on your beliefs, you might use lunar cycles as a time management tool rather than as a source of energy. How many times have you said, "If only I had more time"? Using lunar phases to schedule and plan your activities can help you prioritize your time. Poor time management skills can lead to procrastination, an inability to focus your attention, and issues with self-control. You might feel overwhelmed or have an unrealistic understanding of what you can accomplish in a certain amount of time. If you struggle to manage your time, that barrier can provide insight into where you are experiencing energetic leaks or irresponsible expenditure of your personal energy. Using moon phases to manage your time can be a great resource and can help you achieve your goals in all areas of life.

Using lunar cycles can also help you create the consistent practice of self-care necessary to achieve your goals. Over time, you will better understand what you can achieve during a lunar cycle, create contingency plans for what derails your progress, and achieve a balanced life by analyzing your daily choices and activities. Remember, energy connects everything, and everything you say, think, and do can provide insight into how to change your life.

Moon Phases

New Moon | Waxing Crescent | First Quarter | Waxing Gibbous | Full Moon | Waning Gibbous | Last Quarter | Waning Crescent | New Moon

Lunar Energy

The moon represents powerful divine feminine energy, giving life to matters of new beginnings, transformation, renewal, and release to create balance. Once you attune to the moon's energy and its cycles, you activate her innate powers and embody her natural qualities of grace, creativity, femininity, and change. There is feminine (yin) and masculine (yang) energy, and neither has to do with gender. Giving is a physical representation of yang energy, while receiving is a physical representation of yin energy. If your capacity to receive is blocked—for example, because you are afraid or anxious—then it is impossible to receive, and you are not free. Without being free, you cannot receive things in life, such as love.

Wanting love but being unable to receive it is where loneliness comes from. Going back to the parable, people are beggars who, through their actions and behaviors, beg for affection and attention in sometimes unhealthy ways. We want to not be alone, yet we find ourselves mentally alone, even when we have caring people around us. The feminine energy of the moon encourages us to open our hearts so we are free to receive wonderful gifts like love from others and ourselves.

Your biggest desires do not arrive overnight out of thin air. The process takes time, and you must do your part. Moon work, as described in later chapters, is necessary so you can heal, learn, and grow. Following the phases of the moon helps connect you with nature's energetic source. It increases mindfulness. It opens your ability to surrender your emotions and the outcome of what you want to manifest to God or the universe (or wherever you put your faith) and trust in divine timing. Wild Moon Healing can empower you to find peace and understanding, but you must have faith.

New Moon

The new moon is the beginning of a twenty-nine-and-a-half-day lunar cycle that occurs when the sun, moon, and Earth are in perfect alignment. The new moon, also referred to as the dark moon, is not visible because the sun is behind the moon, so you cannot see it from Earth. Thus, the sky looks dark. The new moon occurs at a specific date and time, but the sky is dark for about three days between phases. Every two and a half days, the moon moves through the constellations of the zodiac. I am an astrology novice, but having knowledge of the key words or phrases associated with each zodiac sign, astrological season, and planetary influence and incorporating these meanings into your Moon work adds substance to the process.

The dark sky influences us to rest, reflect, plan, and create a steady foundation from which we can achieve our goals. Use this creative energy to ponder all your aspirations and ambitions—even what you think is just fantasy—and let the excitement of possibilities take over. Create your intentions.

I use several journaling techniques during the new moon phase. I encourage you to use them all the first time. After that, you can use what you feel is best for you at that moment. The following exercise is the first technique. More details will come later in chapter 8.

Exercise – Intention Journaling

Part of new moon journaling and the Wild Moon Healing process is manifestation, and manifestation begins with intention. This exercise will help you discover what you want in your life, what you feel is missing, and why. This exercise is necessary because creating an intention is more than writing a statement about what you want to create and who you want to be. You are authoring a story about the rest of your life.

First, look back at the 5-5-5 Method exercise. As an example, let's say a memory came to mind of you visiting your aunt at her beach house every summer. Maybe your mind wandered to how in awe you were of her lifestyle of retiring, living at the beach, and living life on her own terms. You realized that memory was important to you because you held her in high regard and always wanted to be like her. However, today, you work two jobs to make ends meet, and you don't know how you will ever be able to retire, much less at a beach house like your aunt's. If that is your dream, visualize it.

Always start a journaling session with a visualization. At the new moon, visualize the dream you have for the rest of your life. In this example, your dream is to retire and live at the beach.

Close your eyes and create a mental motion picture of what you want to achieve. Watch a movie in your head of you succeeding in the future. Keep watching this movie until all your senses are engaged.

Visualize financial success as you retire at your dream beach house. Feel your hair blowing in the breeze as the scent of the salty ocean air lingers. Taste it on your lips. Hear the sway of the ocean as you sit on your porch, watching the sun sink below the horizon. When you are there, in the future, physical sensations of success will manifest in your body. Did you feel a chill as the sun set? Did you smile? Feel the peace. Feel the calm.

Now, open your eyes and write the story you want to live in your journal. Don't leave any details out. Focus on your senses and feelings. Write the entire wonderful story of your life.

You will create an intention statement and supporting affirmations later on in this book, using this story as a guide.

Always end a journaling session with gratitude for all the amazing experiences life will bring you.

Waxing Moon

The waxing phase of the lunar cycle is approximately fourteen days long and follows the new/dark moon phase. It completes its cycle before the full moon. This lunar phase represents a time of transformation and growth. As an illustration of the energy in this lunar phase, imagine your dream taking form as you watch the moon expose a sliver of light in the sky. As the moon grows, the energy supports your intention, bringing it closer to fruition every night. Use the energy to anchor your new moon intentions by jumping into action to make your dream a reality. Then, as the moon grows, use its waxing energy to take note of any issues with your plan, shift your perspective when necessary, and adjust your action plan. Before the full moon, use the energy to go after what you want with your whole heart.

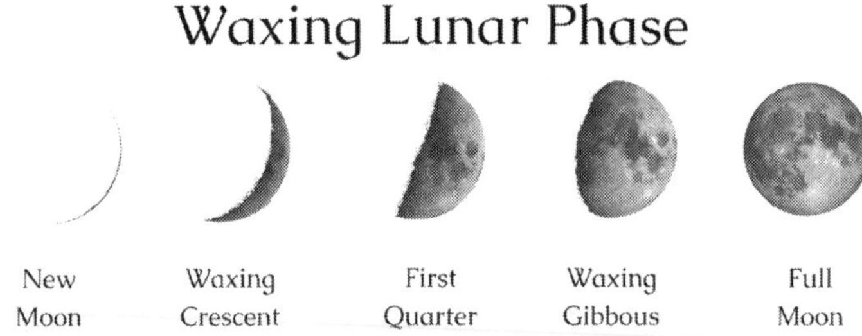

There are three aspects to the waxing moon phase: the crescent moon, first quarter moon, and gibbous moon. The waxing crescent moon takes place right after the new moon. It first appears as a tiny glimmer of hope in the sky. It shines light on your intention and helps it grow through your inspired action. The crescent moon is both gentle and insistent, both grounded and visionary. This is the time to anchor your intentions and think about what you want to manifest.

Reread the story of your future life and the affirmations you wrote under the dark moon aloud. Visualize your reality as if the intentions have already manifested, and take action to secure your intention.

Exercise – Anchor Your Intention

When you have a clear intention, your results will be measurable. Hold a vivid picture in your head of what you want to create so you can anchor your intention. These activities should create excitement and make you feel good.

---

1. Create a task list of action-oriented items you can do right now to help manifest your intention (if you did not already complete this under the new moon).
2. Write your affirmation(s) on sticky notes and post them around the house.
3. Write a positive message on your mirror with a dry-erase marker.
4. Create a vision board using pictures, words, and colors that express what achieving your intention looks like.
5. Schedule time on your calendar to celebrate your daily, weekly, and monthly achievements.
6. If your intention is finance-related, incorporate your affirmations into your budget spreadsheet (e.g., for cash withdrawals, write, "Cash to use for anything I choose," or for deposits, write, "Unexpected money showing up for me.")

7. Shrink your range. For example, a ten-day detox on your inspired action list may seem daunting, but during the detox, there is only one Sunday. "Only one Sunday" sounds easy and attainable.
8. Set a daily notification on your phone to congratulate yourself on your success.

Be creative and have fun. This exercise should make you feel good. So, if you are losing weight, do not hang that old bikini up as motivation; it will not make you feel amazing right now. To anchor your intention, do activities that ground you in the excitement of your goal. Just as an anchor secures a ship, your activity works to secure your success. An anchor can also work as a reminder that you are doing your part and progressing toward your goal.

☪

The waxing first quarter moon is the halfway point between the new and full moons and brings with it an energy boost. With greater light from the first quarter moon, you may see issues with your planned activities. This is a time for learning, so find workarounds to address challenges proactively and productively. You may also notice triggers that steer you away from your goal. Eventually, you will plan for when such triggers appear so you can remain true to yourself and the life you are creating. There is always another way of doing things or resolving a situation; there's always another path to follow. Do not give up.

☪

As the full moon approaches, the moon's energy increases with the waxing gibbous, so this is the time for massive action.

Go after your intention with your whole heart. You may feel tension or stress, or you may worry that your efforts are not working. Evaluate your approach or actions to see what you need to change. If you change nothing, nothing will change. You may also see truths in situations and relationships, or the universe may offer you new perspectives to consider as the full moon approaches.

The focus of this moon phase is to take inspired action in all you do. Live an intentional life. Identify any limiting belief systems. If you are having no luck performing inspired action or restorative activities, you may have a belief system that warrants examination, and Moon work can enhance this review in unimaginable ways. Explore yourself on a deeper level by asking yourself questions. Change your life by working on the only thing you can control: you.

Do not undervalue the process of cognitive labor during this lunar cycle. The effort of predicting a need, identifying options for filling that need, deciding on actions to take, and monitoring the results is all part of taking inspired action. Inspired action requires practicing stillness, restructuring your thoughts, and focusing inward. The inspired action you take creates an energetic ripple effect that emits energy to your immediate environment and beyond. We must elevate our thinking to see and create goodness all around us. The more we change our thoughts, the more our positive energy will create love and joy in our lives and in the world. You never know where the ripples will end!

Exercise – Discovery Journaling

As you take intentional action toward your goals, you might hit snags. To avoid frustration resulting from early setbacks, be vigilant. Refine your ideas and plans as the month unfolds. Throughout this lunar cycle, use the energy to discover why things are not going as planned. This type of journaling involves maintaining a record of everything that is happening in your life. Include your thoughts, feelings, and inner conflicts. The goal is to counteract any excuses you come up with for derailing your progress and then return to a place of inspired action.

Create a daily habit of mentally digesting your day with discovery journaling. Writing things down brings clarity and focus to your situation because you are actively interacting with your thoughts. This type of journaling is not extensive, but it has two parts: one, summarize your day or identify important things that happened, and two, decide how to proceed. Here are some examples of discovery journaling:

- "Met my water intake goal today! Repeat it tomorrow."
- "Stubbed my toe at the grocery store; did nothing for the rest of the day. I forgive myself for not being productive."
- "Argued with a coworker at lunch. Grabbed takeout for dinner. Binge-watched Netflix. Tomorrow, bring lunch in a cooler to avoid my coworker until I can calm my emotions."

There is a lot to learn from the events you capture in your journal entries. However, discovery journaling is not about simply identifying the triggers, snags, or barriers that derailed your success; instead, state what happened, then identify alternate actions you can take to get yourself back on track and living your life on purpose. Trust your inner knowing.

With this technique, you are not solving the problems of your life. The purpose is to identify what went wrong (or right) and refocus your efforts so you can continue taking inspired action toward your goal (and achieve restful sleep). In creating this habit, you can identify a barrier or trigger for which you should build in contingencies in case your plans go awry.

☪

Full Moon

The moon has no light of its own, so when the moon looks most full, it is reflecting maximum light and vitality from the sun's rays. From our perspective on Earth, the moon appears to illuminate as the light bounces off its surface. While full moon energy lights up the sky for several days before and after its culmination, the moon reaches fullness when the sun and moon are in direct opposition on the zodiacal wheel.

The moon is at its spiritual and energetic pinnacle when it is full in its radiance—and that is when she is also most appreciated on Earth. Spiritually speaking—and in relation to the work you started when the sun and moon united at the new moon—the full phase of the moon is a metaphor for fulfillment and completion. At the new moon, you created an intention, and with the full moon, you achieve results (or at least your reality reflects your level of effort).

At the full moon, aspects of the moon and sun combine. The emotional, inner aspects of the moon combined with the life force character of the sun's rays dancing on the moon make this a pinnacle moment. Now you can analyze what might hinder your progress by looking in your shadows. Shadows are nothing to fear. The shadow self includes the parts of yourself that you deny because an outside influence affected you and made you want to hide that aspect of yourself. Shadow work is about investigating your shadows and exploring deep inside yourself so you can heal, awaken, and experience growth. Although your heart yearns for your inner desires and dreams to come to fruition, it can be difficult to find a path forward. The full moon illuminates the world and your metaphorical path—and that includes shining light on the obstacles you are experiencing. The full moon is the best time for shadow work, even though facing uncomfortable truths about the self can be difficult. Everything either contributes to or reduces your personal energy. Through shadow work, you can discover energetic leaks and identify the things that detract from your desired level of satisfaction. Shadow work uncovers the false and limiting beliefs that guide you, so you can learn about your true self and the unique gifts you offer the world. Through Moon work, you will learn lessons that will help you believe in yourself and grow.

Exercise – Emotional Journaling

Things in life will happen, and you will have an emotional response to them. This exercise does not focus on what happened, but rather, how you can learn from your emotional reaction.

During the full moon, identify one negative thing you should let go of during the waning cycle. Do not overburden yourself by attempting to work on everything at once. Pick one triggering situation from your discovery journal to work on. Remember, this process is about you. So, for example, if you wrote in your journal about an argument you had with a coworker, do not write about why this person irritated you. Write about how you reacted. Describe your emotional response to that triggering situation. How did it make you feel? Ask yourself questions, like:

- What offended me about what happened in the lunchroom? Did my coworker's etiquette demand a reaction? Was I holding on to a belief I'm passionate about? Did I not stand up for myself, causing an emotional buildup to explode?
- How did I expend my energy? Was it worth arguing about?
- Did my physical actions contradict my current goals (e.g., grabbing takeout on the way home)?
- What negative habits keep coming back no matter what I do? Are there other times/situations in which I eat unhealthy takeout and derail my progress?

If your response to any of these questions concerns a trigger of yours, then either you are not emotionally ready for this work, or you are not taking responsibility for your actions. For example, imagine you look back at your discovery journal over the last several months and notice that you had a one-off disagreement with a coworker. But under a variety of scenarios, a trend of TV binging shows up. Mindless activity is derailing your progress; everything else is an excuse. Your coworker is not your real trigger, so what is? Without identifying the trigger that "made" you engage in a mindless activity or sink back into an old habit, where do you unravel the mystery of why you engage in mindless activity so often? Even if your journaling reflects that self-sabotaging behavior only occurs after a negative encounter with this specific coworker, what does that tell you about you?

Unearthing the emotions that compel you to engage in mindless activity is challenging. So, write something that engages your feelings. Simply reciting a narrative about your version of events is not helpful. You must engage your feelings. The narrative might be that you were mad. But when you write to unearth your feelings, you may discover that you felt heavy or burdened or like your heart was racing.

Some examples of emotional journaling prompts:

1. I wish I felt confident enough to _____.
2. I wish I could change _______.
3. Because I don't have _____ , I feel like _____.
4. I am so ashamed about _____.
5. I wish I could stand up for myself when ____ happens.
6. I feel powerless when _____.
7. I wish I were brave enough to _____.

I encourage you to complete the exercises under "Full Moon Phase" in chapter 10, so you do not stay in a triggering place. Bringing up these emotions may require support. You don't have to go through this alone. If you don't have anyone in your life you trust, call your doctor.

Waning Moon

After the full moon and during the waning moon phase, the moon seems to disappear a little more each night. This phase signifies a time for gratitude, forgiveness, and surrender. It is a counterpart to the waxing moon phase, when you refined your outward, forward-moving actions. During the waning moon phase, it's time to reflect on how you feel. Practice stillness. Reflect on and surrender your limiting beliefs and energetic leaks in sync with the shrinking moon. During the full moon, you asked challenging questions to evaluate your habits and relationships. Now is the time to discard the things that do not work. Recharge, make room, and prepare yourself for the positive things that are coming your way.

Waning Lunar Phase

Waning Gibbous

Last Quarter

Waning Crescent

New Moon

The waning gibbous moon appears to shrink as darkness overtakes the right side of the moon. With gratitude, consider, "What do I need to release?" Be thankful for the things that protected you in your time of need. These protections provided security and understanding, but they no longer serve a purpose. Reflect on what is blocking you from achieving your goals. Pay attention to energetic leaks or roadblocks that are holding you back. Embrace what comes up, acknowledge it, and then surrender it. You may have to release something you want to hold on to. This is an emotional process, so be kind to yourself.

The waning last quarter moon is the halfway point between the full and new moons. It is a call to go within and seek intuitive answers and heart-driven guidance. Grant yourself permission to forgive yourself and honor your feelings during this phase. Consider revelations about yourself, your situation, and the people in your life. What do they mean to you? Sort out what works and what doesn't work by asking why. Your answer may reveal that it is time to let go of people or remove yourself from certain situations. Minimalist living is an out-of-the-box way to approach letting go of tangible things that block you from reaching your goals. Instead of letting go, establish new healthy boundaries. Asking why can help you deconstruct the rationalizations you use to enable your negative behavior and reframe your mind to seek significance or substance instead of chasing superficial success.

During this time, it is important to readjust your goals and forgive yourself. Forgive every mistake, bad habit, and unfortunate decision you may have made. Forgiveness of self allows you to move on and approach new situations from a loving perspective. During this time, messages about where you need to speak up or change your life will be reflected in your emotions. Be mindful of how you are feeling. Listen for direction and guidance. To make room for positive change, work in tandem with the moon to shed what holds you back from manifesting your desires.

☪

The waning crescent moon is the ultimate phase of the lunar cycle. It occurs right before another cycle begins with the new moon. Exert no effort to control anything. Go with the flow. This is an opportunity to reflect on the entire lunar cycle. What have you learned? What has happened? What has not happened? Review your journal entries to evaluate how you've changed since you wrote them. Take inventory of your current state of mind and the sensations in your body. Let what you discover guide you on what you should work on in the upcoming lunar cycle. Consider how you want to reorganize your time and actions to improve your success with the next new moon.

Exercise – Forgiveness Journaling

As you grant yourself permission to forgive yourself and honor your feelings, there is only one journaling prompt necessary:

"I forgive myself for…"

☪

Lunar Eclipses

A lunar eclipse occurs when the moon moves into the Earth's shadow, blocking sunlight from reflecting off the moon. A lunar eclipse ushers in change, sometimes abruptly. Throughout history, eclipses have inspired amazement and fear, especially the ominous full blood moon. A lunar eclipse does not occur often, so when it does, it shakes things up and gets us out of our comfort zone.

A lunar eclipse is about the culmination of an emotional cycle, encouraging us to let go of emotions that no longer serve us. It is like a cosmic reset switch. Use the energy of this lunar event to intentionally create change and growth. This is the time to make a big decision you have been putting off. Maybe you need to leave behind what is safe to make way for growth. Eclipses reveal opportunities to transform, so breathe through the fear. Be bold and decisive. Rock the boat a little—not by being mischievous, but by taking inspired action according to your true self.

Moon Rituals

A ritual is a physical expression of your intention to create positive change in your life. A ritual symbolically creates space, allowing new things to enter your life. No matter where you are or what you use the space for, you can declare it a sacred space for a moon ritual. This space can be your kitchen table, bathroom, or backyard—whatever makes you feel good.

Remember how the nervous system is your command center? When you perform a practice that makes you feel good, your nervous system releases feel-good chemicals into your system. A ritual should extend your self-care practice. It should be a grounding activity that nourishes you and creates a sense of home and belonging. The process should focus on self-discovery and opening up your energy to attract the things you want in life or that are in your best interest.

To perform a moon ritual, at a minimum, you need to be present and in a clean and quiet space with a pen and journal. Remember, there is no right or wrong in this process. There is only what you feel supports you.

Create a ritual with the intention of using the energetic network to send your goal from your personal energy out into the world and beyond. The network includes your own personal energy, Gaia (Mother Earth), and Source (God/a higher power/universe), as well as the moon. When you think of the change you want to create, all the energy throughout the universe jumps into action to help you transform.

The Hermetic principle of correspondence, "As above, so below,"[8] is a powerful statement that expresses this energy connection. This principle embodies the truth that correspondences flow between various aspects of being and life and distinct levels of vibrational energy. Our universe is made up of the stars, sun, moon, planets, and galaxies. The spiritual universe, where God, angels, spirit guides, and the many wonders of the physical universe live (as above) influences us and affects our daily lives (so below). The human energy system is comprised of chakras, the subtle bodies, and the aura. Our personal energy flows through a vast network of energetic

[8] Hermes Trismegistus. The Emerald Tablet of Hermes.

channels called "meridian pathways" and radiates outward into the world.

Using this principle in *Wild Moon Healing* language, "as within, so without" refers to how our internal communication results in self-care. How you outwardly care for yourself determines your level of inner self-esteem, the root of all your experiences. The energetic influence of our experience creates our self-talk and daily habits (as within), and the level of vibration we internalize from our experiences radiates outward for the rest of the world to see (so without). Your thoughts and actions send a frequency through the energetic network. Accepting how your thoughts and actions interact with everything outside of you creates a desire to break negative behavioral and thought patterns. You want the rest of the world to experience high vibrational energy from you. But you can only accomplish this when you are living in alignment with your authentic self.

During a ritual, be deliberate. Engage your body, mind, and spirit. Design a ritual that honors you and includes elements of self-care and self-love. Your ritual will be most effective when it feels meaningful to you. Perform your ritual with good intentions, so what you attract matches your energy. Wild Moon Healing and creating intentions is not about perfecting a specific ritual. There is an ebb and flow to the process that is unique to everyone. It is not about perfecting your life (because then you are comparing your life to that of another, which is the opposite of manifesting). You want to take an active part in creating your best life, but the ritual does not have to be perfect. It only needs to be perfect for you.

In time, you will find *your* perfect rhythm and movement that reflect your authenticity in tandem with the moon's energy.

Lunar Cycle Rituals

The ritual you create must take into consideration the reflective nature of the moon. The moon reflects the light of the sun, revealing the intention you want to affirm for yourself and announcing it to the world.

You need to decide what you want to work on during the upcoming moon cycle and how to best move ahead with inspired action. If it seems like nothing works out for you, or you are unhappy about an aspect of your life, the universe is telling you that change is needed. Before you can achieve your goal, you must do internal work (but then, healing yourself *is* the purpose of Wild Moon Healing!). By using a ritual in your Moon work, you can amplify the vibration of your energy with intent. Over time, you will create a ritual that feels correct for you.

Incorporate information about the current astrological season to guide your tarot and journaling exercises. Seasons are based on sun signs (birth signs) and the attributes of each sign. You don't have to be born under a particular sign to use its energy, but you have to make the intention to use it. If you can, add planetary influences into your Moon work. For example, knowing what planets are in retrograde when you do your ritual can help you tweak small elements for the biggest punch. Planetary retrograde occurs when a planet appears to be moving backward in the sky, which can make us feel sluggish. Any planetary retrograde is a time for "re-" words, like *refine, reassess, realign, reconnect, refocus, rethink*. For example:

- If Mercury, the planet best known for communication, is retrograde, reassess the way you communicate to discover how you can improve.
- If Saturn, the planet that rules karma, is retrograde, review your past negative behavior so it won't be repeated.
- If Neptune, the planet of inspiration, is retrograde, realign with your purpose by reviewing your fantasies to see if you can turn them into realities.

We perform rituals every day. We wash our face before bedtime and drink a cup of coffee to wake up in the morning. As noted earlier, the best time to perform your Moon work ritual is during the new moon or full moon. However, lunar influences always affect us. It is not beneficial to do any ritual when the moon is waxing. That phase guides you to work toward your goal and evaluate your progress as the energy grows with the moon's glow. It is not helpful to perform rituals under the waning moon; in fact, the only ritual I do under this lunar phase is one to cultivate self-compassion. Gentleness is necessary as you surrender something that no longer serves you, because letting go is hard. Do not beat yourself up. Forgiveness of self requires admitting that there is emotion living within you related to an experience that you need to release. The act of surrender and forgiveness is the toughest part of the process, so kindness is all you need. In the following pages, I have shared what I do during the new moon and full moon phases.

New Moon Ritual

The major restorative activities I engage in during a new moon ritual are meditation, gratitude practice, tarot readings, and journaling.

Be creative with your ritual space. Make it as unique as you are. Incorporate symbolic items that represent each of the elements. Engage all your senses as you craft your space, and add items that reflect your intentions. For example, if your intention is to increase the steps you walk each day, put your walking shoes in your ritual space. Make it yours. Based on your culture and beliefs, you can:

- set up an altar
- light candles
- use aromatherapy
- smudge (burn sage or sweetgrass) to cleanse yourself and your space

- ring bells to clear energy
- consult tarot or oracle cards
- take a bath with herbs, flowers, or oils
- pray

You can include the four elements, using, for example:

- crystals for earth
- music for air
- spices for fire
- a seashell for water

A new moon ritual should set you up for success and support you in setting the tone of your practice through specific activities that are aimed at creating your intention. A new moon ritual sends a clear, flexible message to heaven and the universe.

Exercise – New Moon Summary

Once I finish journaling, I write a summary in the following format because I find it easier to reflect on my intention at a later time. Here are the items to include:

- Counting your blessings (gratitude) maintains your awareness of everything you appreciate, helping you sustain a high energetic vibration.
- Action items express the successes you expect to achieve.
- Summarizing your action items in affirmative language ("This lunar cycle will…") reinforces the desired outcome in your subconscious. Action-oriented "I will" statements express your purpose and level of determination. Articulating what will happen expresses faith and trust.

- Positive "I am" affirmations reinforce your character and align your thoughts and actions with your intentions and true self.
- Write your monologue to inspire healthy self-talk.

The following example is for the intention "I am becoming the healthiest version of me." For more information on form of intention-setting, see the Intention Contract Exercise in chapter 8.

I Am Grateful For:	Action Items:	This Lunar Cycle Will:
My family	Meal prep	Bring me encouraging weight loss
My job	Curb TV time	Provide strength for healthy choices
My life	Wash my face	Enable me to use my time wisely

Affirmations:

- "I am healthy and fit."
- "I am making the best food choices for myself."
- "I am achieving my goals."
- "I am in control and present."
- "I am more trusting of myself."

Self-Talk:

This month, I will see my physical body change. I will use my momentum to see rapid, positive change in my body. I will make mindful, healthy decisions. I will plan and prep meals, so I am well prepared for the upcoming week. I will lose weight by focusing on my diet and strength training. I will read more and not spend so much time watching TV. I will wash my face every night to establish a bedtime self-care routine.

☪

Full Moon Ritual

Full moons offer a time to go inward, seek clarity, and examine your shadows. Therefore, performing self-care activities during your ritual is key. Start off with meditation or a relaxing bath with oils, herbs, dried flowers, or candles to engage your senses. Journaling is the cornerstone activity to finding answers in your shadows. Seek guidance in tarot, knowing that it reads your current energy. It does not have to all be serious.

Sometimes I like to make moon water on full moons. Moon water is water that is charged under the energy of a full moon. The moon can seem mysterious, signifying wisdom, illusion, intuition, spiritual connections, and the things we cannot see. Spiritually, moon water can help you achieve balance and positivity in your life. Making moon water is a meditative experience. My favorite comes from June's Strawberry Moon; I swear, it is sweet! The giant moon that graces the sky in June coincides with the strawberry harvest in North America.[9] To make moon water, all you need is drinking water and a container. Here is a basic recipe:

[9] Its name comes from the Native American tradition, and it reminds us to collect wild strawberries. Folklore states that picking strawberries beneath the light of the moon honors the crops and ensures a bountiful harvest the following year.

Moon Water

- Purified, distilled, or spring water (tap or rainwater will work if it is healthy/safe to drink)
- Glass container (mason jar, large jug, bowl)
- *Optional:* Fruit (dried or fresh), flower petals, quartz crystals, herbs

Step 1. Fill your container with water.

Step 2. Add optional items if you choose.

Step 3. Holding your container, meditate on your monthly intention and what you want to manifest for at least five minutes.

Step 4. Express gratitude to the moon. You can say something like "Thank you, moon, for blessing this water to help me with (intention)."

Step 5. Place your container somewhere it will be lit by the moon—either outside in the moonlight, or inside near a window through which you can see the moon. If the weather is cloudy, no worries. Just as you can get sunburned on a cloudy day, the energy of the moon can move through the clouds.

Step 6. Before sunlight touches the container in the morning, bring your water inside or move it away from the window. If you used a crystal, take it out. Let it dry before you place it back where you keep it. The crystal has not only been charged by the energy of the full moon, but the moon water has cleared it as well. Its properties are ready for you to use as you see fit.

Uses for Moon Water

- Drink it.
- Pour it in tea.
- Cook with it.
- Wash your face.

- Take a bath.
- Mix it with essential oils to create a room mist or cleaning solution.
- Add it to your altar to represent the element of water.
- Water your flowers.
- Sprinkle a little on anything you want to bless.

Tips:

Charge your water for three consecutive days, including the day prior to and the day after the full moon. You can make moon water at any time of the month. It is just my practice to make it under a full moon.

Throughout the waxing and full moon, I evaluate my progress. At this point in my life, I have been Wild Moon Healing for several years, and I am aware of my triggers. Sometimes when I evaluate my progress, all I can do is maintain the awareness that my triggers were engaged (which started me on an episode of binge eating). I share this to encourage you to remain committed to your goals. Being mindful of your actions has a profound effect on your healing. Even if you cannot immediately stop your negative behavior, mindfulness is a window to the reason behind your behaviors. Evolving with Moon work involves gaining awareness of all that you do to help change your perspective. In my case, the perspective shift is that binge eating does not define me, nor do the triggers that led to an episode of binge eating. Just as meditation allows you to observe your thoughts, mindful awareness allows you to witness your behavior. This insight helps you progress toward your goals because awareness is the root of all inspired action.

4

WE CREATE OUR OWN CHALLENGES

Limiting Beliefs Theory

A limiting belief is a state of mind or conviction you consider true that limits you in some capacity—a negative affirmation, if you will. These types of beliefs are false representations of yourself and the world, and they prevent you from pursuing your goals and desires. Limiting beliefs can keep you from doing important things, like applying for a dream job, finding a healthy relationship, leaving a harmful relationship, or releasing the extra weight your body is holding. Limiting beliefs can also keep you from doing unimportant things, like skydiving, researching why a banana peel is slippery, or tasting that weird ice cream flavor. Limiting beliefs rob your life of joy, happiness, spontaneity, and fun.

Certain aspects of life are challenging and out of our control. By learning to respond instead of react, we ensure life's challenges do not become worse. We create our own challenges in life by hanging on to limiting beliefs and expending unnecessary personal energy. For example, medical and mental health issues begin with limiting beliefs, negative feelings, and unhealthy self-talk that are often born out of low self-esteem.

Living a pessimistic life leads you down a path of creating your own challenges. People who expect the worst outcome are more prone to experience a mental health issue, such as anxiety, stress, or depression. This can lead to a lifestyle of addiction (engaging in compulsive behavior because the brain sees it as rewarding), with no regard for the consequences. Addiction is not the pleasure-seeking activity of a person lacking willpower. It is the indulgence of a person with low self-esteem who fears rejection and the opinions of others and who escapes their pain or disguises who they are.

Limiting beliefs can create a medical health issue and/or mental crisis in a person's life because that person gave away their power to distract themselves from a traumatic experience. By teaching people to love their whole selves, restorative Moon work builds a framework to help rid the world of addiction and (avoidable) disease. To help you achieve your intention through opportunities and resources presenting themselves, you must believe you are worthy of what you are manifesting. Manifesting is just a fancy word for "making [it] happen." Bring your magic, have faith, and don't give up. Go after your goal. It will not manifest itself. Manifesting with the different phases of the moon while working through addictions, roadblocks, or barriers helps you not only achieve your goals, but heal your heart.

As I said earlier, energy links everything. Nothing is random. But limiting beliefs make your brain and thoughts become dissociated from your actions and behaviors, so things appear separate. In a disconnected mental state, you do not realize how past experiences relate to your present experience. Your past influences your core belief system, behaviors, and feelings, especially those related to the consequences of your past actions, such as being laughed at as a child. Historical events from your life become unconscious processes that guide your conduct.

Your subconscious mind holds limiting beliefs and drives your actions and behaviors. For example, when you decide you want to lose weight, but experience difficulties in achieving that goal, it is because your limiting belief is driving a behavior that's counter to losing weight. This is what I mean when I say our thoughts (e.g., "I want to lose weight") disassociate from our actions (but I continue to eat unhealthy foods). Our beliefs create boundaries and limitations around what we perceive to be reasonable behavior.

So, what's a healthy boundary? A boundary is a form of self-care, reflecting the amount of love and respect you have for yourself. A healthy boundary is a way of prioritizing your well-being. For example, most people believe that stealing and killing are wrong and that a healthy boundary stops most people from committing these crimes, which not only prioritizes their well-being, but society's as well. So, not all beliefs limit us in bad ways. Limiting beliefs are concerned with how you perceive yourself, your interactions with other people, or the world. A limiting belief tells you what you cannot achieve. When you tell yourself you cannot do something from a subconscious place, guess what? You won't.

"I AM" statements tell other people about the person you are, whereas "I WILL" statements state your purpose. Our internal and external language is powerful. "I AM" statements affect our belief systems. If, for example, you have told yourself since high school that you are not good at math, that could be the reason you cannot stick to a budget. This belief leads you to overspend, and your mounting debt creates stress. You feel the need to escape your debt, so you drink more than you should.

Then, you receive a medical diagnosis of stomach ulcers. This exaggerated scenario portrays what I mean by the connectedness of seemingly random events that reflect unhealthy boundaries. If you don't know who you are, then you have no comfort in what you have done and what you will do in the future. For example, a person who does not know who they are or what they want may drink to excess. Social anxiety stemming from their insecurity may cripple them, so to be around people and appear to have fun, they must be intoxicated.

If you say, "I am tired," you will continue to be tired. So, focus on the fact that at least you are awake, willing, and able. If you say to yourself, "I am fat," you will have a challenging time adapting to weight loss behaviors, so focus on health rather than weight. If you engage in positive self-speak, like "I am kind. I am smart. I am important," I am certain you will bless others with your awesomeness.

Limiting beliefs can come from family traditions, education, experiences, social status, economic standing, or trauma. Our life experiences ground these beliefs in emotion. Limiting beliefs are mere opinions, however, they come from a belief system of subjective, narrow views that people believe to be the absolute truth. As noted earlier, limiting beliefs are born out of our experiences. For example, perhaps you went through a divorce after your significant other cheated on you. Linking your identity to something or someone outside of yourself—in this example, a relationship—creates an environment that grows your limiting belief system.

The limiting belief born from going through a divorce could be "I am not enough," because the experience of losing your spouse to someone you see as younger, smarter, or prettier diminished your sense of self-worth. You associated your personal self-worth with being a spouse rather than being an individual. After the experience robbed you of your mental or emotional strength, your baseline belief became that you are not good enough. Because of this false and limiting belief, you formed opinions that stereotype people as cheaters, and you stopped trusting. This frame of mind keeps you stuck and not only unable to engage in a healthy relationship, but unable to enjoy your accomplishments or special moments in life.

Exercise – What Am I?

Is a limiting belief affecting what you want to manifest? To find out, make a list of areas in your life where you feel challenged, areas you wish were different, things in the past that caused heartache, or times when you may have overreacted. Reflect on the list and write down thoughts that come to mind. Are your thoughts true? This is not an exercise for listing all the negative qualities of a specific person who hurt you. This is about your thoughts about *yourself.* What/who do you believe you are?

Here are some examples of false and limiting beliefs people may believe or tell themselves:

- I am not good enough.
- I am not pretty or thin enough.
- I am too old / too young.
- Bad things always happen to me.
- I am not smart enough / I do not know enough.
- I do not have enough time.
- I do not have enough money.
- I do not deserve to be loved.
- I could never start my own business; it is a pipe dream.
- I am too fat/stupid/ugly.
- All people cheat me.
- I will never find another partner.
- Love is too painful for me.
- I will get hurt.

- I am not good with money.
- I am always broke.
- It is too late in life to pursue my dreams.
- I cannot make enough money doing what I love.
- I'm not the problem. (Denial blocks energy.)
- The economy is bad right now.
- No one listens or cares about what I say.
- I cannot be my real self; I will be judged and shamed.

Saying or thinking these types of thoughts holds you back from achieving what you want. These thoughts are fear-based and prevent you from even beginning. The Wild Moon Healing process supplies you with techniques to become aware of what your limiting beliefs and energetic leaks are and where they come from. Through this work, you can identify the core belief that created your other limiting beliefs.

Limiting beliefs can have negative effects on your mental and physical state, but the good news is that restorative measures can reverse those beliefs. If all you can do during this exercise is consider a specific person who did you wrong, you are giving your power to that person, which is an energetic leak. This exercise helps you identify not only false and limiting beliefs, but also energetic leaks. Practicing this exercise will help you identify what you believe you are ("I am") and what you consider yourself capable of doing ("I will").

Energy

Everything has energy. In our body, energy is the inner "me" as a force in all of us. Energy is language. It does not communicate through words, but it transmits messages. The universe encodes messages based on the frequency of your vibrational energy. Therefore, you can pray without saying a word. Just a tear transmits your energy, and again, no words are necessary. The universe does not respond to your wants, needs, dreams, or desires; it hears your vibration. Unresolved trauma and pain are magnetic, drawing into your life what matches that vibration. You can want or have a basic need that requires attention, but like attracts like, so if your energy is vibrating at a low level based on negativity (e.g., shame, fear, anger, or guilt), you will attract things that match that vibration.

Moon work focuses on healing mentally and physically on the inside to raise the vibration of your energy. Everything starts in the mind. So, to raise your vibration and change your life, you must change your mindset and love your entire self. If your energy is stuck because of past trauma and you are experiencing false, limiting beliefs and energetic leaks, you are vibrating at a low energy. The universe knows it. The people in your environment know it. If anyone has ever given you an uneasy feeling, it is because your energy sensed an energetic presence that is lower than your own.

I believe the contagiousness of yawning is because of an energetic shift in your state of awareness. You can explore shifts in your awareness with Wild Moon Healing principles by evaluating your thoughts and feelings when you yawn. Are you tired or transitioning from a high energetic activity to a lower one? Do you need to get up and move around? Go through the same explorations with laughter. If you find yourself in a lower energetic state and someone attempts to lift your spirits with laughs and challenge your will to remain angry, your energy will shift. You'll laugh. Your state of awareness realized that the time for being angry was over. The experience was gone, and you moved on to a more pleasant one. Again, we see this with depression. Because of a momentary energetic shift, a depressed person can still laugh, thus shifting their depression to an altered state of awareness (happiness or joy), if even for an instant.

Unlike physical energy and the science of physics, scientists cannot measure spiritual energy. Energy is the foundation of all matter, and it is always flowing and changing. The physical body has veins and arteries to help support life via a beating heart, and it has nerves and organs to support our bodily functions. We also have a subtle energetic body that's comprised of energetic pathways known as meridians that flow with prana (or life force energy) and converge at powerful energy centers known as chakras.

Meridian pathways allow energy to flow, like water flowing in a stream, into the chakras. The energy in the chakras moves in a circular motion, and its speed affects the vibration of your energy. Consider the way a wind turbine uses air that flows in various patterns and speeds to create energy/electricity. Our energy flows in various patterns, and its speed is based on either heavy, slow-moving energy caused by energetic leaks and false and limiting beliefs, or light, faster-moving energy caused by preventive or restorative care. Like attracts like, so the more care you practice through the Wild Moon Healing principles, the faster your energy will move, increasing the vibration you send out into the universe and attracting higher energetic experiences and resources into your life.

Subtle energy is an invisible force that drives your potential, affects your actions and reactions, and compels your intentions. Understanding this energy helps you understand why and how life experiences happen and the affect those experiences have on you. Everything is energy, and energy is vibration pulsing at myriad levels. A person's vibration (or the vibration of a place, thought, or thing) is an energetic quality. A vibration is a state expressed by mood, so a cheerful person's energy vibrates at a higher level than that of a person who is angry or sad. The energy of food also vibrates differently. For example, a pescatarian diet has a higher vibration than the standard American diet (SAD). When low-vibrational people surround you or you put low-vibrational foods in your body, your body's energy and the level at which it vibrates at a cellular level are influenced. Low energy can create dis-ease in your physical body. Your vibration affects your emotions and thought patterns, which can create limiting beliefs. Negative energy that affects our personal energy can come in different forms, and these things cause energetic leaks.

Energetic Leaks

Energy is our vitality and life force. Everything in life is either giving you energy or taking it away. An energetic leak is when you spend energy in ways that cause a deficit. With an energetic deficit, you can be moody, ill, unable to concentrate, or tired, among other things. This deficit can only occur when you lose contact with your authentic self. When this disconnect is present, you are susceptible to buying into an external story or narrative that triggers a strong emotional response in you. Energetic leaks create stress and can affect your body, thoughts, feelings, and/or behavior.

When an energy deficit exists, you may experience stress in different ways, such as feeling unappreciated, disrespected, fearful, or insulted. Stress can cause high blood pressure, heart disease, and obesity. It can also cause mild physical symptoms, such as headaches, muscle fatigue, or an upset stomach. Stress can create irritable or overwhelmed feelings that can cause you to overeat, drink in excess, or withdraw from others.

When you worry or feel anxious, your body releases fear hormones, like adrenaline and cortisol. When you zone out in front of the TV, hoping to reduce your stress level, you disassociate from your stress or trauma. Dissociation is a coping mechanism, just like procrastination. What are you detaching from? What energetic leak is making you want to hide from your life?

Energetic leaks can create feelings of stagnation. You do not become stuck because someone is holding you back. You become stuck because you think and do things that hold you back. You say "yes" when you want (or need) to say "no." From a place of fear, you relive past hurts instead of releasing them. You hold on to anger, allow a person to belittle you, or do something you do not want to do.

Imagine that you are a bucket full of water. You are the bucket, and the water is your energy. When your bucket fills (and is not leaking), you feel good. Others see you as supportive because your presence helps them feel good about themselves. It is unavoidable that every thought we have and every action we take cracks our metaphorical bucket, hence the need for sleep to revitalize our energy. However, when your bucket is leaking energy, others around you may feel offended, ignored, or unappreciated. When people feel nourished by your high-vibrational energy or starved by your diminished energy, they deplete your energy. Rather than taking responsibility for their own happiness and well-being, they rely on you to make them feel a certain way.

Regardless of who or what is depleting your energy, energetic leaks expose themselves. For example, if you say or do unkind things, that's a clue that you have an energetic leak. Are you exhibiting the characteristics of a toxic energy vampire? Toxic energy vampires must always be right, have the last word, debate, gossip, or be negative Nellies. These people can suck the life right out of you. It is easy to see such traits in others, but can you see these energetic leak clues in yourself?

Exercise – Energetic Test

We use energy all day, every day, and to regenerate, we need adequate sleep, a healthy diet, and movement. However, when we cannot replenish our energy levels during a normal circadian rhythm, we experience an energetic leak. For example, attempting to sleep in on the weekend to make up for lost sleep during the week is a sign that you are experiencing an energetic leak. In 2017, the Nobel Assembly awarded a Nobel Prize to Jeffrey Hall, Michael Rosbash, and Michael Young for their research on circadian biology and the identification of the clock gene.[10] These genes are components of our circadian clock, comparable to the cogwheels of a mechanical clock. So, if your clock gene is out of balance, your sleep is affected, and you are experiencing an energetic leak.

If you are unsure of whether your energy is leaking, consider your mood. Low-energy moods may be an indicator of emotional issues. Take out your journal and contemplate the scenarios below. Does anything resonate?

- Am I short-tempered?
- Am I sick often?
- Am I sick and tired of being sick and tired?
- Am I always a victim?
- Do I "fly off the handle" at trivial things?
- Do I have a "woe is me" mindset?
- Do bad things follow me, or does it seem like my life never gets better?
- Do I complain often?
- Do I feel the need to "fix someone" by giving unsolicited advice?
- Do I want to prove others wrong?
- Do I ever laugh?
- Do I feel lost or alone?
- Does my mood affect my appetite?

[10] Jeffery Hall et al. "Press Release," https://www.nobelprize.org/prizes/medicine/2017/press-release/.

- Is my life made up of a series of one unhealthy relationship after another?
- Is it hard for me to concentrate for long periods of time?

Be honest and transparent as you figure out what areas of life rob you of your strength. Transparency ranks on par with responsibility and accountability. For example, perhaps you notice you get angry often. You need more information so you can take responsibility for your actions. Investigate further with questions that help you identify your "I AM" statement, such as:

- Am I always angry?
- Am I only angry at work, while commuting, or at home?

After asking yourself a few questions, you may realize that your temper is worse in the morning, from the time you wake up until you arrive at your job. You might think, "Well, that's strange." However, it is not odd at all; it's telling. Probe further:

- Do I like my job?
- Do I engage in challenging work?
- Do I have any conflict with coworkers or management?
- Do I feel appreciated?
- Did I not receive a promotion I was expecting?

When you realize why you are unhappy with your job (or whatever the case may be), your journaling should change to questions that identify what to do next. For example:

- Do I understand why I didn't receive the promotion?
- Am I overqualified for my job?
- Do I have just a "job" versus the career I imagined for myself?

- Do I need more training or education?

Remember, Wild Moon Healing is about you, not about a bad supervisor or coworker. Your statement becomes "I am unhappy with my job." When you identify what you are, you can take control of your emotions and stop giving your power away. But first, you must be transparent with yourself and truthful enough to find answers that can help you change your current experience.

Energy Is Money

Energy is your body's currency, and you only get so much of it, so be careful where you place your attention. Are you gossiping or taking on unnecessary responsibilities? Some life experiences can lift you up, while others drag you down. Life is an investment. Spend your time doing things that provide a good return—things that make you proud. If you squander your energy, you can create a debilitating energy deficit.

As you can see, an energetic deficiency does not have to come from an outside energy vampire; you could be your own energetic leak. By giving away your personal power, having an energy deficit, or holding onto false and limiting beliefs, you create a life box (like a Pandora's box) that places physical and emotional stress on your cognitive function and nervous system. When you build a life box, you limit everything in your life, including your currency (energy). When you feel trapped and don't see other options for your life, you can experience anger or anxiety. Everyone has a life box. Healthy boundaries are the foundation of a life box that allows your energy to flow. When you experience an energetic leak, you build unhealthy boundaries and coping mechanisms and unnecessary walls that fortify your life box. This constricts energetic flow and creates a deficit. Even in a deficit, your daily energy must come from somewhere. That place is your physical body at a cellular level. Low energy creates an environment in which you are susceptible to fear, self-doubt, and physical dis-ease. Energetic leaks are inevitable, but the good news is that you can stop and reverse an energetic leak and recharge your mind, body, and soul.

As noted earlier, stress causes your body to release certain hormones, but your body also produces feel-good hormones, like dopamine, serotonin, oxytocin, and endorphins. Based on how the body reacts to fear hormones, it is logical that being mindful, surrendering your present circumstance, and releasing perceptions of false and limiting beliefs will improve your mood and promote the release of feel-good hormones. Then you can enjoy the present moment. Negative feelings come from fighting against your situation or experiencing trauma, but mindfulness eliminates barriers and helps you become proactive in working to achieve your goals. Self-care practices that work on self-awareness and physical activity can also help ward off dis-ease in the body.

If you feel physical symptoms or mental distress, see your doctor. But also consider the sources of your energy depletion. When you remove an energetic leak (or when you manage its source), your stress decreases, your energetic vibration increases, and you feel better mentally and physically. So, take responsibility for your energy leaks and engage in corrective behaviors that help you create the life you want. If you feel you cannot correct these behaviors, keep doing the Moon work until you can regain your power and control. It will amaze you how calm you can be, even when circumstances trigger a negative emotional response.

Exercise – Self-Doubt Test

Limiting beliefs and energetic leaks are part of life. The key is to identify them so you can overcome them.

For this exercise, ask yourself the following questions and write your answers in your journal. Extrapolate on each answer and provide detailed examples of how, why, when, and where you do these things. Have you ever:

- Allowed another person to make major life decisions for you because you doubted your abilities?
- Shied away from an opportunity because you did not believe in yourself, your capabilities, or your skills?
- Been cynical, jealous, or angry about the success of others, or wondered when it will be your turn to succeed?
- Given up and stopped giving any effort?
- Wondered if you would amount to anything or become a significant person?
- Been late or missed appointments?
- Sought approval or permission to move forward in life?
- Compared yourself to others to discover what is "wrong" with you or what things are missing from your life?
- Put off self-care for the sake of someone else's happiness?
- Found yourself in a perpetual state of learning to procrastinate on leveling up?

If you have done any of these, then you have self-doubt that's fueled by limiting beliefs and energetic leaks, making *you* the most dangerous person in your life. A false belief system and energetic leaks rob you of time you could spend creating your amazing life.

☪

Fluidity of Time

Time is linear; it starts, and it goes on forever. It started before we were here, and it will continue to flow long after we are gone. The concept of fluid time is emotional. Time seems flexible, yet we also deem it as uncertain and unchangeable. Have you ever heard someone say, "Time flies," or "It seems like it was just yesterday" as they spoke of the past? Have you ever felt like time moved so slowly that it seemed to stand still? The notion that time can speed up or slow down expresses its fluidity. People even refer to memories by saying, "Remember that time when...?" Time measures how we spend our energy.

You spend your time wisely when you focus your energy on creating, communicating, and sharing your amazing life and passions. You can tell you've spent your time well through your feelings and emotions. The concept of "spending" time can only happen in the present moment. Just as with the concept of energy as money, it doesn't matter if you used to have money to spend or expect to have more in the future… right now is the only time you can spend what you have.

The inability to remain in the present is an energetic leak. People often live in an illusory mental state created by false and limiting beliefs. Imagining potential future scenarios where you might be happier (fantasy) or where you might suffer (anxiety) without taking inspired action to create or avoid said future situations means you are not present. Remembering only the good times and seeing life through rose-colored glasses (reverie) means you may be out of touch with reality. Thinking about past mistakes or what could have/should have been (regret/

guilt) keeps you locked in a mental prison where you cannot be present. Staying in a place of anger or fear over losing a loved one (grief) can cement you in the past. While the only healthy place to live is in the present, there will always be a past, present, and future.

There is a mural on the ceiling of the Rockefeller Center in Midtown Manhattan titled *Time* that illustrates time as past, present, and future. The artist incorporated the two marble pillars from the building's original architecture into the mural to represent the separation of the "past" and "future" from the present moment. When you are standing under the "past" part of the mural, you cannot see beyond the first pillar to where the "present" and the "future" are illustrated. Likewise, when you stand under the "future" part of the mural, the second pillar blocks the view of the "past" and the "present." Only when you are standing between the two pillars—in the "present"—can you experience the full picture of time. It is amazing how many details you miss when you are not standing under the "present" part of the mural.

There is a lot more to the meaning of the mural, including concepts like balance and the enormity of time in our lives. For example, there is a strong, muscular man with one foot on each pillar. When you walk through the entranceway and look up, the man appears to move as he balances scales that hang from either end of a large piece of wood. He is evaluating all of his choices, regrets, and worries—the choices he has already made that led to failure (or that he could have handled better), and the choices he may make in the future and their effect. The large piece of wood represents the idea that regret and worry are heavy burdens to carry, and that you can only release them in the present moment.

If you are dreaming of tomorrow or remembering yesterday, you are not present. Maintaining a natural presence in this current moment in time is important in seeing all that is happening in your life and all the choices that are available to you. When you lose contact with the present moment, your emotions replace the facts. When you are mindful and aware, your focus increases and your stress decreases. For example, you may still have deadlines at work, but instead of focusing on how stressed the project makes you or worrying about losing your job if your work is not perfect, you could practice being present and just do the work.

Detaching from the past and probable future to live in the present helps you live with passion and purpose. Being present creates openness, allowing you to see and experience things without preconceptions. You can sense the energetic vibration of others and choose whether that energy is worth having in your life. To just "be" is an amazing experience.

Exercise – Take Stock in Life

Taking stock in your life involves being mindful of and reflecting on your current life experiences. It is like practicing gratitude, but when taking stock, your intention is to encourage thoughts about what you want out of life. With this exercise, you must be present and aware and simply observe.

Notice all the blessings in your life, including your relationships, career opportunities, or material things around you that you enjoy. Notice your emotions. Do you feel resentful, regretful, or sad? Appreciate your surroundings. Do not change or influence the emotions in your current experience.

Instead of listing what you are thankful for, with this exercise, take inventory of what you have in your life. Detail everything from the place you lay your head at night to the love you receive from your dog. Look around and record what you see.

Now, return to the top of your list and evaluate each item. Look at yourself honestly. Where and who are you right now? Where can you create change in your life to become who you want to be?

- Have I allowed wrongs done to me to remain in my heart? Do these lingering negative feelings reflect who I want to be?
- What have I sacrificed to get my worldly possessions? Have I sacrificed my relationships, truth, or health? Have I received these possessions at the expense of my youth?
- Do I spend money I don't have to surround myself with things? How do my things make me feel? Do I become angry if something breaks? Do my things take the place of physical relationships?
- Have I received awards for athletic, vocational, or educational life achievements? Have I ever hit a milestone that I was proud of, even if someone did not formally recognize it? Was I able to share my achievements with someone special in a way that I wanted?

As you recognize behaviors in your life that keep you in the past or the future, identify how you can change to be present. The focus is not to make amends, because creating change in your life to influence the behavior of another is giving your power away. The focus is not to devalue your achievements that helped create the person you are today. Rather, ask yourself, "Did I allow a specific moment in time to define me?" Maybe you still live in the glory days of being a high school quarterback. Instead of recognizing how that memory helped shape who you are today (the game is over, who are you right now?), look at your life as a whole. Are you proud of what you see in the mirror? You cannot change your past, and tomorrow may not come. Be who you want to be in the present moment.

☪

Create Life, Not Challenge

Challenge can make life interesting by giving you a dose of healthy competition with yourself and others. However, I used the term "challenge" to mean hardship. But then again, hardship is subjective. A person who perceives growing up in poverty or having a learning disability as a barrier to overcome may approach their life's challenges as a competition, opening limitless possibilities for their life. A person can also view those things as an excuse, which can make their life challenging.

People who see time and life as linear may have a challenging, unsatisfying, or unrewarding life. If something in the sequence of how they define life does not happen, that then creates an excuse to not move forward. To them, it may seem like "just yesterday" they had their whole life ahead of them. They were excited, brimming with possibilities and dreams. But they fell into this linear, mundane routine and lost their luster in life. They experienced challenges and believed they were not up for the competition needed to move past it. So, they gave up. Now, when they look into their future, they may say that there is "not enough time." If that is you, you are still creating your own challenges. Time is uncertain. Tomorrow is not guaranteed. To the forty-seven-year-old reading this book who always wanted to become a nurse, do it! You are not too old. That is a false belief. Society needs you, so it's better to show up late than not at all. There is no finish line; there is only what you use your time and energy to create: today.

Wild Moon Healing is not a linear, start-to-finish process. If you have a lot of emotional trauma to explore, it can be hard. As you explore your trauma, you will gain insight into your behaviors and reactions. An emotional reaction may appear involuntary, but behavior is never involuntary. Your life created it. The formula for every behavior is as follows:

- You have an experience (a traumatic event or an energetic leak).
- You attach meaning to that event.
- The ego assigns an emotion based on the significance of the meaning.
- The assigned emotion dictates the words you used to describe the experience.
- The words that describe your experience (false, limiting beliefs) affect your behaviors and moods.
- Your words become your story, causing you to live against your truth.
- Your story affects the vibration at which your energy radiates, which affects how you use your time and live your life.

The meaning and emotion you attach to a life event leads you down one of two paths. On one path, you're reactionary, relinquishing control of your life to something outside of you. And on the other path, you're responsive, maintaining personal control by accepting responsibility for your experience. As an example, here's a simplified scenario:

> Jan and Peggy go on vacation together. When they arrive, the weather forecast calls for rain all week. Jan does not care about the weather, because fun is on the agenda regardless. Peggy, however, had envisioned plenty of sunshine, so she adopts a doom-and-gloom mindset. Jan is present and makes the best of the situation, but Peggy remains stuck in the idea of frolicking in the sunshine and cannot enjoy the present moment. Jan wishes the

> vacation was longer because she had so much fun that time flew by. Peggy felt like she was stuck in a bad dream and couldn't wait to leave. The shared experience was a rainy vacation, but because they attached a different meaning to the weather, they had unique experiences.

Your emotions and words have a profound effect on your life. All Peggy had to do to experience fun was surrender the meaning she associated with rain. A shift in your focus changes your emotions and words; therefore, your experience will adjust to match your new perspective. Changing your perspective shifts your personal energy, allowing you to create a new story for your life where you control the meaning of a life event.

If you believe something to be true, but it isn't, you are still holding those words and meanings in your subconscious. Peggy believed she couldn't experience a great vacation in the rain. Since she believed a false truth, it became her reality. If Peggy had let go of the belief that rain meant no fun, she could have had an amazing time.

Had Peggy accepted her circumstance and practiced forgiveness toward herself for blaming the rain, she could have changed her words. Acceptance shifts your perspective, and the resulting energetic shifts reprogram your subconscious mind. Had Peggy accepted the rain and acknowledged that she was going to have a rainy vacation, she wouldn't have seen doom and gloom in the lack of sunshine. Acceptance of your situation means you tackle everything with an attitude of "OK, this is how things are. What do I do now?" This was Jan's frame of mind. She found fun ways to spend her time despite the rain. Jan knew how to detach, pivot, adopt a new perspective, and not let a negative experience define her.

Healing from your negative experiences (as this book is attempting to guide you through) allows you to be present and in control of your personal power. You can choose not only how to use your time and energy to create your life, but your reactions in triggering situations, because you choose your thoughts and then respond. By letting go of whatever took up so much of your time and energy, you create space for new things to appear in your life. When you are present, you can make fresh memories to think about tomorrow. It is important to record your memories, so keep your journal handy!

Throughout the lunar cycle, you can journal to uncover truths about yourself, but your focus will change with each phase. For example, new moon journaling identifies what you want, pinpoints why you want it, and helps you create a list of inspired actions you can take. During the waxing phase of the moon, the way you approach your journaling is different. In this phase, you learn from your behaviors to enhance your self-awareness. With a heightened level of awareness and the illumination of the full moon, you can uncover what holds you back and what you need to release. Therefore, under a full moon, you define what you need to let go of through journaling. The energy of the waning moon shifts your focus to forgiveness, enabling you to surrender anything that no longer serves you so you can choose love.

Embrace Change

Wild Moon Healing is about embracing change that comes from breaking down the barriers that hold you back. Through this process, you'll also embrace time, acknowledging that anything worth experiencing happens in the present moment. You can only accomplish these new levels of awareness through self-love and self-acceptance, because the change you are embracing is the change within you.

Change is inevitable. Heraclitus, a sixth-century Stoic philosopher, said, "No man ever steps in the same river twice, for it is not the same river, and he is not the same man." Change is the only constant in life. Everything you experience, all stimuli affecting your visual and auditory sensory receptors, and every conversation you take part in or overhear changes your thoughts and your body. Every day differs from the one before it. Each moment is unique. You cannot repeat or recreate special moments. Progress is about changing your world based on who you are, rather than creating a version of yourself that suits everyone else. Mindful and intentional interaction between your true self and your environment creates profound change and meaningful moments in your life. And this change creates energetic ripples that affect so much more than your personal world. We are always changing, and a consistent practice of manifesting with the lunar cycles puts you in the driver's seat of that change.

5

SOURCES OF ENERGETIC DEPLETION

In the last chapter, we discussed what energy is, how energetic leaks affect us, and how we spend our time. Now we will explore specific ways we create our own challenges in life, resulting in energetic depletion. First, let's look at some of the primary ways we use our energy.

Multitasking

In theory, multitaskers are more productive, but multitasking and taking on too much at once can decrease effectiveness and overall productivity. It is possible to multitask when your activities are in alignment with your truth, of course. But just because you can do it all does not mean you should. Rest is part of the magic of life. Engaging in redundant, excessive, or avoidable activities may lead to exhaustion, and then you won't be able to perform your tasks well, if at all. Don't invest time or resources in one area of your life at the expense of another.

Unscheduled time is an important way to slow down and can lead to creativity. Be like a kid. Look around with your eyes wide open, grateful for all you see, hear, and smell. Use your imagination to see pictures in the clouds. Roll down a hill. Do cartwheels. Go on a scavenger hunt or play flashlight tag. This may sound silly, but silliness and stillness support creative energy flow.

Playfulness is healing because it allows us to reconnect with our inner child. In adulthood, we conduct our behavior in a reasonable, grown-up fashion. The result? We can lose our fun and our passion. We can even lose ourselves amid the hustle and bustle of the responsibilities we take on. To lead a contented life, we need balance. Whether it is balancing alone time and time spent with others, our material life and our spiritual life, or our work and home life, we need time to work, play, love, and create. Even if we can manage it all, balance helps energy flow.

Exercise – "I Spy"

There is a childhood game called "I Spy," where someone says, "I spy with my little eye something that is [name a color]," and the other players must look around their immediate environment and guess what the item is. This game is great for sneaking in developmental learning and to pass the time while on a road trip. The adult version of this game is to spy on yourself to see how you are spending your time.

In your journal, write, "I spy with my little eye…" and list all the things you feel you need to do:

- Complete household chores
- Meet work deadlines
- Drop the kids off at sports, and make sure you know when it's your turn to bring snacks
- Wash the car
- Go grocery shopping, meal plan, and cook dinner
- Engage in hobbies
- Do volunteer or community work

Today, everyone in society seems to enjoy being busy, so your list will most likely grow quickly. Instead of engaging in too much, intentionally select which activities you engage in and the people with whom you surround yourself. How do you select what to engage in when you must do everything? The answer is simple: everything does not have to be done right now, and you do not have to do it all. How did you become the "fixer or doer of all things"? We assign ourselves roles, most of the time unbeknownst to ourselves.

Take a deep breath. Block out free time for yourself, even if it is just five minutes. When you meditate or journal about what no longer serves you or what holds you back from your potential, you discover ways to choose what you want and do not want. Ask yourself, "Do I want to spend my energy this way?" Asking yourself this question means you are making a conscious choice not to overexpend your energy. If you become ill, mentally or physically, because you stretched yourself too thin, the world will continue to turn. Taking on too much means you are putting yourself and your health last. You are no good to anyone when you are ill, or worse!

Choosing = Personal Power
Personal Power = High Vibrational Energy

Excess Emotional Reactivity

How you react in any situation will either deplete or preserve your personal energy. Strong feelings can mean you are taking part in life with passion. You do not want to repress your natural reactions, because then you are preventing yourself from feeling. But you should be mindful of the intensity with which you express your emotions and the impact of your emotions. Ask yourself, "How do my emotional reactions affect me, others, and my environment?"

When you buy into a story and react, you throw your energy at another person. Energy is money; imagine throwing your paycheck into a fire. You may even physically feel your reaction in the form of a quick heart rate or body tremors. Powerful emotions are valid, but you are not obligated to react. In fact, a reaction is what energy vampires are after. They either love to see you upset, or they act as if your reaction to their behavior harms them. Energy vampires will never take responsibility for their actions, so why waste your time and energy reacting to whatever story they are creating?

Know that your emotions are awesome and valid, because emotions serve as inner guidance. Emotions are indicators of an energetic leak; they tell you what you need to pay attention to. Checking in with your feelings makes you aware of your energy expenditure. Being present is the only way to control emotional energy-sucking reactions.

If you realize you are moody or emotional, meditate. Instead of making everyone around you uneasy, evaluate why you feel a certain way. Talk to a trustworthy source. Rather than reacting, rely on your moods and emotions to provide information, and use it to rid yourself of energetic leaks. If you give your power away in unhealthy ways as an emotional release, such as giving in to anger or alcohol, your Pandora's life box will become more complex.

Exercise – Increase Emotional Resilience

I love the saying "Change your mind, and your ass will follow," because that, in its simplest form, is what you are doing when you are Wild Moon Healing. You work on cognitive skills (your mind and thoughts) to change your behavior (your physical self). As you become mindful of the intensity of your emotions, you will realize your triggers.

When you notice your emotions are taking over, step back. Partake in a physical activity to help shift your energy. Whatever you choose to do, do it with the intention of releasing your current emotional state. Your intent is to increase the vibration at which you send your energy into the universe. As a spiritual practice, using intention helps you reconnect with yourself and focus on what you need (or want) in your current situation.

- The simplest activity you can do to change your mood is to stand up, stretch, and focus on your breath. Breathe in through your nose and out through your mouth, carefully controlling each breath.

  Have you ever watched a movie with (or witnessed in real life) a heated argument? One person walks in circles, moving their arms, breathing out through their mouth. They may not realize it, but their body is attempting to de-escalate their emotional reaction through physical activity.

- Go for a walk. In chapter 1, I mentioned that the conscious mind influences the central nervous system, which handles our stress response. Walking increases blood flow and circulation, which has the positive effect of reducing a reactive response.
- Compliment someone. Doing or saying nice things from the heart not only makes someone else's day, but it makes you feel better too. Have you ever been considerate to someone who was unkind to you? It feels good.
- Thank someone who has supported you. Tell them you appreciate them. Write a letter, mail a card, or send a text message. When you send out positive energy, you increase your own energy and attract more positive energy into your life.

Strongly Held Beliefs

Beliefs or opinions are not energetic leaks in themselves, because we live by and act on what we believe in and are passionate about. But we still need to create a culture of personal responsibility. When you hold on to beliefs, they harden your heart. Being convinced you are right makes you incapable of opening your heart and connecting with others. This binds and restricts your actions, helping you become irresponsible and intolerant of others in your social sphere.

Personal responsibility is not the same as social responsibility. Personal responsibility means that a person chooses, instigates, or otherwise causes their actions, and then takes responsibility for managing them or dealing with the consequences. Social responsibility is an ethical framework that enables people to act in a way that benefits society at large. Many times, people feel they have a right to express their opinions or react emotionally in a public setting, which can affect others negatively. When others' opinions have power over you, you may need to heal from their expressed beliefs. Because opinions are feelings, they are neither correct nor incorrect; they are simply the story someone wants to express.

There is no place for the opinions of others in the Wild Moon Healing process, because you are creating your own story. Your feelings and opinions are valid. Feelings are a product of the current knowledge, experiences, and mental programming that form your opinions. Therefore, they are subjective. Regardless of whether your viewpoint is biased, you are responsible for the actions that derive from your feelings. However, this does not mean you should change your beliefs.

Honoring all beliefs does not mean you omit your own. It means showing compassion and empathy toward others who believe differently from you. When a belief is held strongly, it becomes a conviction, a sentence you impose on others, condemning them for their beliefs. Everyone deserves to have their own beliefs. Everyone deserves love and compassion. No one needs to force another person to understand their circumstances or beliefs. Social responsibility is not a right to attack others because you judge that their belief is an act of intolerance or that it comes from discrimination, negative stereotyping, or prejudice. However, you are subject to personal accountability. You must show "good behavior" based on your belief system. Lead by example, without shaming others.

Commit to showing, through how you live your life, what personal responsibility and accountability look like. Everyone will respect your authenticity as you change your behavior to match your truth. The best way to create change is by trusting your intuition. Let your intuition guide you, as it is your road map, and your beliefs define the passion and purpose that guide you on your path. Strongly held beliefs or false, limiting beliefs can guide you down the wrong path. The process of Wild Moon Healing stills the mind so you can discover what is right for you and learn to trust your intuition.

Exercise – Strengthen Your Intuition

Life is a learning process. You do not want to stop learning, even if you are learning about beliefs that are different from your own. Learning about what makes you and everyone else unique opens you up to a new level of appreciation for all that is around you. Earlier, I stated that if you remain in a perpetual state of learning without taking inspired action, you avoid moving forward. But also remember that sometimes inspired action is only a cognitive function; you don't have to physically move your body to perform inspired action. In this respect, appreciating your and others' individuality is inspired action. Letting differences shine through, just being and admiring, is the inspired action we need at times. Learning about different beliefs allows you to understand the world better, minimizes intolerance and stereotyping, creates an opportunity for you to meet interesting people, and can stimulate your mind by exposing you to new experiences. If you stop learning, or cannot act on what you learn, you stop living.

Strongly held beliefs prevent you from learning and repress your intuition. When beliefs become emotional, they dominate your inner guidance system. Strongly held beliefs are loud, so to reconnect with your intuition, you must quiet yourself. Have you ever done something because it is what you were taught, because your parents did it that way, or because people have always done it that way...

but it left you feeling unsettled? That is your instinctual voice, nudging you to look beyond what others consider acceptable, normal, or ordinary. By listening to that voice, you reconnect to your inner knowing.

Take a few deep breaths. Breathe in through your nose and out through your mouth. Create the intention that you will learn how your intuition communicates. The flow of subtle energies guides your intuition. If you get goosebumps or feel a stirring in your gut, that is a message from your intuition. Intuition uses emotions to portray significant messages to your conscious awareness. Sit down. What feelings or sensations come up? This may not feel rational, but trust and acknowledge your body's wisdom. Now, have fun with the sensations to strengthen your intuition.

- If your phone dings with a notification as you sit, concentrate before you look at your phone. Guess who the message is from. What is it about? Are you correct?
- Lay a deck of playing cards face down on a surface. Sit with the energy of the cards. What feelings and sensations come up? Can you feel which card you are about to flip?
    - Start small. Pull out five red and five black cards. Mix them up and lay them all facedown in any order you choose. Now, try to flip only the black cards.
    - Next, pull one card from each suit, lay them facedown, and try to flip only the spade.
    - Pull all the court cards, lay them facedown, and try to flip only the jacks.

- ○ Pull out sequential cards of any suit, mix them up, lay them facedown, and try to flip the number five card.

Graduate in steps, increasing the difficulty of your card combinations. Eventually, lay out all fifty-two cards in the deck and flip a two.

Feel the sensations in your body. Notice how you feel before you flip the correct card as opposed to how you feel before you flip the wrong card. For example, perhaps you get a tingle in your right forearm if you are about to turn the wrong card. What's your "tell"?

Don't doubt yourself. Follow your intuitive hunches. The more you practice, the stronger your intuition will become.

Feeling Self-Important

We must love ourselves, and self-love does not affect others negatively. However, if self-confidence turns into a need for you to elevate yourself above others, you have moved beyond self-love. Inflating your opinion about your personal characteristics, stature, or wealth is egotistical. To be absorbed in yourself in a self-centered way may show issues with self-esteem.

Poor self-esteem is a growing problem in the modern world. Just consider social media. Developers of apps that allow users to manipulate pictures of themselves have monetized their lack of confidence and self-acceptance. When a person feels they must filter themselves on social media, they portray a reduced sense of self-worth. If you have unresolved negative core behavioral or thought patterns, your inflated ego allows obstacles to sidetrack you, which diminishes your sense of self-worth. The ego can be belligerent, refusing to accept responsibility or take criticism and underestimating challenges.

It is the ego's job to feel important. Its survival depends on it. For that reason, egos seek drama (or create it) to put you at the center of attention. The ego mind cannot be in the present. It lives in the past or the future, where regret or anxiety reign free. When it feels exposed, your ego creates negative situations to keep it busy. It encourages worry and supports change for the sake of change, and then you allow an irrational emotion, like fear, to make you abandon your path. When you manifest with the moon, you engage in activities that help you discover your truth and explore how to create meaningful, effective change.

When the actions, words, or behaviors of others attack your sense of belonging, make you feel unimportant, or offend or upset you, the ego needs to redirect its focus. So, it creates dramatic situations to hide your fear, doubt, and insecurity. The ego shifts focus away from your self-care practice, the present moment, and the facts to create a "What about me?" scenario. There is nothing wrong with feeling important, but we need to regulate our egos.

Having a delicate ego is a sign of an energetic leak. The ego can turn you into a victim, or you might develop a superiority complex to justify your behavior. An unbalanced ego mind affects your decisions, moods, and character, and people's actions are a measure of their character. How you react to others is also a measure of your character. When you act with your personal interest in mind and take everything personally, you become an energetic vampire. Being aware that your ego is involved with your actions can have the profound result of improving or repairing relationships in your life.

Exercise – Mirror Meditation

Everyone has an ego. The mind has imperfections and traps. Moon work is a tool to help you achieve self-love over self-importance (or the opposite, self-loathing). Dr. Tara Well, a self-proclaimed mirror-gazing expert, developed a technique using a mirror and meditative techniques.[11] The mirror teaches us about ourselves. Our own reflection can help increase self-esteem and emotional resilience, regulating the ego.

Most people would describe someone constantly looking at themselves in the mirror as either conceited or egotistical. For example, let's look at people who are addicted to selfies. They take hundreds of identical photos with the purpose of capturing that perfect photo they believe will gain the most attention. The other extreme is always taking pictures but never being in them because they don't want attention. These types of behavior describe people who have a challenging time looking at and seeing themselves on the inside.

Gazing into a mirror in this meditative exercise forces you to give yourself attention, instead of seeking attention from outside sources or hiding from it altogether. This meditation will not turn you into a narcissist. What it will do is help you stay present and grounded in reality so you can better manage the intensity of your emotions and reveal your authentic self. A mirror can help you surrender the ego that gauges who you are based on your perceived notions of others and tells you that you are never enough or just a pretty face.

---

[11] Tara Well. "What the Mirror Can Teach You About Yourself: Advice from a Mirror Gazing Expert," https://www.mindful.org/what-the-mirror-can-teach-you-about-yourself-advice-from-a-mirror-gazing-expert/.

Find a quiet place where you can be alone—a place that has good lighting, so you can see yourself. Use a fixed mirror, something you don't have to hold in your hands. As you gaze at yourself, place one hand on your heart and breathe. Notice the sensations in your body—your heart rate, your body temperature, etc.

Notice your expression. Are you critiquing your appearance? Notice the outward signs and signals that your body is sending you. Is your skin dry? Are your eyes red? Are there wrinkles on your face? Is your body asking for your love? If so, acknowledge your accomplishments and all the ways your body has shown up for you. We often mistreat ourselves, but the body is designed to always heal itself. Your body has never given up on you.

Look at your physical body. Thank it. Say things like:

- "I appreciate you."
- "I'm amazed at how you support me."
- "You are not a problem to be solved."
- "You are my home; I honor you."
- "I respect and love you."
- "There is no other like you; you are a rare gem to be admired!"

Now, look inward. Lean into your reflection. Look directly into your eyes.

- Do you see past the superficial?
- Do you see the trauma you carry around?
- Do you see your desires, your unmet expectations?
- Do you see your anger?
- Do you see your pain and struggle?
- Do you see all your hard work?
- Do you see your truth?
- Do you see yourself, but still don't recognize your reflection?

Acknowledge everything that comes up. Notice your feelings as you look into your eyes. Struggles and negative emotions make us tired. Are you tired? Do you feel heavy?

Now, get out of your head and back into your body. With one hand still on your heart, place the other on your stomach. Breathe. Notice how your stomach and chest rise and fall with each breath. What's the message?

- Do you have the same problems digesting your food as you do digesting your emotions?
- Do you have the same problem moving your joints as you do moving past your emotional pain?
- Do you have the same issues with your eyes as you do seeing the truth in your situation?
- Do you have tension in your shoulders as you carry burdens you should put down?
- Do you have excess weight as you carry emotions and beliefs that weigh heavy on your mind?
- Do you have dry skin that's asking to be quenched as you deny your adventurous spirit because of your responsibilities?

Your body is talking to you. What is it saying? What is it asking of you? Recall that this book is intended to help you create a life you love. Let your body tell you what healing activities you need to do to break through the behaviors, habits, and thought patterns that are holding you back from reaching your full potential. Instead of searching for your worth in the opinions of others, see yourself as you are. You are an amazing creature. You know what you need.

Check in to evaluate your feelings and appearance and talk to yourself. When you have a conversation with your body while looking in a mirror, you can see how your self-criticism affects you. By doing this exercise, I notice an increase in self-care behaviors that are more nurturing and accepting of myself. The mirror offers a perspective you cannot access inside your head. It makes it harder to lie to yourself when you truly see yourself.

☪

Unclear Relationships or Boundaries

Healthy boundaries are a critical part of self-care. Creating boundaries is an educational process that helps you establish limits that teach others how to treat you and behave around you. They tell people what they can expect from you. Without boundaries, energetic leaks will be part of your daily life. You will experience feelings of depletion. You will allow others to take advantage of you and take you for granted. With your energy depleted, you may feel resentful, hurt, or angry.

Signs that you are in a relationship with unhealthy boundaries include:

- Your relationship is difficult or filled with drama.
- You may have a challenging time making your own decisions.
- You fear letting down a partner, friend, coworker, or other individual.
- You fear your partner telling you to be quiet if you express yourself.
- You feel guilty, have anxiety, or are often tired.
- You are a passive-aggressive victim because you fear abandonment or rejection.

Hanging out with a person for a long time without being sure of what they want, need, or feel but hoping it will "all work out" drains your energy. Hanging on to a relationship that's well past its "expiration date" out of fear of being alone drains your energy. Being in a relationship where you are indecisive because your partner makes all the decisions (leaving you wondering who you are) drains your energy. Being a person who strings others along is a powerful energy drainer, too.

Behavioral signs of weak or unclear boundaries include people-pleasing or saying yes when you need to say no. You know that person you always go to for help because they always say yes? Stop being selfish. Give them a break. If you are reading this book and you are a "yes person," you will learn to say no when it is appropriate for you as you heal your energetic leaks. Being in a relationship with unhealthy boundaries does not mean you cannot say no. It could mean the other person does not respect your no or yes responses. This calls to mind the adage, "Good fences make good neighbors." A fence does not protect you from your environment; your neighbor can still be too noisy. But a fence prevents visitors from entering your property without notice or permission. This is what healthy boundaries do.

Healthy boundaries tell people, "This is who I am." Before you can communicate your truth, you must discover who you are. Ongoing inner dialogue that does not descend into self-shaming, nitpicking, judgment, or finger-pointing is self-exploration, allowing you to discover who you are. Once you can do this with yourself, you will communicate better without nitpicking, judging, or pointing the finger at your partner, family, friends, or strangers.

People seem to have a challenging time enforcing personal boundaries with themselves. The intention or goal you create with the new moon will lead to an action plan that will help you solve this issue. The action plan: setting and maintaining personal boundaries. Does your action plan include meal planning to help you eat healthy foods? If yes, why go through the drive-through for dinner? Does your action plan include establishing a budget to help you get out of debt? If yes, why run errands all weekend, spending money just because there are good sales? We run over our own boundaries every day. If you can't respect your own boundaries, how can you expect others to respect them? We teach others how to treat us through the way we treat ourselves. Though maintaining your boundaries is important, be careful not to become too rigid with them; that can lead you down a path toward isolation.

Boundaries are crucial for creating a firm foundation for healthy relationships with yourself and others. People with strong emotional health create healthy boundaries, but boundaries also create emotional health. Healthy boundaries are always safe (they keep you from the abuse and selfishness of others), flexible (they are situational), and able to create connections (they help you work through problems and maintain relationships with yourself and others). Speaking your truth by establishing healthy boundaries is possible with Moon work.

Unconscious or Excessive Speech and Gossip

Listen more, speak less. When you speak, do so with care. Hear no evil, speak no evil, see no evil. Listen to those three monkeys and be careful what you say, listen to, and watch. Drama, gossip, or complaining does not have to come from you. Just being around it, seeing it, and hearing it will deplete your energy.

Listening to others is a way of respecting a relationship boundary, because when you do so, you give value to the person speaking. When you take in what a person is saying, it is a sign that you care. The act of effective communication (where you balance speaking and listening) influences a healthy relationship. Drama, gossip, bickering, and complaining create noise made up of useless words.

There is a beautiful Sufi tradition that invokes mindfulness and awareness of our words called the Four Gates of Speech.[12] Before engaging in conversation and asking four gateway

---

[12] Michelle Cross. "Four Gates of Speech," https://www.michellecross.co.uk/four-gates-of-speech/.

questions about truth, necessity, kindness, and timeliness, we become mindful and aware:

- Is this thing I want to say true?
- Is it necessary or helpful if I say it?
- Can I say it lovingly?
- Is it the right time to say it?

If you answer "no" to any of these questions, it is best to leave your words unspoken. Likewise, if you hear words and feel that their message is untrue, unkind, or unnecessary, end the conversation. If you cannot find the words to stop a conversation in a healthy way, put your hand up. (Holding up a hand is a universal action that represents a red octagon or stop sign). You can visualize a stop sign entering your situation to end the conversation. I have done this, and it works, even with energy vampires!

When you must be around energy vampires, you can protect your energy by crossing your arms below your chest to protect your solar plexus chakra. The solar plexus is your power center, and by protecting it, you protect your energy. Remember, intention is everything, so be mindful when crossing your arms so your action matches your intent.

Everyone should incorporate the Four Gates of Speech into their self-speak. Being kind to yourself and suspending self-judgment are very important when healing.

When you speak less, you do more. Imagine intentionally not speaking for five minutes a day. Your silence would total 150 minutes, or two and a half hours, a month. What could you do with this extra time? Doing is always better and more productive than speaking. Therefore, we must take inspired action on our intentions. Otherwise, we will achieve nothing. Unconscious speech or gossip is mindless and accomplishes nothing. However, active listening is an inspired action that can improve personal, social, or work relationships.

Tips for improving your active listening skills include:

- Make eye contact with the person speaking to you.
- Watch for nonverbal cues. Body language mirrors your thinking mind, and if you are not paying attention or are uninterested in the conversation, people can tell.
- Visualize what the speaker is telling you.
- Paraphrase rather than give unsolicited advice ("So, what you are saying is…").
- Ask clarifying questions (but avoid yes or no questions). It is a conversation, after all.
- Don't change the subject abruptly.

Being Tested

Throughout the healing process, the universe will test you to confirm whether your decision making is true to your authentic self. When an intention manifests, but not in the way you envisioned during your new moon process, do you take what you can get, or do you intuitively know that the situation is not yet in your best interest, so you wait to see what the universe will bring next? Having trust and unwavering faith—knowing that what is best for you will manifest in your life at the right time—is an integral part of the Wild Moon Healing process.

The universe knows who you are and what is right for you. So, when your energy vibration tells the universe that you are lacking in faith, it will test you. Some people mistake these tests as "God Winks." A God Wink is an experience or "coincidence" so profound and so aligned with your needs that it seems like divine intervention. A test from the universe is more like a temptation; it seems great, but it does not align with your truth. For example, perhaps you meet a new lover. Thinking you have found a perfect relationship, you ignore some of your boundaries. To maintain that relationship, you act against your long-held beliefs and create new false, limiting beliefs. If you jeopardize any part of yourself for a relationship (or anything else), you are not living authentically and have lost faith that what you want and deserve is on its way. Thus, you failed the test. Passing the "test" or saying no to temptation requires faith and patience. You must know your truth so you can choose what is correct for you.

There are immeasurable meaningful moments, both good and bad, between life and death. These moments create our lives and influence us. Being responsible and authentic to yourself leads to risks, and of course, none of us wants to hurt, fail, or be judged, so we build protection mechanisms. When we protect ourselves from risk (or avoid it altogether), we miss opportunities and experience regret or discomfort. Since our experiences create our lives, wouldn't you like your life to be filled with positive opportunities, resources, and people appearing in bold, unexpected ways? Such synchronicities can generate outcomes that will make you happy and that you can be proud of. So, why settle for less than you deserve? Settling never equates to happiness. Take risks! Risk healing from the inside out. When you do, you will notice encouraging changes in your life.

You can ask God or the universe to help you recognize tests and see blessings when they appear. Freedom looks different for everyone, so it is essential that you take responsibility for discovering what and whom your authentic self is so you can realize what your freedom looks and feels like. That way, when it arrives, you won't mistake it for a test.

Exercise – Convert Desires into Beliefs

If you feel the universe is testing you or you are stuck in a cycle, you may have to convert what you wish for into beliefs. For example, if you are seeking a healthy relationship and you keep meeting the same type of person (who is not right for you), you may have to create a new belief system.

This exercise is a visualization to help you align your desires with your faith. Most people visualize the story of their life in terms of what they want to happen, rather than believing it is going to happen. If you want to succeed at Wild Moon Healing and create your best life that's abundant in health and joy, you need to make the mental shift from dreaming to believing. Instead of thinking in terms of hypothetical outcomes or in forms of wishful thinking, convince yourself that you are predicting the future. If you have been working on strengthening your intuition, you will have an easier time with this.

Go back through your journal and locate the intention journaling you completed under the new moon. Before you started journaling, you visualized what you wanted to create as a movie or a recording of your life in the future. Go back to that visualization. Press play and watch it again. Contemplate all the details as they unfold. The movie already exists because it has already happened; you have simply not experienced it in the physical realm yet. The reason you feel excitement and joy, feel your hair blowing in the breeze, hear the ocean roll up on the sand, or taste the salty air is because it is a memory. Your visualization is the universe gifting you with a vision of your future self, a glimpse of your future life.

Believe in this gift. But you must do your part to make sure that movie becomes your experience. You must take inspired action toward your goal now. Examples of inspired action include:

- Open an IRA, or start contributing to your employer's retirement plan.

- Explore properties for sale at the beach you want to live on to help set a realistic expectation of property values and expenses.
- Create a budget and follow it so you can retire.

This is how you create your future. The more you believe in the outcome, the more inspiration you will find to act on.

☪

Misuse of Divination Tools

As noted earlier, all your choices up to this point are the reason why you are where you are in life. They are why you behave the way you do. Yesterday's choices no longer matter. A promise of tomorrow does not exist. All you have right now is the knowledge of whom and what you want your future self to be. But using divination tools alone cannot create this future for you; you need to do the work.

Using divination tools in a disempowering manner represses your intuition. How do you use these tools incorrectly? Instead of tapping into your personal energy and knowing your truth intuitively, you use divination tools as the truth rather than as guidance. If you want to know your future, manifest with the moon and start choosing differently. Create your future through inspired action.

Divination tools can help guide you on your path if you use them to tap into your personal energy and intuition. These tools are only as effective as the parties using them. Tools such as tarot cards and pendulums work off your energy. When you are seeking messages from oracle cards or a psychic or medium reading, remember that diviners use metaphysical tools to read your energy and help you tap into your intuitive knowing.

As your energy changes, the tools you use provide different information.

If a clairvoyant you are working with speaks with certainty about your future or provides information about your future as if it is the will of God and is going to happen, they are distorting the message you were meant to receive from the tools. Every choice you make and every action and inaction changes the trajectory of your future. If a lightworker misuses tarot cards or reads their own interpretation into the configuration of an astrological chart, the sitter (the person receiving the reading) may misinterpret the message, or worse, may accept what they heard during the reading as truth or unchangeable destiny.

Other Energy Leaks

While false and limiting beliefs create an environment that makes us susceptible to depression or addictive behaviors, addictions, habitual behaviors or patterns, and a mismanagement of time or sexual energy are all energetic leaks. Too much of anything means there is an emotional need that is not being met. Chasing "the answer" or the perfect path causes energetic leaks as well, because you are not listening to your inner knowing, nor are you enjoying what is around you in the present moment.

Exercise – Protect Your Energy

Everyone should focus on maintaining their vitality and life force, making the best use of their time, and creating an abundant life. When you lose focus on creating your life, energetic deficits will become your new normal. Symptoms of depleted energy levels manifest physically and mentally. A deficit can first appear as a feeling of mild dis-ease in the body, but if you do not protect your energy, a more severe energetic deficit can result from low self-esteem, anxiety, or addictive behaviors, which can lead to a life-threatening dis-ease and even death. You cannot eliminate all energetic leaks from your life; unexpected trauma occurs every day. However, addressing energetic leaks and protecting your energy is the only way to balance your life and maintain good health.

Effective ways to protect your energy include:

- Quieting your environment – Free your time from social media; it's an echo chamber of negativity that protects energy vampires from rebuttal. You cannot engage in a healthy dialogue in that type of hostile environment. Alone time to still your mind without electronic devices is healthy.
- Visualizing – See yourself creating an energetic bubble that's powerful enough to contain your personal energy. Hold your hands parallel to one another with your palms facing one another about six to eight inches apart. Move your hands together and apart, without bringing them completely together, and feel your energy. Once you feel it, visualize a ball of energy between your hands. Use your hands to make the energetic ball grow. Push it above your head, out to your sides, down below your feet. This becomes your energetic boundary, and you will only mindfully give your energy to what you allow in your space. You can make it as big as you want and let anyone or anything inside it that you choose. Let your bubble change color like a mood ring so you can learn to recognize the frequency of your personal energy and acknowledge your feelings. Know that this energetic boundary always exists. Say

out loud, "I create my energetic boundary with the intention of protecting myself from experiencing energetic leaks. I am safe. My energy is contained."

- Creating a handle – Establish a slight physical movement (the way Samantha Stephens in the television series Bewitched[13] wiggles her nose to make things appear or disappear) as a way of acknowledging that you are engaging your energetic power. This prompt will help you work on awareness and intention. If you feel a heavy energy nearing or entering your personal space, squeeze your hand, tug your right ear, or tap your left leg twice to tell yourself you are aware of the negativity. By doing this, you're telling your subconscious mind that what you do next will be with the explicit intention of protecting yourself from that energy.

If you have anxiety or experience anxiety attacks, the prompt you establish will help bring situational awareness to what initiates an increase in your anxiety or triggers an anxiety attack. Let's say for example that your prompt is to tap your left palm below your pinky finger with the middle finger on your right hand. Every time you start your prompt, notice if a negative energy has entered your personal space. Did your environment change? Did something change in your mind? If it was just in your mind, what were you watching or listening to at the time? What kind of conversation were you having? Pay attention to your thoughts.

Are you sure the energy entering your space is negative, or do you fear that the person who has entered your space will judge you? Do you have

---

[13] *Bewitched.* Directed by Harry Ackerman. Created by Sol Saks. American Broadcasting Company.

something to say? Are you unsure of how to say it? As you do this more and more, how does it feel when you experience negative energy versus when you experience an anxiety episode? Perhaps when you experience anxiety, you notice that your heart rate increases and you perspire. But with negative energy, maybe you turn your chin toward your left shoulder. What is your physical response?

- Using an energetic rubber band – I first learned a version of this technique from Carol Tuttle at the Carol Tuttle Healing Center.[14] Visualize everyone and everything that drains your energy. Imagine that all the energetic vampires in your life are in the same room as you. It is noisy and chaotic. Throw a huge rubber band around them. They are too busy robbing you of energy to notice. Start walking backward while holding the rubber band with your dominant hand. When you are ready, release the rubber band with the intention of returning their negative energy. All the gossip, complaining, and disrespect snaps back to the person who originated it, relieving your stress and restoring your energy.

  The first time I did this exercise, I stretched the rubber band out and imagined myself walking back toward the vampires and releasing the tension on the band because I didn't want to hurt anyone. The truth is you cannot hurt anyone doing this exercise, just as their negative energy cannot hurt you. If someone doesn't live up to an imagined exception you hold for them, it can hurt your feelings, but they did not hurt you. You are not returning or inflicting pain on anyone. You are just returning the negative energy from whence it came to fix your energetic leak.

[14] Carol Tuttle Healing Center. https://course.liveyourtruth.com/hc/.

- Engaging your deflector shields – I also learned a version of this technique from Carol Tuttle.[15] Imagine shiny metal shields surrounding and protecting you. Any time you sense negative energy entering your personal space, engage those shields and reflect the negative energy back toward the person sending it out. If they do not leave your personal space, you will notice them becoming flustered by their own stifled energy.

Protecting yourself from and overcoming energy leaks will help you plug into untapped potential and clear the barriers that are holding you back from living your best life. There is no reason for you to take on negative energy from anyone. Take steps to correct your energetic leaks so you can release any negative self-images or limiting beliefs you hold about yourself.

[15] Ibid.

6

MENTAL AND EMOTIONAL WELLNESS

Preventive Care

Wild Moon Healing is not only about healing mental and physical health issues, but also about prevention through restorative activity, self-exploration, and self-discovery. This inner work is how you identify energetic leaks and false, limiting beliefs before negative influences create lack or struggle in your life. Prevention of mental or emotional unrest is an act of surrendering emotions to avoid dis-ease in your body. Practicing mindfulness and achieving self-awareness before false and limiting beliefs or energetic leaks deplete your energy reservoir helps teach the art of surrender. This involves checking in with your body daily and asking yourself questions about how you feel. Get to know yourself. What do you want?

Everyone at every age should learn the skill of surrendering their emotions. Even if you have not experienced a severe trauma or loss, any type of distress or injury affects your body's command center, making both your experience and your need for healing valid. Why? Because it is not just trauma that creates barriers in our lives. Any insignificant negative thought or feeling can turn into an obstacle if we do not release it. For example, say a teenager feels tormented because their body does not look like the bodies of the models they see in magazines. That feeling did not begin with trauma. It began with a perception or thought that requires surrender. To overcome this, the teenager could flip the script in their head and identify what that model has in common with them. You must let go of comparisons and rationalizations, just as you must let go of anything else in your life that is holding you back. Your testimony is your story. Your feelings are always valid. Do not compare yourself to others.

Preventive care is comprised of activities, like keeping up with your annual physicals; monitoring your blood pressure; and getting an annual skin check and regular colonoscopy, mammogram, or vaccination. Undertaking restorative activities and taking preventive measures for your mental and physical health are part of promoting a healthy lifestyle. Lifestyle is an enormous factor in overall wellness.

Mental Health and Sleep

Your level of mental health is closely related to your level and quality of sleep. A lack of sleep takes a mental and emotional toll that can create physical health issues, such as depression. The Harvard Medical School claims most Americans are sleep deprived, but only ten to eighteen percent of adults in the United States population experience daytime grogginess. Whereas, of those with conditions like anxiety, depression, bipolar disorder, and attention deficit hyperactivity disorder (ADHD), fifty to eighty percent experience daytime grogginess.[16] If you experience persistent sleep issues, it is time to talk with your doctor, but there are things you can do on your own as well.

If you are sleep deprived, especially if you experience daytime grogginess, it is time to make some changes. The big three sleep interrupters you should avoid when you have issues sleeping are caffeine, nicotine, and alcohol. Limit (or stop taking) naps throughout the day, establish a nightly routine, avoid caffeine, and turn off blue-light-emitting devices about an hour before bedtime.

Promote Wellness

You can stop physical, emotional, and mental health issues before they cause problems in your life and the lives of others by promoting wellness and good mental health for all. Wellness programs:

- help people with high-risk medical factors change their lifestyle to improve their quality of life.
- help healthy youths and adults be compassionate role models and encourage healthy lifestyles in others.

To encourage healthy lifestyles in yourself and others, you must understand that:

- expressing your feelings and emotions is healthy and necessary.
- communicating in a healthy manner involves an exchange of deep thoughts, ideas, and feelings that makes everyone feel safe.

[16] Harvard Health Publishing. "Sleep Deprivation Can Affect Your Mental Health," https://www.health.harvard.edu/newsletter_article/sleep-and-mental-health#:~:text=Sleep%20and%20mental%20health%20are%20closely%20connected.%20Sleep,likely%20to%20have%20insomnia%20or%20other%20sleep%20disorders.

- creating healthy boundaries that honor personal beliefs (without attacking others who believe differently) is essential for physical and emotional health.
- discovering what you believe, value, and enjoy is an investment in your life.
- having fulfillment, meaning, and purpose will help you fall in love with life.
- practicing self-care is a necessary part of life and is not selfish, as it prevents you from needing medical care.
- engaging in self-exploration and self-discovery is necessary to identify yourself as an important individual.

Through educating yourself and others, you can help shift the stigma around mental and emotional health from shame and disgrace to dignity and self-respect. Love, compassion, and empathy encourage emotional and mental well-being. Our ability to experience compassion and empathy develops during childhood, based on the level of love and nurturing we received. If you love someone, compassion and empathy come naturally; however, they do not require love. Compassion and empathy are the ability to put yourself in another's shoes and imagine their feelings without experiencing them (albeit still having an emotional experience). You don't have to love that person, and you don't have to feel sorry for them or pity them. Instead, you share in their pain or negative experience and give them space to feel how they feel.

Compassion and empathy can motivate you and affect both your behavior and the behavior of others; ergo, they support your personal wellness, increase your energetic vibration, and promote increased self-esteem. The energetic elements of self-worth (our emotions) are at the root of all behaviors. Therefore, emotional and mental wellness can help defeat addictive behaviors and certain forms of depression.

Addictive behaviors are born from low levels of self-esteem, and the ultimate purpose of Wild Moon Healing is to teach you to love yourself and your life. You can achieve your highest potential, but you must believe you deserve it. But what if, as you learn these skills, you teach the next generation these skills, too? What if today's young people grow up in an environment that supports them emotionally? What if they are present and grounded from the beginning? What if they learn how self-care promotes self-love and self-acceptance while honoring and respecting the uniqueness in others? What a wonderful world it will be when no one needs to *learn* to love themselves, because they have the skills to support their emotions and the knowledge of preventive care and wellness. Constructive behaviors help you develop strong self-esteem, fight against addiction, and prevent dis-ease.

We can heal our behavior and change our lives at any age, but by teaching our children about their emotions and how to surrender to them, we can prevent or reduce issues such as AUD and type 2 diabetes from developing later in their lives. We cannot preach abstinence, healthy eating, and physical activity to children while excluding mental and emotional wellness components. Activities like meditating, journaling, practicing gratitude and mindfulness, and engaging in physical movement like yoga teach our children to listen to their bodies and achieve mental and physical wellness. We should also teach our young people the value of personal development, which comes from learning outside of a classroom. When children are curious, and the adults in their lives encourage them to pursue their individual interests and passions, they will not only live value-added lives, but such pursuits will set them on a lifelong journey of discovery, health, and abundance.

Making health a priority means changing the way people characterize mental and emotional wellness.

Mental Wellness and Teens

One of the biggest and scariest challenges parents and caregivers of teens face is mental health issues. Teach your children positive coping skills, such as breathwork and meditation. Allow them to explore creative outlets, like music or drawing. Encourage movement and outdoor activities, and start these routines at an early age. Educate teens on mental wellness. But before you do any of that, heal yourself. Be the change. Be the example.

Stop the Stigma

A stigma is a stereotype that creates negative attitudes and beliefs toward people who appear to be disadvantaged from a circumstance or illness, such as depression or obsessive-compulsive disorder. A stigma is a false, limiting belief. The stigma of those with a mental health disorder is that it affects their credibility. Mental health should never do that. People, including narcissists, weaponize the word *stigma* to destroy others, or they use it as a control mechanism. Stigmas discriminate against and isolate people. No wonder people do not wish to talk about them! If you have a migraine or the flu or break ribs, people are sympathetic. They understand those types of illnesses. But mental illness is another story.

People don't like to talk about what they don't understand or what they feel others will not understand. A person diagnosed with depression, for example, may double their challenges because depression can lead to behaviors that could cause physical health issues. The most well-known health issues are emotional, like feelings of sadness, guilt, or hopelessness. Another common physical aspect of depression is the inability to focus or concentrate on tasks at hand. But this health issue is emotion-based and causes physical illness as well, such as an upset stomach, pain, and fatigue. Pain can be debilitating, but which came first, the pain or the depression? These are things to investigate. People with depression learn to live with this illness or cope as best they can. It is difficult to find professional help, and it shouldn't be that way.

Some people believe seeing a therapist is a luxury. That is the way it seemed to me. When I was looking for a mental health professional, I was quite disappointed. It's not that I couldn't find one; there were other factors playing against me. I was taking a lot of time off work to deal with my physical health. It was difficult to find a therapist in my area who had availability, but when I did find someone, they wouldn't work with my schedule. In my mind, I thought that if I made an appointment and took even more time off from work, I would lose my job. Combine that fear with my depression, and I reached an elevated level of anxiety, fearing that I wasn't going to survive. Would I have lost my job? Most likely not. But this type of mental warfare is what a false belief system creates. What we say in our heads creates our worry and anxiety before there is something to stress about. We need to see the stigma of depression for what it is: a limiting belief. When we can move past the stigma, we can start the necessary conversations for healing.

Part of practicing preventive health care is talking about the issues that plague us. Open discussions about topics such as body image and depression will help stop the stigma attached to them. You are not alone in your struggle, even if you feel that way. For example, people should feel safe discussing feelings of shame related to eating disorders or urinary incontinence. But embarrassment can prevent people from mentioning it to their doctors. Have you ever thought things like "If only I had done something different. I should have changed my behavior sooner. I should have been aware of the signs. If only I had known I was not alone in my struggle. I should have spoken up sooner"? Had you been able to take part in an open dialogue about any experience without feeling humiliation or guilt, do you think the condition of your mental and physical health would be different today? For example, the 22 A Day counseling movement is helping to bring awareness to post-traumatic stress disorder (PTSD) and veteran suicide,[17] but vets still are not speaking up. From now on, preventive care needs to include open dialogue on hard topics.

How do we stop the stigma?

- Talk. Get comfortable talking about mental health... *your* mental health.
- See a doctor. Treat it like any other physical condition. Take time off work, see a doctor, and create a care plan.
- Speak up. If you hear anyone make a stigmatizing remark, state some factual information to educate them.
- Document your transformation. Moon work will help you identify and document how your life became what it is today, whether good or bad. Moon work will also transform you, and journaling will help you document your journey toward wellness.
- Support people. Studies from the National Institutes of Health[18] find that lower-income countries have a higher level of wellness support, and while higher income countries address stigma with good intentions, they fall short of making wellness support programs available to their citizens.
- Express compassion. The restorative activities discussed in the next chapter will influence your life and raise your vibration. With an increased vibrational energy, you will help those around you… even if you don't realize it.

Human Rights

Every human being has an inalienable, fundamental right to discover their authenticity. No one can tell you who you are.

[17] Military Veteran Project, https://www.militaryveteranproject.org/.

[18] H. Stuart. "Reducing the Stigma of Mental Illness," https://www.ncbi.nlm.nih.gov/pmc/articles/PMC5314742/.

You may become familiar with yourself and choose which parts of you to share with others without shame. Having a sense of purpose and engaging your creative center helps you develop your individuality. Correcting the major causes of energetic leaks supports individualism. For instance, when you hold powerful beliefs to the exclusion of all other belief systems, you leave no room for others who believe differently to express their authenticity. You have a responsibility to honor others for their uniqueness, just as you have the right to know your own. Honoring others does not mean we deny our own convictions. We can all coexist.

During the civil rights era, the U.S. Equal Employment Opportunity Commission (EEOC) was established and created Title VII of the Civil Rights Act of 1964, making it illegal to discriminate against someone based on race, color, religion, national origin, or sex. They say an employer cannot discriminate against someone's authenticity. Because countless individuals feared being themselves in the face of discrimination, governments had to create laws to enforce something that derives from natural law. We human beings should protect the rights of individuals to be authentic. Now, our society as a collective has the ability to free people from a millennium of repression. But it is up to each of us to do our part.

The only thing in life we can control is ourselves. We need to use that power to engage in self-exploration and self-discovery to become what is now protected in the United States and other countries: our authentic self. Live your sincere truth through the actions in your day-to-day activities; may they reflect your beliefs through love and understanding. Let us manifest with the moon to become our true selves, so we can be mindful and intentional in creating our lives while supporting others to do the same. As we grow and step into our power, we may wish that our loved ones could enjoy the same benefits of change we are experiencing. From that place of love, we may want them to change. But the only way to influence others in a way that does not create shame or hostility is to live by example. As you grow into your authenticity, that truth may not be the same for others. Let them see that spark in you and be curious, rather than pushing your change onto them. We can only love someone through their storm; we cannot force them to create change in their life.

Let's all live well together and enjoy abundance and good health.

Body Image and Self-Esteem

Our bodies are an outward expression of our subconscious minds. Living in a weight-equals-worth culture has created the notion that body dissatisfaction is normal and that we can fix our bodies. Society needs to treat negative body image as a mental health concern. Our thoughts and feelings on a subconscious level direct both our behavior and how we treat our bodies. Negative thoughts about our bodies can lead to neglect, abuse, and feelings of shame. Normalizing ways people can honor and respect their bodies while celebrating the differences, uniqueness, and individuality of every body will help people appreciate the skin they're in.

The phrase *body image* describes the way we think and feel about our bodies. Our unkind thoughts and words about our bodies lower our self-esteem and create unhealthy relationships between us and our bodies and between us and the food we consume. Negative body image results from comparing our physical selves to unrealistic ideals, which also lowers self-esteem. Low self-esteem creates the subconscious atmosphere for negative self-speak and an unending cycle of striving for perfection. While that struggle is real, "perfect" does not exist. It is subjective, an illusion.

Buying into that illusion is an energetic leak. It does not matter what your ideal body looks like. If you do not feel you measure up to the standards you set for yourself, you may develop unhealthy self-talk, and you may take unhealthy measures to control your weight or change your appearance. Such unhealthy measures include things like disordered eating, which can lead to depression. The term *disordered eating* refers to irregular eating habits that are harmful to the body and a person's self-esteem. A medical diagnosis of an eating disorder is different, but only from the narrow perspective that a doctor has made a diagnosis and established a treatment plan. Disordered eating may include signs and symptoms like:

- Dieting frequently
- Feeling anxiety around certain foods or food groups
- Skipping meals
- Eating extra meals/snacks in secret
- Engaging in rigid meal and exercise routines
- Being unable to control food intake or recognize when you are full
- Being so preoccupied with body image that it affects your daily life
- Counteracting the consumption of "bad food," such as a slice of pie, with exercise, food restrictions, or fasting or purging
- Using pills, including herbal/natural supplements, and laxatives to lose weight

Some people rationalize their behavior and do not recognize that their poor wellness and eating habits have become chronic. Causing harm to your body may be a symptom of mental or emotional stress that is caused by false, limiting beliefs that live in your shadows.

You cannot outrun your shadows. Karma can come swiftly, but it often takes time, as do the effects of mistreating, neglecting, and abusing our bodies. Everything you put in your body causes chemical and biological reactions. If we mistreat our bodies, there will be consequences. It is amazing how, when we do not practice self-care, our bodies withstand so much abuse and neglect. One day, our bodies will hold us accountable for our neglect. The accountability or karma for being irresponsible with our bodies sometimes arrives as excess weight or dis-ease. Sometimes, the damage done is too excessive for physical healing. Our bodies always speak to us, supplying us with valuable information that's necessary for wellness. If you do not take its message seriously, you will continue experiencing challenges in your life.

The circumstances of a person's disordered eating are as unique as their story. Therefore, everyone cannot address challenges with body dissatisfaction and unhealthy relationships with food in the same way. Two people standing next to each other can share an experience, but the emotions each person attaches to the experience and how they process it will be different. Every life experience up to that point creates a reaction. For example, if two people experienced religion differently in their past, they will not respond to a shared religious experience in the present moment the same way. Say two best friends in junior high school, Mary and Sally, go to Bible study every Wednesday evening. Mary dresses to hide her body, and her parents do not let her date. Sally dresses in the current fashion for her age, and her parents are not as strict. During their senior year of high school, Sally becomes pregnant. At one Bible study meeting, the sermon is on premarital sex. Sally's takeaway is that she has committed a sin and is now unworthy in the eyes of God.

Religious shaming generated a subconscious message that made Sally think, *If someone looks at me disrespectfully, it is my fault*, and *My decision branded me unworthy of love.* These young girls' Bible study group may have taught them a lot of things, but it did not teach them to respect their bodies. Instead, they continued to struggle with the body image belief systems their society imposed on them. Religion should advocate for mental and emotional wellness, self-respect, love, and compassion. As it is, it does not address many false, limiting beliefs about our bodies, leaving vulnerable young women like Sally and Mary to struggle with their body images alone and without help from their church or spiritual community.

Since our bodies are an outward expression of our subconscious minds, any type of negative body image can lead to mental and physical health conditions. Negative body image affects women and men, girls and boys. If we promote mental and emotional health in our young people, they will grow into adults who are confident in who they are, what they want, and what they stand for. They will make choices that honor and respect their bodies. By learning to love and accept yourself, you'll unleash your authentic self. When you are standing in your truth, you will feel comfortable in any place or situation.

Exercise – Do I Love Myself?

Exploring your thoughts about your body can expose some of your false, limiting beliefs and provide insight into the ways you neglect or abuse yourself. Everyone should discover the opinions they have about their bodies.

Take out your journal and use one or more of the following prompts to help you uncover ways you can heal your negative body image and low self-esteem. The goal is to learn how to love yourself!

Whether you believe you struggle with negative body image or not, begin your journey of Wild Moon Healing with a simple question or journaling prompt.

- I hate my body because…
- When I look in the mirror, I see…
- The things I like about my appearance are (make a list)…

- The things I appreciate about my body unrelated to appearance are…
- Experiences that make me feel good about myself are…
- My best quality is…
- When I think of food, I…
- My experience of clothes shopping is…

Draw a picture in your journal of what you think others see when they look at you, if you cannot find the words.

This type of questioning will help you discover how you limit yourself in your body image struggle and start you on your journey toward self-love and self-acceptance. The answers must be honest and transparent, and the questions may not be as simple as they appear.

If you have difficulty, start the process with fact-gathering questions, such as:

- How often do I weigh myself?
- How does the number reflected on the scale make me feel?
- What kind of self-care habits do I engage in?
- What feelings come up when I look in the mirror?
- What positive and negative things am I doing to change my body?

My Story – Living with Depression

On my personal journey, I learned that addressing my mental and emotional wellness was the key to my overall health. Writing about my depression is difficult because the words elude me. My family has a history of depression. My mom was one of the two-thirds of people with depression who do not seek proper treatment. She was never able to crawl out of that dark hole, and it broke my heart. When you are depressed, you feel trapped, unable to move forward with life. From my perspective, Mom did nothing to better herself, change, experience new things, or complete her education. She had hobbies she loved, but she did those activities alone and rarely socialized.

I observed her experience through the years and identified her symptoms, but I did not see them in myself until I was to the point of crying for (what seemed like) no reason. So, what makes my story different from my mom's? How is it that I was able to climb out of that dark hole when she could not? The answer is not just that I wanted to feel different (I am sure Mom wanted to feel different, too), but our experiences of depression were different. I took inspired action, searching for ways to create a unique life experience and find answers for myself. Had I kept doing the same thing and thinking the same way, nothing would have changed.

I went through all the "normal" procedures. I saw my doctor, received a prescription, and searched for a mental health provider. Wild Moon Healing was born because of the lack of excellent physicians who could treat emotional issues. My quest to find happiness created an arsenal of what seemed to me at the time to be unorthodox approaches to wellness. How could writing help my depression and the physical issues caused by it? But journaling has provided me with so many insights, and I realized that when I connected to the information I was writing, I felt better. Over time, I realized that the new feeling became my baseline emotion. Every breakthrough I experience elevates my energy even more. So, how do I put that experience with depression into words?

The best way I came up with to tell my story of my depression and figure out how to "fix" myself was to journal and describe my life through a sort of timeline, starting with a few years prior to my diagnosis of depression. I could have gone back farther, but this part of my life paints a telling image. While journaling,

I did a "data dump" from my mind straight onto paper. This type of journaling removes emotions and encourages you to simply list factual events of your past.

Exercise – Timeline Journaling

Even if you are not depressed, take the time to journal about the factual events of the last five years. The information you uncover when you look at your life from the perspective of "This is me today. How did I get here?" is valuable when you are unearthing false beliefs and energetic leaks in your life.

Timeline journaling is the simplest form of journaling. There is no emotion involved. It is a data dump of actual life events, and they don't need to be in chronological order. List events related to your work, family, school, hobbies, etc. Detail all the things going on in your life, resolved or active. Remember, list everything you have been through. Include your achievements. We must celebrate our successes, but as you have discovered on this journey called life, for every success, there is sacrifice along the way.

Journaling is an outlet to help you uncover, process, and understand your thoughts and feelings. Even if your journal is only comprised of notes, bullet points, lists, or pictures you have drawn, over time you will make connections of how your emotions, behavioral patterns, and experiences are linked to and affect you in the present moment. Putting ink on paper instead of using an electronic or voice-recording device helps coordinate your left and right brain activities, leading to richer content. Our ego minds complicate things through judgment and overthinking, so try your best to describe your life experiences without judgment.

Here are some prompts to help get you started. Over the last five years:

- What have I been doing?
- What changes has my family encountered?
- What challenges have I faced?
- What type of schedule have I kept?
- What did I accomplish?
- How have I improved myself? Have I engaged in a new hobby, gone back to school, etc.?
- How have I surprised myself?
- How do I spend the majority of my time?
- How have I let myself down?
- Have I lost anyone or any pets?
- Have I changed jobs?
- Have there been any recent additions to my family, including fur babies?
- Have I visited any interesting places or tried new things?

After reading all the things I had written in my journal, I concluded that my life before my depression diagnosis was stressful. Between my job and graduate school, it was like I was working two full-time jobs. My life before the diagnosis was also lacking in self-care. Everything I ate during the three years of graduate school was takeout, so I could keep pressing on with my to-do lists. I rarely socialized, but when I did, I drank too much. I quit smoking, which was a good thing, but between stress and no self-care, quitting aided in me gaining a significant amount of weight over a brief period.

The stress I put on myself in striving for a perfect GPA, not to mention being the mother of a deployed Marine, created a unique anxiety. I became sedentary, sitting behind a computer for both work and school. After amassing school debt, I realized I needed a career change. I was unhappy with what I was doing with my life. Even when I learned about a tragic military accident hours before the news reported it, I did not call anyone. I sat on my couch, crying and staring at my phone, waiting to hear from my son. I knew that if I'd called anyone or asked a friend to come over, they would have said rational things like "He's fine. He will call soon." In the end, I learned that the Osprey my son was in had landed, and he was a first responder on the scene of the accident.

No one who is depressed wants to hear positivity when the possibility of the worst news of their life is looming; that's how the depressed mind works. A rational mind would want comfort and support when something bad is going on in someone's life. A depressed mind cannot see past the worst-case scenario, and it wants to be in this dark place alone.

Before my diagnosis, I experienced the fear and heartache that every military mother experiences, and I also lost our family pet, Sox, our beloved cat of over eighteen years. These experiences are related because when I lost Sox, I was alone for the first time in my adult life. I'd had my son when I was quite young, and I never had the time to learn who I was, what I liked, or what I wanted to do with my life. So, being alone with not even a pet to care for, no fulfilling pastime to fill my days, a master's degree I did not celebrate completing, and no idea how to figure out how to change my life and improve my emotional issues all left me feeling intensely lonely.

In chapter 4, I discussed energetic leaks and how certain actions and behaviors affect our mental and physical health. And here, I've identified my major energetic leaks: stress, anxiety, overworking, lack of self-care, loneliness, not socializing enough, poor eating habits, and physical inactivity. Add in the external, out-of-my-control stressful events of being a military mom, losing our family pet, my mother's failing health, a family history of depression, plus the physical symptoms of dis-ease I was experiencing, and no one should be surprised that depression became an issue for me.

Before I was diagnosed with depression, I often could not think of a reason to get out of bed on the weekends. I never missed work. The intense loneliness of not having anything to do or anyone to do it with kept me in bed a lot, but it did not come on suddenly, nor did my major health issues. My body was talking to me way before my doctor diagnosed me with depression. I realized my doctors were treating the physical symptoms of illnesses I created because of my lifestyle. I had to take responsibility for everything—what I ate and drank, my thoughts, the time I spent watching TV instead of being active. The entire state of my life was because of the decisions I had made.

Even my good choices, like going to graduate school, affected me. The stress of schoolwork is one thing, but I put high expectations on myself to prove (to myself) that I could excel in academia. One semester, I had an issue with my professor, and I felt he should have apologized to me. Since he did not, it took a long time for me to get him out of my head and refocus on schoolwork. I wasted six weeks of a twelve-week course brooding over being accused of plagiarism, which ultimately I proved I was not guilty of.

A sidenote on expecting a human being to do the correct thing: In my case, I expected my professor to apologize, and he did not. Realize that no one owes you anything, ever, no matter what the circumstance. The time you waste seeking closure or being upset because a person did not apologize to you is time out of your life that you will never get back, and that is your fault. When you choose to move on for yourself, life will become better. You cannot control anyone but yourself.

One of my "ah-ha" moments was realizing that "wait equals weight." Any time I spent waiting on a person (physically or figuratively) to do what I considered to be correct led to my binge-eating disorder. Waiting tells me that I am unimportant, that I do not matter. These false, limiting beliefs created a negative self-image and contributed greatly to my depression. In my life, I often use food to feel better, but food only fed my negative feelings and created a lifelong unhealthy relationship with it in the form of an eating disorder.

My professor was not the first person to make me feel insignificant. My family members have been guilty of this as well. For example, my sister has a loose concept of time. She is often late for meetings and gatherings and is unapologetic whether she is five minutes or five hours late. Having no regard for time conveys an energetic message to the people waiting for you: they are not important; they can wait. I remember the day and hour that my unhealthy relationship with food turned into a full-blown eating disorder, although I didn't know it at the time. Not knowing my truth or recognizing my need to feel important to my sister, whose actions reinforced time and time again that I was unimportant, caused me to hit a breaking point. This incident was different; the outcome hurt, and I tried to eat my feelings away. This time, though, I was not waiting on my sister by looking at a clock.

Just like in the situation with my professor, I was waiting for my sister to do the *right* thing. I know what it feels like to not be considered, because I felt that I was unimportant to someone whom I wish cared more about me. This time, I witnessed my sister treating her three-year-old son in the same way, in a dangerous situation, and I became short-tempered. My internal conflict caused me to explode as I witnessed my nephew crying in the hallway, hungry and listening to his mother and her boyfriend argue. The message I received was that my nephew was not important. It was not my business to intrude, so I waited for my sister to act in a way that showed my nephew he did in fact matter. She didn't, and I could not take witnessing my nephew's basic needs being ignored, so I reacted instead of responding.

A verbal altercation turned into a physical one. In the end, I helped no one. My sister married a verbally abusive narcissist with an addiction issue, and her son paid the price. They are both out of that situation now, and I love them dearly, but I want you to focus on me in this story. Remember, Wild Moon Healing is all about you, not the story or other people. My reaction did not express healthy boundaries or values, communicate my needs, or positively (or safely) resolve the situation. I did not realize this at the time, but my false belief that I was unimportant drove my actions. And the same out-of-control, mindless behavior that drove my actions created my binge eating.

Looking at my life up to the time of my depression diagnosis, binge eating was my companion; it was always there for me. All in the same month, my professor accused me of plagiarism, my son was deployed, and I lost Sox. In the three months that followed, I binged more than ever. I gained eighty pounds. I needed to gain control. My life was at stake. Several years into my healing journey, I had another "waiting" experience with my sister as we traveled together for a family event. With no regard for anyone else's time, she spent hours getting ready. Since we were traveling in the same vehicle, I was trapped. Eventually, we began our day and did the things we'd planned. However, as we were making our way home, I wanted to do one more thing. I asked her to call our uncle so we could stop and see him since his house was on our way. She said, "I really don't think we have enough time for that." My entire demeanor changed in an instant, because I'd sat for hours that morning as she found enough time for herself. But I did what I always did then: I internalized it.

That night, while driving through the mountains, I saw the most beautiful moon I'd ever seen. That legendary harvest moon was also a super moon, and that night, it seemed so close I thought I could touch it. Its beauty calmed me. However, when I got home, I binged. Only this time, I'd been on my healing journey for several years, and the energy of that beautiful moon made this bingeing episode significant.

My healing journey had changed me more than I'd realized. As I binged on my feelings, I was aware of my behavior and my trigger. Although I was aware of my bingeing, I couldn't stop. That was when my huge "wait equals weight" breakthrough happened. My brain finally connected how waiting (literally and figuratively) on people was a trigger for me. I was able to identify that I felt unimportant and insignificant. My awareness of my actions did not mean I magically stopped bingeing. However, my awareness helped me reduce the duration of that episode purposefully and mindfully by engaging in restorative activities that got me out of my head and back into life.

I've used all the reflective journaling techniques in this book to heal. With timeline journaling, I was able to see how the three years I spent in graduate school were so focused on one thing—graduating—that I disregarded myself as a human being because of it. I neglected my self-care physically, mentally, emotionally, and spiritually. I was hypervigilant about going after a goal that had nothing to do with my core values, and I was pursuing an unfulfilling career that was not relevant to my life purpose. When you are chasing your purpose, you tend to take better care of yourself and the things you value in life—or so I have discovered. I forgive myself for feeling angry and upset during triggering events, for not seeing that I was depressed, and for having no awareness of my false, limiting belief system.

I knew I was losing control, but I wasn't aware that self-loathing from the false perspective of feeling unimportant was the source of the problem. I'd had an unhealthy relationship with food since adolescence. I'd lost my brother when I was thirteen, and since then, I'd felt unimportant to family members. My birthday was forgotten that year (two weeks after losing my brother), and as a result, I came to falsely believe that I played an insignificant role in my family. Even though my rational mind knows that to be untrue, the thought is still there in my subconscious, and it resurfaces when I think about my forgotten birthday. But was that moment in time when my unhealthy relationship with food began? While I saw and acknowledged how my mother used food to cope with her emotions, I could not see how or when the same behavior started with me.

Considering the stressors in my life while I was in graduate school, it makes sense now that I lost control of my ability to choose what and how much to eat. When you mistreat your body so badly that it shuts down (in my case, in a matter of months), it exacerbates an already unstable health issue. The false belief system that made me mistreat myself was created from a message I received time and time again in my life. The false messages we subconsciously think about keep showing up in our lives because our reality is created from what we think of most. We attract new experiences that reinforce these messages again and again. The limiting beliefs become strongly held and cause havoc in our lives. So, unlearn your unhealthy belief systems, relearn new ones that serve you by doing Moon work, and start attracting positive experiences. Timeline journaling is a solid, uncomplicated way to do just that.

The difficulty with timeline journaling is that you must analyze the data dump of what happened in your life and take responsibility for your actions, even if you lose control like I did with binge eating. I needed to acknowledge that I alone am responsible for the state of my physical and mental health. Back then, I let outside influences set the trajectory of my life. To reach the conclusion that I am responsible for my own weight, I had to be transparent with myself and accountable for my depression and the life I created with my belief systems, habits, actions, behaviors, and thoughts.

I believe most cases of depression are like diabetes. While type 1 diabetes is genetic, people can often avoid or manage type 2 diabetes by making healthy decisions about their diet and physical activity. As with type 2 diabetes, most cases of depression are from lifestyle and personal choices. If you take steps to return to a life of healthy physical and mental activity when you are depressed, you can change your life.

My lifestyle and personal choices created the perfect Category 5 storm. Because of my personal decisions, actions, thoughts, and behaviors, my life came to a screeching halt. I realized that because I was attempting to create change from a negative place, it never worked out. Negative energy only creates more negative energy. When you manifest with the moon, however, you learn how to shift your energy by incorporating restorative activities into your life.

Everyone experiences negative emotions, and all emotions are valid. We will and should experience them all at one point or another. If you fake too much positivity, or if your friends and family tell you not to feel *that way*, a false belief could arise, telling you that your feelings are not valid. Negative emotions do not go away if you ignore your feelings. Earlier, I discussed unclear boundaries, where a person says yes to everything in order to people-please, often to the detriment of their own health and well-being. Anyone with depression does the opposite. We say no often. I would decline offers to do things, or when I accepted, I'd back out later. We want to be active with friends and family, but our subconscious program keeps us stuck. Talking about depression is important. Speaking up and establishing healthy boundaries with yourself and others helps you engage in life the way you want to.

Exercise – Honesty

You did splendid work in your timeline journal, but now you must look inward. Whether or not you suffer from depression, take an honest look at your life, decisions, actions, and reactions. To heal in the present, you need insight into your past. What energetic leaks were you experiencing prior to your negative experience, depression diagnosis, job loss, or failing marriage? By looking at your timeline journal, can you see where you created your own challenges? If you experienced events that were outside of your control, how did you react? Your reaction can provide valuable insight into your current life. Reactions always tell us about the false beliefs that limit us, and they expose any energetic leaks we may be experiencing. These insights are key factors in revealing what you need to surrender.

To surrender, you must first feel and experience the emotion you assigned to your life event, then forgive yourself for every decision you made from this dark place so you can let it go and make room for positive things in your life. Through journaling, you will start a conversation with yourself and your feelings (depression, grief, or another emotion), and you will see where it goes. Allowing feelings to surface can be hard, so be prepared to reach out for support if you need it. Use the following journaling prompts to be honest with yourself. If words don't come to you, that's OK. Keep doing restorative exercises, and your body will tell you when it is time to return to this exercise.

Complete a three-to-five-minute breathing meditation to honor your body and see where your mind wanders, then read the statements below aloud. What comes up for you? These statements are intended to help you take responsibility for your life and lovingly accept the parts of you, including your actions and false beliefs, that play a role in your situation. You have to accept the part you played in order to forgive yourself. Surrender it all so you can create space to heal and move on.

- I forgive myself for not taking better care of myself.

- I forgive myself for not knowing how or being able to talk about…
- I forgive myself for…
- I forgive depression (or grief, regret, etc.) for…

There is no shame in seeking professional help to assist you with your difficult emotional circumstances or taking a prescription medication to treat mental health issues. Seeking and accepting help is empowering and could be the cornerstone of living a life free of depression and emotional chaos.

7

RESTORATIVE WORK

Restorative Theory

As you have seen, healing with the moon involves emotional and inner child work (i.e., restorative work). It is about bringing unconscious blocks to your conscious mind so you can surrender them. This is how you heal, grow, and achieve the life of your dreams. I break healing down into four parts that work in tandem with the lunar cycle:

- Under the new moon, you learn to understand yourself and figure out what you want and why you want it.
- Inspired action is the theme of the waxing moon, providing you with an opportunity to analyze why things did or did not work out and how you react in certain situations and around certain people.
- The full moon supports the emotional revelations you should honor to encourage healing.

- The waning moon provides the perfect time for reflection and surrender before you start the cycle over again.

Be gentle but honest with yourself. Honesty is the best (and only) approach to learning things about yourself that hold you back. Be easy on yourself, but stand accountable. Own the state of your life so you can create change. It is difficult to acknowledge that we create our own challenges, but that is part of becoming responsible for your life. To experience healing and growth, you must ask yourself thought-provoking questions. As you learn more about yourself, your energy, and your thoughts and feelings, you can relax, knowing that this process works.

Restorative thoughts speak to your mind from your heart. Think, for example, about the ripples a pebble creates after it's tossed into a pond. Every thought you have, every word you say, and every action you take has some effect on your life and environment, and the effect goes beyond what you can visually see. Energy connects all things, and the ripples we create are comprised of both positive and negative energy. We all leave our personal imprint on the world.

We are filled with energetic ripples from our ancestors and all those who were here before us (the collective energy). We cannot imagine the magnitude of the impact our ripples will have. Discover and maintain your authenticity. Keep growing through inspired actions to ensure you are leaving only positive ripples in the world. From time to time, we all have issues with keeping a schedule, backsliding on our commitments, procrastinating, or going back to old habits that hinder our Moon work progress. Be aware that you can stifle your process by thinking negative thoughts about your behaviors and missteps in your progress, even if you are not aware of these thoughts. For example, if you have emotional reactions associated with things, circumstances, or people, can you link them to your negative thought patterns? Elevate your thinking to see and create goodness all around you. The more you change your thoughts to positive ones, the more your positive energy will create love in your life and in the world.

Your reality grows out of what you think of most. Unhelpful thought patterns differ in subtle ways, but they all involve distortions of reality and irrational ways of looking at situations and people. Our conscious minds may be busy building a shelter for safety, only to become our personal prisons. For example, protective thoughts may be necessary during a specific experience, like a physical injury or the death of a loved one, but hanging on to these thoughts can create limiting beliefs that no longer serve you beyond the current circumstance. Limiting beliefs can develop from things like fear, guilt, grief, prejudice, social anxiety, or others' expectations and judgment. Such limiting beliefs can make you a victim and create negative habits that stifle your energy and your forward movement. If you hold on to them, they will affect your current life.

If you want to see progress in your journey toward wholeness, you must put in consistent work. Remember, you are restructuring your thoughts both mentally and emotionally, so you need time to experience things and develop understanding. But with practice, positive and rational thoughts will come to you effortlessly. You will experience synchronicities, and positive things will manifest in your life. The more restorative activities you engage in, the more you will experience growth and the more often you will attain your goals.

Restorative Activities

Whether you are practicing preventive care or restorative therapy, healthful activities will affect your life and improve your overall health. Wild Moon Healers relate mental and physical health to one another in ways many people do not understand. Change starts with you, so manifest the healthiest version of you by taking care of yourself and making your well-being a priority. As your vibration increases, you will feel better, and therefore, attract better. You will attract people who love, accept, and respect you. Experiences that stimulate you and make you feel good will start showing up in your life.

When you struggle through barriers while working on your intentions, you are vibrating at a low frequency. By being honest with yourself, you will discover where your negativity, false and limiting beliefs, or energetic leaks come from. You'll know what things you do, thoughts you have, or people you have in your life that are not healthy for you. Restorative activities will enable you to release these lower-vibrational elements, and that will increase your vibrational frequency.

Because you and the world around you are always changing, restorative measures should become lifelong habits. Energy is always shifting. Therefore, you should adjust your restorative activities to match your energy. Think of restorative activities as an arsenal in your toolbox. Not every tool will work for you in every situation. Some tools might work at first, but then you may need to switch things up, permitting your conscious mind to explore the deeper meanings of your thoughts, actions, and behaviors.

Restorative measures are a continuous educational approach to healing. You should never stop learning. You'll keep growing in life by learning more about yourself and others. Therefore, restorative activities are inspired actions you should incorporate into your daily activities. Inspired action comes from a place of excitement and involves activities that are aligned with your truth, your authentic self.

In the following pages are some examples of ways we can restore, nourish, and cultivate a higher level of energetic frequency.

Restore the Physical Body

Healthy Eating Habits

Everything has energy, including the food you eat. When your doctor tells you to "eat the rainbow," he or she wants you to eat a wide variety of fruits and vegetables that contain the vitamins and minerals your body needs. When your diet is comprised of whole, colorful, fresh foods, you are engaging your energy to match the high vibration of the foods you eat. A balanced diet supports your body in becoming energetically balanced.

What part of your body also has the colors of the rainbow? Your chakra system. This energetic infrastructure supports our mental, emotional, and spiritual well-being. We associate each chakra with physical qualities and emotions that express themselves in diverse ways, depending on the vibrational level of your energy and how it flows.

One way to support your physical and emotional well-being is to eat a healthy, balanced diet. Eating Standard American Diet (SAD) foods like processed meats, prepackaged foods, fast food, fried food, soft drinks, and red meat and a diet high in sugar, refined carbs, or saturated and trans fats is a primary cause of obesity and type 2 diabetes. Consuming a SAD diet is a sign you have an energetic leak. It could also be a sign of depression. Why? Because you're most likely always on the go, too busy to grocery shop or cook. This is a clue that you might not be making time for self-care.

Mindful eating is a fitting example of how you can use mindfulness in your life to support healthy habits. This form of eating helps satiate you with less food, and it inspires healthful food choices. A component of mindful eating is meal planning, which is a great self-care practice that supports you in eating intuitively and enjoying mealtime. Meal prepping is a perfect mindful exercise that encourages healthy eating habits. It involves dedicating time to think about the food you eat well before hunger strikes. When you shop, choose high-vibrational whole foods, like fruits and vegetables, to elevate your body's energy. Mindful, intuitive eating promotes compassion and trust of self because you will choose foods that support your body.

Mindful eating can free you from an unhealthy relationship with food, helping to correct disordered eating patterns. It eliminates external and internal distractions. Distracted eating results in overeating and weight gain. People who consume a low-vibrational, non-nutritious diet or go on frequent yo-yo diets often have excessive exercise habits, use meal replacements over proper food, and have disordered eating traits and a negative body image. Our vibrational energy equates to our level of self-esteem. To boost your self-esteem and heal from your negative body image, apply a mindfulness practice to develop healthy eating habits and a positive relationship with food.

Physical Activity

Physical activity is any movement that uses your muscles and requires an expenditure of energy. To move your energy, you need to move your body. Movement affects chi, our physical and spiritual potential energy. If you do not move, your chi will become deficient. Inactive lifestyles cause chronic illnesses and even sleep issues that can keep you immobile. Like attracts like, so physical movement attracts and promotes energetic flow.

Inactivity increases early mortality from physical issues, such as cardiovascular disease or diabetes. The mindless activity of moving less and sitting more lessens your awareness of your body. Just standing up, going for a walk, taking the stairs, cleaning the house, or planting a garden can help you engage your self-awareness. Engaging in these simple activities can lead to the habit of regular exercise or movement, which is the best thing you can do for your overall health and energy restoration.

A sedentary lifestyle appears to use little energy, so in theory you should have plenty of energy in your reserves, right? Wrong. Too much physical stillness slows bowel function and weakens joints, among many other things. This damage, caused by doing nothing, uses your energy reserves to repair it. To someone experiencing chronic pain and physical mobility issues resulting from a sedentary lifestyle, saying that you should "move more" may sound like an energetic leak. But that chronic pain is karma from a lack of self-care. Your body can only do so much on its own. Push through the pain, because physical activity keeps your energy flowing in your body. As a person with chronic pain and mobility issues, I've learned to do what I can. It is better than doing nothing at all. It helps remove blockages where your energy may be stagnant and helps you move beyond feeling stuck in life.

The best physical activity to manifest with the moon is yoga or Qigong. The practice of moving into stillness allows you to experience the truth of who you are, create awareness of your physical body, and become more balanced and centered. Yoga can decrease your blood pressure and resting heart rate, decrease pain, and increase your immune system function. For those with mobility issues, ask your doctor about chair yoga as a possible activity for you. Each pose builds self-awareness because you are moving mindfully, and when you hold the positions, you notice what your body is telling you.

Supplementation

Optimal cognitive function helps you regulate mental health and achieve a state of wellness. Supplementation can balance neurochemicals, like dopamine and serotonin, to create and sustain happiness and well-being in the body. When there is a compromised command center and the body cannot sustain hormonal and chemical balance, supplements can help maintain ideal levels of neurochemicals.

Good nutrition, digestive health, hydration, and time spent in nature increase cognitive performance. Focusing on restorative activities, like healthy eating habits and increased water intake and outdoor recreation, can help improve nutrient absorption and your body's ability to build neurotransmitters, the chemical messengers of the brain. The transmitted messages are human feelings, thoughts, and actions—even consciousness itself.

When these messages are not balanced, stress, anxiety, and depression can spike, especially during the holidays and the darkness of winter months, when vitamin D levels decrease from lack of sun exposure. The end of daylight savings time in the fall means people wake up in the dark and go home after work in the dark. Too much darkness enables mindless behavior, including mindless eating. Besides supplementation during these months of the year, a sunlamp can positively affect mood. Talk to your doctor about supplementation and what might be best for you.

Practice Self-Care

Self-management involves you focusing on your role as a practitioner of your own health. The most significant tool in achieving good health is self-care. This is when you prioritize your health and physical, mental, and emotional well-being. You take responsibility for supporting good health, preventing disease, or coping with an illness. Self-care is about intentional, proactive care for your physical, social, mental, emotional, and spiritual well-being. To achieve balance, though, you must evaluate and work on all the categories of well-being:

- For your physical health, you need to get enough sleep, eat a healthy diet, and exercise.
- Social health is about spending quality time with friends and family.
- Mental health means suspending self-judgment and practicing compassion for yourself, while challenging your mind by learning new things, reading books, or completing a puzzle.
- Spiritual health is about praying or connecting to Source and doing things to develop a deeper sense of connection.

- Emotional health is about finding healthy outlets to process your emotions, like talking with a friend.
- Intellectual health is about engaging your brain and finding new ways to expand your personal knowledge and skills.
- Environmental health is about achieving satisfaction through inspiring, supportive, and encouraging surroundings.
- Vocational health is about having personal satisfaction with your occupation.
- Financial health occurs when your current and future financial situation brings you satisfaction.

A cyclical approach to well-being is necessary, because you cannot work on everything all the time without jeopardizing your health. Wild Moon Healing helps you create a cyclical practice so you can check in with yourself, practice self-care, and evaluate your well-being in these categories all month, every month. Achieving a state of wellness means you can cope with life's difficulties, maintain emotional awareness, and engage in a healthy relationship with yourself and others. Reaching a state of wellness is how you cultivate positive feelings in your life. We express emotional wellness as confidence, emotional and behavioral control, responding versus reacting, and resilience.

Do not mistake self-care for vanity or selfishness; it is neither of those things. Any healing practice starts with the soul, and every soul should engage in self-care. Let nothing get in your way. You are worthy of happiness.

Restore the Mind

Be Present

Practice being present. If your mind is rooted in the here and now, an event from yesterday or even seven years ago (a fear-based reaction) cannot affect you. Likewise, a potential future event (an anxiety-based reaction) cannot affect you. Those types of thoughts are not real, because they do not take place in the present moment.

Fear and anxiety prevent you from living in the present and experiencing the wonderful things that are right in front of you. Being present when you do emotional journaling allows you to focus on your reaction and explore why you reacted to a situation the way you did. When you are present, you become aware and accountable for your emotions and actions, making you able to control them better in the future.

In the present moment, you can see things for what they are, but do you always grasp the poetic sense of it all? For example, say you are on a road trip when the rain finally stops. You decide to take a break and stretch your legs in a cornfield. If you are in a present state of mind, you might notice the music created as the wind blows the corn tassels, how the sun's rays glisten as they bounce off the raindrops falling from the leaves, and how the stalks bow after a hard rain as if to say, "Thank you for the nourishment." But if your mind is a million miles away, you will miss all that beauty.

Thought Stopping

Your thoughts are powerful, so you need to monitor them to make sure you are using your energy in useful ways. By practicing mindfulness, you'll gain awareness of not only physical sensations but also your thoughts, feelings, and emotions. There is a natural rhythm to the process. Something happens in your body. You feel a twinge and think, "I shouldn't eat that because I'm fat." You acknowledge it without judgment. However, looking for negative thoughts or behaviors in order to correct them will keep you focused on negative things, and as a result, create the potential for more negative thoughts or behaviors.

This purposeful expedition to seek, find, and correct any negative thoughts or behaviors so you can rid yourself of them is called "thought stopping." This is the opposite of being mindful, and therefore, it is an unproductive activity. The intent is noble, but remember, your reality grows from what you think of most. Concentrating on everything you want to change in your life is not inspiring, so the actions you take from this mindset will keep you where you are. Instead, think about what and where you want to be rather than what and where you no longer want to be. To progress toward your goals, you need to not only keep your eye on the prize, but embrace the feelings you want to have when you get there. Thought stopping only embraces the past and the negative.

Personal Development

Personal development is another restorative activity that encourages mindfulness. This does not have to involve formal education, but it can. There is a free blog, podcast, book, or YouTube channel for whatever you want to work on in your life or learn to do. To help maintain positive energetic flow and release any fears you may have, be sure to turn your learning and research into inspired action. Procrastination, or the lack of inspired action, comes from false, limiting beliefs, such as "I do not know enough," "I will not be good at it," or "It is too hard." Sheer curiosity can lead to amazing personal growth. Find something that excites you and learn about it, then incorporate what you learned into your daily life.

Inspired action should not feel like work, so if something excites you, learning about it is a fantastic way to develop passion for yourself and motivation for your life. Always recognize yourself for showing up. Take pride in what you do. The universe always meets your efforts halfway, helping you move closer to your goal.

Get Outside

There is no better way to get to know yourself than by connecting with nature. Being in nature has its own magic and healing powers. The sun is the best source of vitamin D, which your body needs for optimal health. Spending time in nature boosts physical, spiritual, mental, and emotional health, helps you stay grounded, and cultivates a sense of inner peace.

Being mindful and present removes barriers so you can enjoy the moment. Stop, take a deep breath, and let your surroundings fill you. It is not just about getting fresh air, though. It is about experiencing nature to enhance your well-being. Outdoor adventures improve cardiovascular and muscular health as well as enhance coordination, confidence, and concentration.

Reconnecting with Mother Nature enriches your life by increasing your environmental awareness and respect for nature and by improving your understanding of the relationship between people and the environment. Being in outdoor settings can force you to limit your tech time as well. It encourages curiosity, adventure, and exploration, and you'll likely discover unusual places. You can disconnect from your normal obligations and stress and reconnect with nature and people. With growing obligations in life, adults can lose curiosity and their sense of fun. By connecting with nature, you'll regain a natural curiosity and a passion for learning.

Active Meditation

Meditating while in motion is about connecting, being present, and engaging in daily activities. You notice what is going on in your body as you perform a task. This practice can add zen to your busy day. Examples are preparing food, cleaning, and showering. You are present and notice how the activity affects you. This is a great practice for those who have a hard time with stillness and those with chronic pain or mobility issues, where sitting for prolonged periods is difficult. Use all your senses, and don't focus on the task, rather the energy it brings.

Using the example of a meditative shower to start your day, notice how the water caresses your skin and the smell of your shampoo. Listen to the sound of the water and notice how it makes you feel. To energetically use this practice, visualize the water carrying all your worries and burdens away and watch them go down the drain.

Exercise – Walking Meditation

A great exercise that combines nature, mindfulness, and meditation is a walking meditation. Ideally, you will want to be outside barefoot. In cold climates or during the winter months, this may be harder to accomplish, so you can do this inside when you must. As with all meditation, you want to experience an awareness of your body, mind, and breath to help you relax. With walking meditation, you'll bring your awareness back to your footsteps instead of your breath when your mind wanders.

In a setting of convenience or your choosing (grass, sand, etc.), stand tall and imagine a path in front of you. Start walking the path slowly. Focus on the sensations in your feet with each step. One step at a time… stretch through your toes as you push off from the ground. Lift one foot, move it forward in the air, place your heel on the ground, and apply weight as you stretch the toes on the opposite foot.

This practice is not meant to be strenuous; it is relaxing. Find a pace that works best for you to connect to your body and mind, not to achieve a good workout. By pace,

I mean, you should breathe in through your nose for two steps, out through your mouth for three steps. Breathe, heel, toe… Breathe, heel, toe… whatever works for you to find a rhythm between your body and mind.

Be aware of the sensations in your body. Is there any pain in your shoulders, knees, or hips? Are you walking correctly? Are your emotions causing you to walk faster than you should? Find your rhythm. Walk as long as you need to without losing your breath or straining.

☪

Restore the Emotional Self

Affirmations

Affirmations are positive "I AM" statements that are spoken aloud with the intention of inspiring and motivating the conscious and subconscious minds. Using affirmations helps us address challenges and overcome self-sabotaging and negative thoughts. Repetition of positive declarations strengthens self-worth. When you repeat encouraging sentiments to yourself, your brain detects your thoughts as a reward, so your nervous system releases the happy hormone, dopamine, into your system.

Your thoughts direct your actions, and positive thoughts will win in this scenario. Anyone can say positive affirmations, but if they think the activity is stupid and will not work, it won't.

Exercise – Creating Affirmations

Affirmations are words, and words have meaning. The meaning you assign to words affects your energetic vibration.

Affirmations are positive declarations that can help you release the surface-level false, limiting beliefs you hold in your subconscious mind. For an affirmation to work for you, you first need to believe it is true or possible. Then, you must commit to repeating the statement. Remember, repetition adds power to this exercise. The more you say an affirmation, the deeper your belief in the statement grows.

Practicing affirmations can engage your creative center, and connecting with your innate creativity can positively affect your subconscious mind.

Write your affirmations so they have significance in your efforts to work toward your goal. Your affirmations should:

- focus on your intention.
- be achievable.
- be positive.
- be in active voice and in the present tense (e.g., "I am," "I can").
- express how you want to feel.
- be meaningful.

For example, if you are manifesting a promotion at work, don't write an affirmation stating, "They will promote me to district manager." First, this uses passive voice, and it is in future tense. Second, remember that the process of Wild Moon Healing is about you and only you. You cannot control other people's actions or feelings. So, a good affirmation to match your intention is "I am ready for career advancement." This changes the statement to active voice. The energy you put out into the universe with this statement creates limitless opportunities beyond just a promotion at your current place of employment.

When you begin Wild Moon Healing, you don't want to create an affirmation like "Wild Moon Healing will heal me." Wild Moon Healing teaches *you* to heal *you*. A good affirmation when you first manifest with the moon is "I respect the process, even though I do not yet understand it."

The best affirmations, though, are the ones you create yourself. The more you discover about yourself, what you want, and what your purpose is, the more this process will become creative and inspiring.

When you are ready, take out your journal and go to a quiet space where you won't be disturbed. Close your eyes and put one hand on your chest. Breathe. Just be for a few minutes, until you feel ready to start creating your affirmations. When you're ready, let your thoughts flow and write them down.

When you feel happy with the statements in your journal, write them again on sticky notes. Post them everywhere… around your home and office, in your vehicle, and on your calendar/day timer. Create reminders in your digital calendar and alarms on your electronic devices. As these notes and reminders appear to you throughout the day, take time to acknowledge them by reading them aloud. Notice any changes in your body as you recite them. Let your affirmations empower you and change your life!

Emotional Freedom Technique (EFT)

EFT is a healing technique that involves tapping key meridian points on your body to clear old limiting beliefs and reprogram new ones. It is a mindful holistic activity that helps you change your thinking from negative to positive. Meridians are the energetic highways in the body through which our energy flows. Tapping into this energetic flow helps you release old patterns, and releasing old patterns helps increase your energy flow.

The *Journal for Evidence-Based Integrated Medicine*[19] suggests that EFT is a powerful healing modality that had significant results in helping people with mental and emotional trauma that caused anxiety, depression, and post-traumatic stress disorder.[20] You do not need in-depth knowledge of meridians, chi, chakras, or traditional Chinese medicine to use EFT. You can research specific tapping points on the head and face and learn how to sequence through them to eliminate symptoms, like negative emotions, cravings, compulsive thoughts, and poor habits.

Some educational resources to help you begin tapping include:

- Donna Eden[21] has been teaching people how to work with their body's energy to stay well and prevent illness for four decades. Her co-authored book *Energy Medicine*[22] is a great resource to learn about energy and how to use it to heal.
- *The Tapping Solution* by Nick Ortner[23] is a terrific book to learn the practical application of EFT.
- I first discovered EFT through Carol Tuttle, author of *Mastering Affluence*,[24] which teaches you "how to be the master of your own well-being" through six areas of affluence.

---

19 Katharina Blickheuser et al. "Clinical EFT (Emotional Freedom Techniques) Improves Multiple Physiological Markers of Health."

20 Ibid.

21 Donna Eden Energy Medicine YouTube channel, .https://www.youtube.com/channel/UCn_yr5l2SQJdW6llBOI1I9Q.

22 Donna Eden, Energy Medicine.

23 Nick Ortner, The Tapping Solution.

24 Carol Tuttle, Mastering Affluence.

Thought Journaling

As part of your journaling practice during the waxing moon, rather than focusing on an event that triggered a negative reaction, the people involved, or your reaction, concentrate on what you were thinking of before or after the event. This helps you acknowledge how your thoughts and emotions affect your reactions, instead of blaming a situation or person for making you react. Authentic power comes from awareness.

Exercise – Thought Journaling

This practice takes time to master because you need self-awareness, the ability to be honest with yourself, and a sense of accountability. This type of journaling is not about people, places, or things. The focus is on your thoughts and emotions before and after a triggering event. A triggering event is an experience that started an episode of compulsive or damaging coping mechanisms or resulted in a physical confrontation. It is anything that upsets you.

Do not journal about how mad you are at yourself because you ate an entire bag of chips after your coworker upset you. Focus on how you felt *before* you were angry. Were you already thinking about how the situation would go because you believed this person to be rude, inconsiderate, or intolerable? Were you upset before you had a bona fide reason to be? Our individual opinions about the character of others sometimes nudge us to judge a situation before we know all the facts. Our judgments affect us on an emotional level. Let's say for example that two days after the inciting event, you realize you have done no Moon work because you have been brooding over the situation, even though it is no longer relevant. The event has concluded, and everyone but you has forgotten it. Why are you still hanging on to those negative feelings?

Before resorting to a self-sabotaging or destructive coping mechanism, focus on your thoughts. You may gain insight, like "This person is an emotional trigger for me, no matter what they do or say. Their mere presence is unsettling."

The only thing you are looking for is insight. You are not analyzing, judging, or labeling anyone.

You can learn to train yourself to respond in a way that keeps you grounded in any situation by applying the Four Gates of Speech[25] to your emotional journaling practice.

Here are prompts that can be helpful in exploring your thoughts:

- Is this thought helpful in any way?
- Is this thought true? Can I prove it is true?
- Is this an old story my mind is playing out of habit?
- How can I make the best of this situation?
- How can I see this in a different way?
- What can I be grateful for at this moment?

Seek Help

I discussed this a bit earlier, but it bears repeating: *Asking for help is not shameful.* It is empowering. You are being vulnerable when you seek help because you are admitting that you're unable to do or understand something. Vulnerability often triggers

---

[25] Michelle Cross. "Four Gates of Speech," https://www.michellecross.co.uk/four-gates-of-speech/.

fear-based emotions based on a foundation of shame or guilt. When you rise above these stifling emotions, step into your power, and take action, you may feel uncertain, and the fear of unwanted outcomes can hold you back. The empowering part of vulnerability is on the other side of fear, but you must go through it. There is no way around it.

The opposite of fear is empowerment, which motivates change and increases your self-esteem. When you seek help, you empower others to support you so you can regain a sense of self-control. If the support you receive enables your dysfunction, it becomes part of the problem and will cripple your recovery and healing goals. Why? Because when you allow someone else to enable you to continue behaving in a manner that does not benefit you, you relinquish your responsibility for your welfare and hand it over to someone else. Enablers permit your unhealthy behavior to continue without consequence to you. When there are no repercussions for unhealthy behavior or when someone offers you a "safety net," you surrender personal responsibility for your actions, and in a distorted sense, enablers provided you with an outlet to blame someone else for your current experience in life.

Enabling is the act of removing or fixing obstacles for a person. This diminishes the opportunity for the person to hold themselves accountable for their actions. Empowerment comes when an individual seeks support or help while taking full responsibility for their actions.

Helping someone gain control of their behaviors and life is empowering. Helpers address specific disruptive behaviors, communicate expectations, and make sure that consequences follow negative behavior. Enablers avoid confrontation at all costs. Enabling also comes from those who lack strong personal boundaries. It is a fear-based action, as enablers fear what would happen if they didn't help someone. They may spend money they don't have or take time off work when they shouldn't just to keep helping someone whose situation never changes. Enablers lie to protect or cover for someone. Everyone's involvement with enabling comes from a negative place. The help-seeker is stuck in a negative life experience, and the enabler responds to their predicament out of fear. It is so hard to hold someone you love accountable when they're doing something that may cause them harm. But enabling unhealthy behaviors perpetuates a negative situation because you do not achieve a different result by enabling the same situation. In the end, help comes from the self, not from others.

It is up to you to improve or change your life. Only you have the answers you seek. But it is also acceptable for others to provide you with support or help while you are on your healing journey. Proper help creates an environment where you can help yourself. Often, others can help you experience a shift in your perspective, which will shift your energy.

Restore the Spirit

Reiki or Acupuncture

Disruptions in life force energy can cause physical pain and other problems. Acupuncture is rooted in the belief that essential life force energy runs through each of us. This technique balances energetic flow through your meridians. A practitioner will check your meridians to assess the vitality of your life force energy. Then, they will insert thin needles through your skin in strategic locations on the body to help release stuck energy. Reiki is an energetic practice of moving energy to restore energetic balance. You can do Reiki on yourself or go to a practitioner.

These healing modalities guide the body toward holistic healing using your own energy.

Sound Healing and Aromatherapy

Sound healing therapy uses sound vibrations from percussion instruments, Tibetan singing bowls, tuning forks, Laughing Buddha bowls, or the human voice, among other things, to relax the mind and body. Sound therapy helps release stifled energy in your body and induces a state of comfort and harmony that's necessary for healing.

In my sound healing experience, I felt the calming, soothing vibration of a singing bowl from my hand to my elbow. The vibration of a Laughing Buddha flat-base bowl was unlike anything I had ever experienced; it resonated throughout my entire body and lasted for hours. The practitioner I worked with said that sound healing can change your DNA. I cannot attest to that, but the vibration from a Buddha bowl has a powerful effect on our vibrational energy, which may help us heal from trauma.

Aromatherapy is a holistic treatment that uses incense or natural plant extracts known as essential oils to promote health and well-being. When you diffuse essential oils or use them topically, their aromatherapy can produce a state of relaxation and relieve stress.

Tarot, Oracle Cards, and Pendulums

Tarot cards, oracle cards, and pendulums are holistic tools that can help you clarify your vision and make sense of things, such as how your past is influencing your present, what is happening in your life, and how to best move forward. When you use tarot, you access your personal energy to tap into your subconscious mind and inner knowing. You use the imagery on the cards to access information that's stored in your subconscious mind to enhance clarity and self-reflection. These metaphysical tools help you connect with your intuitive knowing. Remember, your energy flows like a river, changing constantly. So, the messages in the cards will change continually as well.

Oracle decks are excellent guidance tools for self-care rituals and are easier to learn than tarot. Although limited compared to tarot, oracle decks supply the "big picture." Tarot is structured and provides detailed personal information or insights, but it also takes time to learn. So, if you are new to card reading, oracle decks are a good place to start. Their guidance can provide you with helpful affirmations and practices to use on your self-healing journey. Use tarot cards if you want a detailed reading and oracle cards for general advice/information. Both can be used to connect with your mind.

It is possible to use a pendulum for guidance on its own or with an oracle deck. You can create a pendulum by suspending a weighted object from a chain so it swings freely. You can use a piece of jewelry, a crystal, or a small household item to make your own pendulum. If you purchase a pendulum new, you should cleanse it and program it before using it. You can clear its energy by holding it over sage smoke for a few seconds, laying it in a bed of sea salt overnight, or holding it under running water for a few seconds. If you use water, make sure it is safe to expose the crystal on your pendulum to water. Water has the potential to cleanse—or destroy—your crystals. Do your research so you know how to properly care for your crystals.

Exercise – Programming Your Pendulum

To program your pendulum with your energy, hold it in front of you and swing it in one direction, back to front or side to side. State out loud, "This motion represents 'yes' answers." Then swing the pendulum in the opposite direction and state out loud, "This motion represents 'no' answers." Then swing the pendulum in a circular motion and say, "This motion represents 'I don't know' or 'maybe' answers." While getting answers to open-ended questions is tricky, it is possible. To do this you can, for example, offer a variety of answers, and tell your pendulum to spin in a circle while you ask the questions and stop spinning when you say the correct answer.

Whenever I have finished using a pendulum for guidance, I always hold my hand under it to stop the swinging and express gratitude.

☪

Seeking guidance from cards and pendulums can be helpful, but remember, you create your future by choosing differently right now. Do not leave your future up to the cards; they cannot create change. They can only show possibilities based on your current energy. Learn from the messages they provide, then take inspired action to change your life for the positive.

Express Compassion

If you have concern for another person's situation, you can energetically feel their pain. Compassion is a nurturing, mother-like emotion that inspires you to care for other people. Caring for others is what makes the human race unique. Expressing compassion and helping others is what humanity is all about. Compassion empowers you to appreciate individualism in people you meet and compels you to help anyone you feel you can support, regardless of your differences. That energy ripples through space and time, increasing society's vibration. You, and everyone around you, bring unique gifts to any situation, so through understanding and kindness, you can see the potential of every moment.

Be an active participant in your life by viewing the world through your heart. Deceptions of false, limiting beliefs from the fragile ego stay in your mind, but your heart has the intelligence to lift your spirits, see the truth in people and situations, and cultivate compassion for all living things.

You can express compassion and say no to a situation that is bad for you at the same time. But be careful about showing compassion if you have issues with healthy boundaries, because it may compel you to fix a situation that is not yours to fix, creating an energetic leak.

Have Faith

The consequences of a lack of trust or faith can be significant and can affect your healing progress. Trust is the foundation of every relationship, including the one you have with yourself, and the source from which your strength grows. Faith is a relationship with something greater than yourself; it is your strength. A lack of trust ends communication. A lack of faith that something is working for your greater good can cause you to backslide into habitual, unhealthy behavior patterns.

Even if you are giving your power away to drugs, alcohol, or food, find a source of strength in something greater than yourself. Faith is necessary to heal. Know that God, the universe, Gaia, your mom, or whatever you believe in loves you. I understand that when you do not feel secure or safe, having faith can be difficult. The restorative activities listed in this chapter (and all the exercises in this book) will cultivate an environment of trust in your life by instilling compassion, empathy, and gratitude, which can open your heart to a relationship with God or Source.

Wild Moon Healing is based on autonomy, because no one can do this work for you. There are resources you can refer to for help, but the responsibility for your life is yours alone. Holding yourself accountable is empowering. Asking for help or working with a buddy who has similar goals helps you stay accountable. If things are not working out as you had hoped, know that the universe is at work for your greatest good and is helping to create the best possible outcome. But you must believe.

Phase 2

MANIFESTING WITH THE MOON

8

NEW MOON PHASE

Explore and Discover Self

Self-discovery is an intimate, personal journey for everyone. Each phase of the lunar cycle is an opportunity to explore and discover more about yourself from different perspectives. Becoming the person you are right now is occurring naturally, although you are not aware of the process. Without awareness, you are not in control; it's just happening. Purposefully harmonizing the progression of becoming who you are with the natural rhythm of the lunar cycle develops awareness. Awareness of your personal growth through the process of self-exploration and self-discovery begins with the new moon. Why the new moon? The energy of a new moon brings a fresh start to another lunar cycle, encouraging new beginnings and presenting you with a clean slate you can use to learn something new about yourself.

Self-discovery is a developmental learning process. You've been doing it all along. Learning is the active practice of creating an infrastructure that is comprised of data (your knowledge) and context (your experience). Accumulating knowledge and experiences forms your beliefs and behaviors. As you live your life, this cycle repeats itself. If your experience is negative or if the knowledge you gain is false and you keep living mindlessly, your beliefs and behaviors will become negative or flawed. To fix this, you'll need a reset. The new moon is that reset.

Every new moon presents an opportunity to tap into her renewed energy and restore yourself, mind, body, and soul. During this lunar phase, you have a chance to discover what you know and question your understanding. Are your beliefs and behaviors consistent with your truth, or are they draining your energy?

New Moon Tools

Intention is a powerful tool. So, do all you do with intention. There are ways to help you discover your true intentions. In this section, we'll talk about some valuable tools that can help you quiet the ego mind and create a powerful intention under the new moon. Use these tools prior to doing the exercises in this chapter to help expand your responses beyond what your thinking mind can conjure up. The first of these tools is meditation.

Meditation

Meditation can improve your intention-creating process. The best way to discover what you know and figure out who you want to be is to be still. In a mindful, intentional way, block out all outside interferences, including noise, activity, and distractions. Practice the *Listen to Your Body* exercise from chapter 2; it will help ready your mind for the intention-setting process.

Gratitude

Practicing gratitude is an essential part of the intention creation process and is a habit to be encouraged. An article by two students attending Berkeley University documented their research study, which looked at the benefits of gratitude in those struggling with mental health.[26] Their study showed that expressing gratitude helps release toxic emotions, even if you do not share it with others.

Following your meditation, with a calm mind, think of the things you appreciate. To foster positivity for the intention-setting process, follow the *Gratitude Journal* exercise from chapter 2, listing at least five things you are grateful for and why. Knowing why you are grateful gives you insight into your subconscious mind by helping you identify the things you value in life. Defining your values helps create healthy boundaries and align your actions with your purpose. Also, by practicing gratitude, you are subconsciously signaling to the universe that you are ready to align your energetic vibration with your highest good.

Express gratitude for the creative responses that come up during this new moon work. Trust that everything that comes up is right on time.

Physical Expression of Gratitude

To expand your energy level, express your gratitude in a physical way. Actions speak louder than words, so show gratitude to others through small, random acts of kindness, such as:

- buying a coffee for the person behind you in line.
- smiling at people.

[26] Joshua Brown. "How Gratitude Changes You and Your Brain," https://greatergood.berkeley.edu/article/item/how_gratitude_changes_you_and_your_brain.

- showing respect to others. Respect is gratitude. Say "Thank you" or "I appreciate you," or hold a door open for someone.
- volunteering in your community.

Expressing gratitude leaves a positive energetic footprint. The more you express gratitude, the more profound your energetic footprint becomes. Adding a thankful vibration to your new moon intention helps focus your thoughts toward achieving your goal. Meditation and gratitude help release daily stresses from your mind so you can look at big-picture items. With focus on the daily grind, you lose the essence of what life is all about. For example, perhaps you need to make sure your daughter gets to school on time. As the dog wakes you up, you realize your alarm did not go off. The house is in chaos. But you and the kids throw on clothes, grab a piece of fruit, and rush out the door. It doesn't matter that your daughter's socks don't match and you've turned her night shirt into a stylish outfit. Slow your mind, meditate, and find your blessings.

Affirming Prayer

Regardless of whether you are religious, there is power in prayer. Using prayer or affirming language as you communicate with God, the universe, your angels or spirit guides, or whomever else you believe in will aid in the realization of your intention. Express your thankful heart. Ask that your spiritual guides assist you in your new moon intention-setting process. A significant factor in creating change in your life is believing that it is possible. A person with faith believes something will happen, even if there is no tangible evidence. Strong faith refers to your conviction. So, believe your intention will come to pass, regardless of the circumstances or what other people say.

Affirming prayer is a way to confirm that all things are working out for your greatest good. It acknowledges the progress toward what you are creating. Praying can help you feel grounded and more connected to God or Source, activate your intuitive center, and attract more positivity into your life. People pray to God, their ancestors, Spirit, their higher self, and the universe. Pray to whomever feels authentic to you. Prayer works because the petitioner keeps an open mind and is receptive to the prayer's magic, its energetic spark.

As with everything, you want to pray with intent. You can pray with:

- Prayers of allowing – Everything you do, do with an open heart. You must surrender the outcome and believe the best possible future is ahead of you. You can pray, "Thy will be done" or "Please resolve this situation for the highest good of all involved."
- Prayers of gratitude – Everything you do, do it with a thankful heart. Prayers of appreciation will attract more of what you appreciate.
- Prayer of confirmation – Everything you do, do it with a positive heart. As with gratitude, you are thankful when you confirm it, but this type of prayer shows appreciation for a positive situation in your life.
- Prayers of inquiry – Everything you do, do it with a curious heart. If you can't see it, ask for guidance. Some people ask their guides to change their present situation. Only you can create change in your situation, so ask your guides to change your perspective. Through this type of prayer, ask to see things differently or ask for help in seeing the lesson.
- Prayers of expansion – Everything you do, do it with an energetic heart. This type of prayer is a way to leave your energetic footprint in the world. Create positive energetic ripples. It is all about you sending all your love and healing energy to anyone, anywhere in the world. Pray big. Pray for entire continents.

Add all these aspects of prayer into one. Expressing yourself through words in a prayer is a release. If you cannot find the words, cry with the intention of receiving healing energy. You are still releasing, which creates space and allows the universe to give you a boost to restore flow and balance to your subtle energy system. Prayer is not perfect. There is no one way to pray. Do it your way.

☪

Perfectionism

Perfection is an idea, a screenshot if you will, that stands still. In a single moment, someone may achieve their idea of perfection or what they believe others will perceive as perfect. But in this scenario, you should take a picture, because perfection is fleeting. (I believe the "perfection is achievable" concept came from the phrase *picture perfect.*) Life is fluid. Moments pass.

Perfectionism is subjective. It is a false narrative that imprisons your mind. It is an energetic leak, an unattainable goal. Why? Because it is a comparison device you use to portray parts of yourself negatively. You assess yourself (or your performance in any given situation) based on negative information alone. Being "perfect" suggests you judge your own value by relying on the opinions or approval of others. When you do this, you put the beliefs and needs of others before your own. This lowers your self-worth, blocks your energy, and robs you of personal freedom.

When setting a new moon intention, figure out what you want to be rather than what you have to do. This fosters success and excitement because you are not comparing yourself to anyone. This mental shift changes your focus from the dreaded things you must do to be perfect, which drain you of the energy necessary to become the best, most awesome YOU who loves yourself and life. When you know what you want to be, you will come up with creative, enjoyable ways to achieve your goals.

Exercise – Discover What You Know

During the new moon, get to know yourself better through emotional journaling. Ask yourself a series of questions and see where they take you without judgment. Simply write or draw what comes to mind. The answers come from what you know and believe right now about yourself.

Your self-discovery questions could look like:

- What do you love about your life?
- What do you know about yourself?
- What are you unhappy with?
- What do you want to create?
- Whom do you want to be?
- What do you want to do?
- What do you want to explore?
- How do you want to feel?
- What is important to you?
- What do you miss from your past?
- What do you want to learn or accomplish?
- What does your future life look like?
- What personal interests do you want to explore?
- What is your purpose in life?
- What do you find inspiring?
- What meaningful thing that adds value to your life have you given up to have your current life?

Each question should lead to more probing questions. When you discover what you want to create in your life, explore your motivation. Ask yourself, "Why do I want it?" Make a list of insights into your purpose or rationale. How do the things on your list make you feel? If your list upsets you, are you striving for something based on a false, limiting belief? Or are you coming from a place of fear? Uncovering your motivation allows you to discover what you know and believe. This process can help you determine if what you think you want is correct, or if you should shift your energy to work on a different area of your life. When you believe, you identify what you need to work on, and you create an intention.

Creating an intention will affect your life, so dream big. Dream of a future you love, so your dream inspires you to act. A simplified scenario might be:

- Q: What do I want?
  A: Ice cream.
- Q: Why do I want ice cream?
  A: To make me happy.
- Q: Will ice cream make me happy?
  A: Yes.
- Q: Do I think I will still be happy after I finish my ice cream?
  A: I don't know.
- Q: Do I believe eating ice cream will help me achieve the goal I'm working on in this lunar cycle?
  A: No.
- Q: Why am I unhappy?
  A: I'm not sure.
- Q: Can I identify a specific emotion other than "unhappy?" Am I bored or lonely?
  A: I miss my friends, so I feel alone.
- Q: What if I called my friends to see if they wanted to grab an ice cream with me?

A: Oh, that would be thrilling, even if we don't get ice cream.

If the thought of having company makes you feel happy, you need to spend time with a friend. It is OK to still want ice cream, but do you see how the ice cream itself will not make you happy? Wellness starts in the mind, so thinking about what you want from an emotional perspective will allow you to dig deeper into your motivation. This information is necessary to create a new moon intention.

☪

Intention

An intention is a mental statement that represents your commitment to yourself as a guiding principle for who you want to be. An intention helps to align your mind with your heart. Setting an intention helps you live a life of purpose, where every decision you make, every second of every day, is about being true to yourself. When you lack intention, life happens to and around you. By setting an intention with every new moon, the receptivity of your thinking mind will become activated, and your energetic frequency will elevate. There is power behind knowing what you want and attracting the opportunities and resources that are necessary for you to reach your goal.

Creating a new moon intention involves more than discovering what you want and your motivation for wanting it. You can explore other ideas and perspectives or ponder all your aspirations and ambitions. Even if you feel like your dream is just a fantasy, let the excitement of all the possibilities take over. The work you do during the new moon encompasses the substance of what you know and believe. You need to rest and reflect during this initial work so you can plan a foundation that will support you in achieving your goal.

As portrayed in the previous simplified scenario, the key of intentions is to create the "right" intention. This requires knowledge (or acceptance) of your false, limiting belief system and your energetic leaks, both of which deplete your energy. For example, if you look in a mirror and think *I am fat*, focusing on losing weight cannot be your goal. If you tell yourself you cannot make money doing what you love or if you doubt your abilities, starting a new career should not be your focus. You will lack the inspiration required for action if your goal depresses you, reminds you of everything you are not, creates a "cannot have" or "need to give up" list, or if it makes you think about what is not possible.

The correct intention for you comes from your inner knowing, your true self. False beliefs overshadow your authentic self. When you are living authentically, you do not think about others' opinions, and you are not afraid to go after what you want. Your intention excites you. When you are on the life path you are meant to be on, you will commit to the change you want to create in your life.

The purpose of finding the correct intention for yourself is to create a plan to change your life and start moving forward. Newton's first law of motion states that "an object at rest stays at rest" and "an object in motion stays in motion." He was referring to throwing a ball in relation to gravity's pull, but in the same way that gravity affects the trajectory of a ball, our thoughts, actions, reactions, words, and choices affect the trajectory of our lives. You can only become what you give yourself the power to become. You can only achieve what you believe you can achieve, and you can only live authentically when you control the trajectory of your life. The more the energy within you flows and radiates outward at a high frequency, the more receptive your life will be to change. Higher frequencies signal to the universe that you believe what you want is possible, and then everything will transpire for your greatest good to manifest your dream.

While the moon has its magic, manifestation is an imperfect process that's unique for every individual because it requires action. You can create whatever you want to create in your life, but you must also heal and learn to love your entire self. Learning about who you are and acknowledging all the unique parts of yourself will make you whole, and your power lies in being whole. The frequency at which your energy reflects into your outer world comes from your subconscious. It matches your baseline emotion, i.e., how you feel right now. Your personal energy is expressed through your words and actions and affects you and those around you. If your emotions and behaviors come from a false, limiting belief system, you'll want the intention you create to have a positive effect. You'll want it to improve your baseline emotion and limiting beliefs. When limiting beliefs or negative emotions pop up, you can turn them off; you can detach from the emotion and feel freedom instead of stagnation. The ability to do so lives in your brain.

As discussed in chapter 1, when both sides of your brain coordinate activities, it can process and connect thoughts better. From the perspective of healing from limiting beliefs and negative emotions (or just healing from your struggle in general), left brain and right brain activities are important, too. The right brain is where you engage your imagination and creativity. This is where you want to gain control and access your intuitive center, so you know what is correct for you. The left brain is logical. Your ego mind will tell you things like "Don't give up," "Don't give in," or "I don't want to fail; keep going." Giving yourself a pep talk like this may seem reasonable, but look at those words from the deceitful ego's point of view. The ego is telling you what *not* to do, creating an environment of energetic deprivation. A deprived person is not free, because the thinking mind is focusing on *disadvantages*. These types of thoughts affect your willpower, creating feelings of imprisonment or restriction and leading you to perform actions that produce results that are contrary to what you want to achieve or create.

Let's say, for example, that the strongest feeling you have is the need to lose weight. First, let's examine the wording of the intention "to lose weight." This statement makes you think about the foods you cannot have and the dreaded workouts you must do (once you figure out how to fit them into your busy schedule). It keeps the focus on what you *do not want*: excess pounds. This creates a mental environment of deprivation and lack. Therefore, your actions become counterintuitive to reaching your goal, making it hard for you to lose weight.

It is easy to spend our lives doing things we feel we "must do." We get caught up in a day-to-day grind, doing things at the expense of ourselves, our happiness, our relationships, and our health. We lose ourselves in the stress of everything that has to happen. We lose sight of what our heart wants. We lose our fun, become depressed, or get sick. Doing things when we lack personal passion or inspiration creates an energetic deficit and affects our physical bodies. Creating an intention or setting a goal helps us focus on what matters, preventing busywork and cultivating an atmosphere of mindful work so we can create the life we want.

All amazing accomplishments start with a vision, or an intention of what you hope to achieve. Right now, you can create your intention and choose a course of action to change your life. You can choose differently to find happiness within yourself. You can change direction as many times as you need to. Want your change or accomplishment to be amazing? Dream big, even if you do not have the resources to achieve your goal. (By the way, most of us do not have the resources when we start out.) By creating a clear, detailed intention and working on your action plan, there will be no stopping you! Add phrasing like "the best possible outcome" to the end of your intention to keep yourself open to wonderful possibilities you could never have imagined on your own.

You are going to ask yourself a lot of questions during the entire lunar cycle to get to know yourself. When you ask the correct question, the proverbial lightbulb will go off and ignite your creativity. If you experience frustration or become emotional, engage in restorative activities. Meditate, express compassion, or get outside to clear your head.

Exercise – The Correct Intention

Probably the most difficult part of getting to know yourself is recognizing if you are creating the right intention. You may go through many lunar cycles with the intention of going after what you want, but if the universe is nudging you to work on what you *need*, you will experience frustration while working toward your identified goal. If you ask yourself what you want and a huge list downloads in your head, it is OK to ask the universe for clarity. Remember, you are not manifesting material things; this is about you. Still yourself. As you think about what you want, feel into it. Is a specific item, subject, or task calling for your attention?

In keeping with the "lose weight" goal, let's say you know you want to lose weight, and that is taking all your focus. Set your intention in a manner that conveys a strong tone to your subconscious and the universe. For example, does it feel different in your body to say, "I honor my body" rather than, "I need to lose weight?" When you engage in "need to," "have to," or "should" activities, you engage in a deprivation mindset, your energy lowers, and you feel heavier.

Repeat this phrase out loud:

"I need to lose weight."

Notice any sensations in your body.
"I need to lose weight."
Your posture may slump a little.
"I need to lose weight."
See what thoughts occupy your mind about losing weight.
"I am fat." "No one will want me until I lose weight."

Negative thoughts are limiting beliefs, so make a note of the way you talk to yourself. Write notes in your journal about what you observed.

☪

Now, shift your focus by repeating this positive intention:
"I honor my body."
Notice any sensations in your body.
"I honor my body."
Did your posture change while repeating this phrase?
"I honor my body."
Pay attention to the thoughts that occupy your mind around losing weight.
"My body tells me what it needs." "My body deserves love and patience."

Write notes in your journal about what you observed. Then, list all the ideas you can come up with on how you can respect your body.

☪

Honoring your body is empowering, and becoming empowered makes it easy for your inventive mind to engage and start revealing ideas about the actions you can take to achieve wellness. Soon, you will think things like *Sure, I can park farther away from the grocery store to get extra steps in. That's easy.* A positive mind becomes creative. Maybe you will start Hula-Hooping while watching your favorite TV show. This way, you are not depriving yourself of an enjoyable activity, and you are changing a sedentary activity into an energetic one. It is empowering to feel you are gaining rather than losing. When your intention makes you feel good and you choose what is correct for you, it is easy to create resourceful ways to support your momentum.

Keeping with the weight loss example, losing weight is just one way of honoring your body. The list of restorative activities in chapter 7 provides great ideas for practicing self-love and self-care. Focus on how improved health will make you feel. Ask yourself, "What activities do I want to do when I am healthier?" "What experiences do I want to have when I am stronger?" Create an empowering vision for your future as a healthy, cheerful person.

Whatever your intention is, make sure you have a vivid picture of how you want to feel when you achieve your goal. Why? Because plenty of people lose weight and are still unhappy. With good health as your focus, you can create an intention statement that reflects positive action, such as, "I honor my body while I become stronger and healthier."

Exercise – Create a To-Be List

Once you establish a positive intention that ignites your creative mind with all the different ways you can go about achieving results, you need to visualize your intent. This process should make you feel free and exhilarated, so if your intention leads to a dreaded "to-do" list, you are focusing on the wrong thing. Instead of creating an "I have to do [something]" list, focus on creating a "to-be" list, a list of nonmaterialistic things you want to be, to create excitement. For example, do you want to…

- be fluent in another language?
- be happy?
- be more energetic?
- be more loving to yourself?
- be more helpful to other people?
- let go and be silly and playful with your kids?
- be part of a healthy, loving relationship?
- be a student and go back to school?
- be financially stable and abundant?

Creating a "to-do" list could mean you are striving for perfectionism from the "I have to" or "I should" prison, whereas a "to-be" list is a mindful exercise of self-exploration. At any age, you can engage in the childlike wonder of deciding what you want to be when you grow up. We all have the right to be our perfectly imperfect selves and do what we enjoy.

Take out your journal and list all the things you want to be.

Exercise – New Moon Journaling

I encourage you to journal throughout the manifesting process each month. Journaling helps you analyze your daily activities and choices to further your healing. Through the use of prompts or predetermined questions, you can use journaling during the new moon as a data dump of the things that are going on in your mind.

Journaling is unique for every individual, so do not stress about grammar or semantics. Just write. If a thought appears but does not seem to make sense, this is your intuition guiding you. Without judgment, write all the thoughts that come to mind. When you are journaling, multiple things may come to mind at once. Make a bulleted list. Draw pictures to express yourself. If a word, color, or feeling comes, express it. Just go with it. Ask yourself questions for every issue, circumstance, or trauma that enters your mind. Identify feelings that come to mind in your journaling. Write down the people that come to mind. If you feel led, write down how you think others feel about you and how you see yourself.

When analyzing what you wrote, think of your journaling as artwork. Ten people can look at a painting, listen to a song, or read a poem and feel differently about it. Your words are like a poem; every word can have multiple meanings. For example, let's say the word *blue* came to mind, so you wrote it in your journal. Instead of staring at it like it is going to explain itself, think about it. What is blue? Perhaps there is blue in your physical environment—the color of your walls, the sky—or maybe there's a blue jay outside your window. Blue jays are pretty and vibrant, but they can also be mean. Do they remind you of a person in your life? How does that person make you feel? What feelings or sensations come up when you think of the color blue? Do you feel cold? Are you feeling blue? Are you unhappy or depressed? Are you truly depressed, or are you exhausted or feeling pressured? What is keeping your spirits low?

This type of self-exploration through journaling gathers data. It does not have to make sense; just write what comes to mind. During your first cycle of Wild Moon Healing, you may have no clue what you are doing. The answer to your questions could be, "I don't know." In the end, you want to have identified something about your life that you can improve, something new you want to learn, or something you want to be. By reading this book and starting this process, you have already set the framework for wanting something different for your life. Identify in your journal what you want to change. Intentional living encourages us to define our priorities and goals. By the end of the month, your journaling should have supplied you with insight into what you want, what you want to do, what you want to stop doing, or what you want to change, so adjust your intention as necessary.

☪

Exercise – New Moon Journaling Prompts

Using predetermined prompts will help you improve your journaling experience by encouraging you to query yourself to gather more detailed data.

Asking "why" questions and identifying the behaviors that hinder your progress will make you think and process details. Ask questions like:

- "Why do I do [this] when I know it is counterproductive to my goal?"

- "Why do I have trouble saying no when I need to, or when I start a new productive behavior?"
- "Why do I have a tough time sticking to a new routine?"

Besides your "why" questions, these prompts can help pull specific data from your memory:

- What trigger (person, place, situation, or thing) happens in your life when you stop endeavoring to change or fall back into your old habits?
- Can you name the point at which you started the behavior pattern you wish to change?
- What emotions come up when you think about what you want to change?
- Is your goal focused on an outcome of gaining attention, appreciation, or respect from outside sources?
- Are you manipulating a person with your intention?
- Why does a person's recognition matter to you?
- Do you blame anyone for your behavior pattern or circumstance?

This type of questioning will help you identify the energetic blocks that are holding you back from realizing your dreams. Your brain will tell you when it is time to stop questioning yourself. Write all your responses in your journal; you will come back to this on the full moon.

If journaling sparks negative feelings or you find yourself in a dark place, seek help. Call your primary care physician, the National Suicide Prevention Hotline at 1-800-273-8255, and/or 988, or if you are in the UK, call Samaritans 116 123. If depression or addiction plagues you, Moon work will help, but you must also seek help from medical professionals. There are treatment plans out there that can work.

To increase your energetic vibration, visualize what your life will look like when the shackles of your energetic blocks are removed in a safe, effective way.

☪

Exercise – Visualize Your Intention

Creating an intention is more than writing a sentence about what you want to create in your life. You are authoring a story about the rest of your life. The exercises up to this point have helped you gather information that can direct you toward the right goal for you. With an idea of what you want to work on manifesting in your life, you need to visualize the dream you have for the rest of your life. You need to feel as if your intention has already come to fruition.

When you visualize your new story as if it has already happened, you anchor your intention. Feel, hear, smell, taste, and see what life is like in your new reality. See the people in your story. Do you see family and friends? Do you see a person you want to meet? Where are you? Are you retired, moving, starting a new career or job? Use all your senses. Attach emotion to your vision. How do you want to feel in this new story of your life? Be specific and detailed.

You know you are going to honor your body. Now, see in your mind's eye what that looks like. What does it feel like when you take care of yourself? What activities are you doing to take care of yourself? Do you have more energy? See yourself doing all the activities you love and enjoying them with no pain or mobility issues. In honoring your body, you'll be able to see all the things you appreciate about it and all the ways it shows up for you. As you honor your body, see yourself losing weight. See yourself enjoying a shopping spree or buying a bikini. What does that experience feel like? Who is supporting you on your journey? Are you confident enough to audition for a play or try your hand at wallyball? What does true confidence feel like?

Now, take out your journal and record your visualization. Write your vision as if it is a memory to reinforce that you believe it.

Exercise – Intention Contract

You've stilled your mind using a new moon tool and enjoyed self-discovery activities. Now it is time to write out your intention. You know what you want your future to look like, but the focus of your new moon intention is on what you are going to do during the next four weeks to help you get closer to accomplishing your goal. Begin by writing an official contract you are entering into with yourself. This document establishes healthy boundaries for you. As you have seen, there are many aspects to consider when creating boundaries and building a self-help paradigm that works for you. One of these is the concept of time and how to use it to your best advantage. An intention contract helps you make better use of your time.

Intentions help you learn more about yourself regarding time, so you can establish stronger boundaries going forward. By this, I mean you learn what you can realistically accomplish in one lunar cycle. You will learn how you currently spend your time and how you could use it better. If needed, read more about time in chapter 4 and redo the *Take Stock in Life* exercise. Make sure your intention contract has you spending your time on things you truly value. As you progress with your Moon work, your intention contract will set you up for success by encouraging you to spend your time efficiently on things of value. In creating intentions, you may find that you fall into one of two categories regarding your time.

- Modest – You do not realize your full potential, so you create a weak contract, leaving yourself too much time to fall back into bad habits.
- Overzealous – You do not have a realistic idea of what you can accomplish, so you burden yourself with a contract you cannot fulfill.

A Sample Intention Contract
[Date] New Moon

What am I grateful for?

1. I am thankful for the weight loss resources my doctor provided me.
2. I am grateful for the supportive friends and family in my life.
3. I appreciate my friend for getting me a free ten-day pass to her gym.

This lunar cycle will…

1. bring me fast weight loss results.
2. bring me the strength to make healthy food choices that will curb my cravings.
3. enable me to use my time so I can do workouts (upper body for now) and read more instead of watching so much TV.

Action Items

1. Meal plan and prep on Sundays.
2. Wash, cut up, and portion out fruit/veggies/food as soon as I shop.
3. Daily: set aside time to work out, fascia blast (working connective tissue in the body), and meditate.
4. Curb TV time.
5. Wash my face every night.

Affirmation(s)

I am healthy and fit. The choices I make will help me lose weight. I can achieve my weight loss goals. I make healthy choices.

Dialogue

This month, I will see my physical body change. I have the momentum to see rapid, positive change with my body and emotions. I am in control and I'm present, so I make mindful, healthy decisions. I will plan and prep meals every Sunday so I am well prepared for the upcoming week. I will lose weight by focusing on my diet and adding strength training and blasting to my schedule. I will read more instead of spending so much time watching TV.

Create an Inspired Plan

You cannot visualize and dream forever; otherwise life will happen while you are busy making plans. With your new moon intention, you'll see it, feel it, and plan it, then prepare to take inspired action to achieve it. Once you have an unclouded vision of what you want, think about the inspired action you can take in the current lunar cycle to help you make progress toward achieving your goal. Be creative! Invent fun activities you can enjoy. The more fun you have and the more you give your inner child playtime, the more magnetic you'll become.

Make sure the action items you decide on are achievable. If you are not a morning person, for example, creating an action item of getting up at 6:00 a.m. daily might not be ideal (at first). Start by changing your bedtime routine and aiming to achieve your action item at night. Say an affirmation like "I deserve to sleep so I awaken refreshed," "Today I worked hard, and now I deserve to rest," or "I embrace my dreams" to reinforce your new nighttime routine. A good night's rest will assist you in your goal of getting up earlier in the morning.

Remember, this is not an effortless process. You need to trust your inner self to guide your intentions. Let your confidence and thoughts run wild. Have faith. Trust. Surrender the outcome to the universe. You don't need to know the outcome. Why? Your way is not the only way. What you think your perfect ending is supposed to be could be based on a foundation of false beliefs and energetic leaks. Focusing on a desired outcome means:

- you exclude all other possibilities, and that suppresses opportunities from the universe.
- you have overly narrowed your focus and will miss other blessings.
- you may have become narrow-minded. Narrow-mindedness leads to missing out on resources that might have led you on a fulfilling journey.

If you focus on what you want to change, what you need, or what you want to accomplish without surrendering the outcome, you stifle your energy. Nothing can manifest. You need to get out of your own way so the manifestation process can begin. To start the manifesting process, you must release the specific ending you want for your story. Releasing the outcome:

- is an act of faith, meaning you are not resisting how God (or the universe) will bring you blessings.
- allows you to focus on how you want to feel. Focusing on feelings as an experience instead of an outcome creates space for endless possibilities and attracts everything for your highest good.

When you surrender an outcome, you might not get what you thought you wanted, but you will receive what you need and what is for your highest good or the highest good for all. Not only do you want to believe that an amazing blessing is on its way to you, you also want to be thankful, feeling as if it has already arrived. From this perspective, your thoughts will affect your nervous system, releasing feel-good hormones that have a motivational role in your body. And you need motivation to create change.

To create change, you need to create a plan. Failing to plan is planning to fail, worry, be paranoid, or obsess. Intentions alone are wants, dreams, and wishes that alter your energy. An intention without action is just an unrealized idea or a lost opportunity. By itself, an intention is not enough to accomplish anything. Action without clear intent is a waste of time. When the powerful forces of a vivid intention and inspired action align, their combined energy radiates at a high frequency, and the universe conspires in your favor.

9

WAXING MOON PHASE

Inspired Action

The major theme of the waxing moon phase is *action.* To live an inspired life, you must *act.* Inspired action is intentional doing. Inspired actions are things you do because the incredible story of your life you wrote under the new moon motivates you into action. You felt the story of your future—emotionally as well as through your senses—and you experienced it viscerally in your visualization.

Your dream for your future must inspire you to take a giant leap toward your potential. Inspired actions are like building blocks. To make progress, you must do [this] before you can do [that]. As an example, it would not be wise to enter an Ironman Triathlon just to see how you do. First, you must train. The scariest part of this process is the moment you decide to change or desire something different. Doing something new (or doing it in a new way) to create change in your life is the simple part.

Knowing something is missing in your life, being conscious that an addiction controls your life, or yearning for something different can be intimidating. But courage is not the absence of fear. Being courageous means moving forward even though you are afraid. Bravery is putting in honest effort even though you are unsure of your ability.

Taking inspired action does not just change the trajectory of your future; it transforms you. It is a bold move to leave behind passiveness and mindlessness and dare to improve yourself. Inspired action defines your character as you accept yourself, be yourself, and love yourself so much that you learn from your action (or inaction) and craft a life with meaning.

Meaningful Actions

Actions that mean something to you are contextual. They connect your goal with your abilities. Under the new moon, you discovered the problems you are having in your life. You explored your interests and concerns. This added meaning to your Moon work. When something has meaning, it gives you purpose, which grabs your undivided attention. Attention brings awareness to things you want to change in your life, but that alone will not hold your curiosity long enough to create change. To hold your attention, the most pertinent information you can focus on is your *why*. Knowing why you are making a change charges your desire; you'll want to do more to create change. Changing means something to you, so you'll yearn to act. Just wanting to change your life isn't enough. You must take action.

To take action that leads to meaningful change, you must be open with yourself. Transparency is the only way to design reasonable actions that will positively affect your success. In discovering more about yourself, you open the door of self-trust. You hide nothing. I am not referring to sharing with others; this is an internal process. Releasing ambiguity in the way you talk to yourself is a necessary life skill to develop because it spurs personal growth.

As you go through the process of Wild Moon Healing, you will learn more about yourself. Your thoughts and emotions can create illusions about who you are (for yourself) and how you believe others view you. Do you know who you are? Or do you believe in the illusions you have about yourself? What lies do you tell yourself about who you are to gain a false sense of confidence? For example, people who habitually lie overestimate their ability to convince others of their lies.

Untruths will catch up with you one way or another. The lies we tell ourselves have no meaning and create distrust. Think about a time when someone was not honest with you. From the point you discovered their dishonesty, you questioned everything else they said. You couldn't believe them even if they spoke the truth.

Looking back, has there ever been a time you told yourself you could do something, but you underestimated your ability and hurt yourself… or you went after something with confidence, but didn't get it? From that point on, on a subconscious level, did you believe yourself to be a liar? Was that true? Of course not. You should explore to gain clarity and perspective on your circumstance. Transparency allows you to believe your thoughts and stop second-guessing yourself. Transparency sheds light on your motives and character, which creates opportunities for personal growth and adds even more meaning to your life.

Once you are truthful with yourself and you notice the mindless activities you engage in, you will gain insight into your energetic blocks, barriers, triggers, or limiting beliefs. Without judgment, use that information to level up in meaningful ways. When you create inspired, meaningful actions, they will:

- shift your mindset from "Here's an idea" (action item) to "I can do this."
- confirm to your brain that you are creating positive change.

- raise your awareness of what is achievable and realistic.
- define the negative patterns or beliefs you can overcome.

Meaningful actions are measurable:

- Can you confirm that the action occurred? Did you do the identified task?
- Did the action align with a key part of your goal? You knew the change you were making, and your action needed to reflect the eventual outcome.
- Did the action positively influence your self-talk? The action should have changed your perspective and helped you realize you needed it to achieve your goal.

So, what does a meaningful action look like?

- To improve health, add a small salad to every meal to increase your vegetable intake (even at breakfast).
- To increase endurance, add one mile a week to your walk to adjust to the increased distance.
- To earn a promotion, complete the required training.

Fresh beginnings require you to do something new, stop doing something old, or let go of something or someone in your life that is holding you back. That is easy to say, but not so easy to do. Rather than asking yourself, "What will I do to get it?", ask yourself, "What do I want, and how will I change to get it?" The former frame of mind suggests that you live against what is correct for you (do you want to win at all costs?), which creates chaos, crisis, and stress. When you live against your truth, you are lying to yourself and creating internal distrust. A willingness to change shifts your thoughts and energy toward personal responsibility. Accountability adds meaning to your life and fosters self-trust and personal growth. Whatever your goal is to attract and create positive change in your life, you need an authentic approach that is significant to you.

Start living your dream through meaningful, inspired action, but do not reprimand or judge yourself if you have a challenging time starting the new routine or if your attempts at change are unsuccessful. Sit. Still your mind with meditation and think about why you are having issues. Be truthful.

Thinking Action

Thinking under the waxing moon phase helps you make progress. Restructuring your thoughts can help peel away protective layers and create a path for physical action. The challenge is how to prioritize mental activity over physical activity. If your goal is to increase your endurance, for example, you may already be aware of how long it takes you to run a mile. So, by adding one mile a week, you can schedule your life realistically to achieve that goal. How can restructuring your thoughts be worked into your schedule? You need to schedule time to reflect on and digest the changes you make in your life.

As you learn more about yourself, you'll need time to process your personal insights and decide how to create more change in your life. You cannot plan an "ah-ha" moment (that moment when all your thoughts make a connection and shift your energy), so you must work your action plan and reflect inwardly. You can accomplish many things in your mind, but be patient. We underappreciate the mental energy we use to think, plan, decide, and problem-solve because the energy exerted is invisible. Be careful, though. Too much cognitive stimulation can turn into mental overload or overwhelm, and a negative thinking process can lead to anger or anxiety. Overthinking is an energetic leak you can use as an avoidance tactic, and it can cause you to slip away from your action plan and procrastinate.

Procrastination is like rocking in a rocking chair; you may be moving, but you're going nowhere. Your conscious and unconscious thoughts can keep you stuck. It is also hard to focus on any task in which your life lacks clear direction and your actions have no meaningful purpose. Even if you believe you are intentionally using procrastination to delay something (although this is not a tactical maneuver), it is still your enemy. You cannot turn procrastination into positive action. It means there is a disconnection between your present self and your future self because of the negative speak going on in your head.

If you are stuck in a cycle in which your actions are not progressing you toward your goal, or you are moving in a direction that does not serve you, you need to evaluate your progress and devise an alternate plan of action.

Evaluate Your Progress

Making progress is like learning a dance: you act and step forward, then hesitate and step back, then tell yourself to "just do it." But then you overstep, stumble backward, and contemplate starting all over. Progress is based on emotions, thoughts, and perceptions. You'll likely go back and forth between "I can do this" and "Nope, I can't do this." No one can force or plan personal progress; it happens organically. Everything you do in life either works or does not work. There are no feelings, judgments, or criticisms; it is what it is. But when you get the hang of it and learn a new dance, it's fun, encouraging, and inspiring.

I don't know about you, but I have never had a bad idea in my life. If there was an issue with anything, or if something didn't work out the way I thought it would, or if the result was undesirable, my error was not the amazing idea. The error was in my execution of the idea. When this happens, you must evaluate both what worked and what did not work. Do not keep doing something on your inspired action list just because it's working or because you've always done it that way. The "if it isn't broke, don't fix it" mentality can prevent you from seeing new opportunities, freeze inefficiencies in place, and inhibit needed change. If you keep doing the same thing because it worked once, you can fall into a mindless routine. Routines are safe, but boring.

Routines and habits stop the dance. You cannot experience self-growth in an uninspiring environment. Often, when we engage in a habit, we are not invested in what we are doing and lack introspective reflection. When you fall into a routine that's comprised of several regular habits, you do not consider the fact that life is always changing. Therefore, your repetitive actions may not always remain relevant. However, a habit is an automatic, repetitive action, and it could be relevant. Several examples include respecting time (disrespect of time is a pet peeve of mine), keeping things tidy to help maintain a stress-free environment, or meditating just before bedtime. Why do you think a particular action yielded a positive outcome? If you have the habit of meditating prior to going to bed, and the sleep app you use reflects improved sleep and you wake up easier in the morning, you have yielded a positive outcome because of the relaxing effect of your habit.

The profound effect of an action could have been a one-time deal, while at other times, you can stumble onto a lifelong habit that will take you places you never imagined possible. For example, perhaps your passion for learning led to the habit of reading daily for learning and personal growth. Then, you thought you would do something new, and instead of reading a new book, you mastered a new language. Now you freelance as an interpreter, making more money than you thought and with the freedom to create your own schedule.

The importance of evaluating your progress is that it helps you determine whether a habit is inhibiting your progress or whether a routine has blinded you to more resourceful ways of doing things. When you evaluate what did not work, be honest and responsible, and don't judge yourself. Why did it not work? Then, decide on different activities or new approaches that will help you achieve success. If something is working, evaluate whether there is a better, more efficient way of doing it or if it would benefit you to do something different.

Alternative Action

After setting your intention, you focused your energy and resources on implementing a meaningful, inspired action plan to progress toward your goals. If something did not work out as planned, maybe your triggers and energetic leaks have a stronger impact on your life than you realize. If that is the case, add more restorative activities to your daily life, like personal development, physical activity, or mindfulness. But this is not always the case. Maybe your actions had a concentrated effect on your progress and shifted your energy. When you make progress, you and your environment change, requiring a strategic overhaul of your inspired actions. You need a mind frame of "OK, what I've been doing so far got me to where I am. Now, what do I have to do to level up and experience further growth?" It is important to check your progress.

Exercise – Check Your Progress

When we cannot maintain our personal boundaries, we lie, make excuses, and procrastinate. Perhaps your health goals include an action item to walk around the block after work every night. Last week, it poured for five days straight, so you did not go for your nightly walk, and you gained two pounds. It is doubtful you gained two pounds last week just because it rained. It is also doubtful that you gained two pounds because you did not walk the number of steps you normally do. Without being critical of yourself, explore why you fell off your action plan. For example, even though it rained, ask yourself:

- What did you do instead of walking after work?
- Did you have a backup plan for indoor activities should you need them?
- Did you replace walking with a sedentary activity?
- If you watched a movie (as we all do on rainy days), did you bring snacks to the couch with you?
- Was it a healthy snack? Did you measure your snacks, or did you eat mindlessly?

Mindless eating increases caloric intake. With increased calories and less physical activity, you gained two pounds. Now that you've identified the facts, how do you remedy this situation so when it rains again, you don't gain more weight? Having a backup plan for your action plan is the most proactive thing you can do when considering inspired action. So, when it rains, what kind of alternative actions can you take? You could:

- choose to eat "movie food" purposefully and accept the outcome of that decision.
- watch a movie after dinner with no additional food.
- go to the gym.
- purchase a treadmill to use during inclement weather.

The options are endless. Just choose your alternative action and accept how that action will influence your progress before you do it.

Exercise – Update Your Intention Contract

Action without clear intent, doing something "just because," or engaging in mindless activity confuses your energy. It lacks an agenda; therefore, you get nothing done. Mindlessness creates inactivity and backsliding, while mindful, inspired action is restorative. It supports you as you progress and experience positive change, improvement, healing, and growth in your life. Meaningful action launches your energy so you can create something new.

When you created your new moon contract, you made a list of all the things you were going to implement, continue doing, or stop doing. Once you check your progress, you may find that the best thing to do is to change your contract and establish new, healthy boundaries with yourself. Your list of actions tells you how to engage to reach your goal. Add your contingency plan. Make your action items more specific. Make sure your activities are realistic and actionable right now so you can create change.

Nothing happens overnight, but if you don't do your part, nothing will change. Living purposefully means following your action plan.

Live Intentionally

To live intentionally means to be present and in the moment, so you can make better choices for yourself and live a life in which you matter. It is not about the result of any inspired action. Living intentionally is about the journey and the way you move through life. Deliberate action creates a road map for your life, where you are free to go in any direction you want. Being purposeful in this journey helps you establish and enforce boundaries. To live intentionally while exploring and discovering things about yourself provides a deeper sense of satisfaction with your life. As you discover who you are, the things you identify as important in life may change and redirect your choices and life path. The more you live intentionally, the more your intuition will "speak up," and you will know what is correct for you.

Living intentionally is a mindset that brings more awareness to your daily life. Therefore, as you learn to listen to and trust your inner knowing, you will notice the way you are living and if your choices are the best for you. Intentional living means you make conscious decisions that align your actions with how you want to show up every day to move toward your goals. There are only two ways to live: you either move toward your goals or away from them.

What if you don't know what you want, but you know what you don't want? Moving away from something you don't want is not the same thing as moving toward your goal. Recall the concept of thought stopping mentioned earlier, where you focus on negative thoughts and behaviors in order to stop them. In a similar fashion, moving away from what you don't want keeps you focused on that. When this occurs, panic and fear can set in. Panic reinforces negative behavioral patterns, such as conflict avoidance, blame shifting, or sacrificing your personal needs. These behaviors will never move you toward your goal. Feeling terrified makes you want to flee, and that response could run you over the edge of the cliff. To live intentionally and go after your goals, you cannot focus on uncertainty, what you don't want, or the probability of negative outcomes. Remaining focused on what you want reinforces behavioral patterns, such as consistent self-care, healthy boundaries, and personal accountability. Living intentionally means identifying what you want, then starting meaningful, inspired action.

Exercise – Cultivate Awareness

The key to living intentionally is being aware of all that you think, feel, do, and say. No matter what you are doing, think about it. Gaining self-awareness increases your ability to pivot should you need to make changes. Self-awareness is about observing:

- Thought patterns – What words would you use to explain your current experience? How would you describe yourself? What expectations do you have for yourself and others?
- Emotional patterns – Do you understand your feelings? Do you react? Do you avoid difficult emotions, situations, or people that make you feel uncomfortable?
- Behavioral patterns – Why do you do what you do? Why do you continue to do things you swear you won't do again? What triggers you? What motivates you?

Living mindfully develops your awareness so you can control triggering reactions that could create negative consequences. Being present, mindful, and truthful with yourself nurtures your awareness so you can choose your actions and respond in healthy ways. Asking questions enhances your awareness, and there is no right or wrong answer. For example:

1. Be mindful of the media you consume. What are you reading, listening to, engaging with, or watching? How does it make you feel? Is it relevant to your life? Are you learning from it? Is it relaxing or

mind-numbing? Should you change to a more relaxing or constructive media source? Why or why not?

2. When shopping (for groceries, clothes, whatever), ask why before you buy. Do you need it? Can you afford it? Do you think those cookies will make you feel better? What are you foregoing if you buy those cookies (your weight loss that week)? Just because those great boots are on sale does not make purchasing them correct for you. Why do you want the boots? Do you think they will make you look better or feel better about yourself? Boots have no effect on character, which is where true beauty comes from. Are you attempting to divert attention away from your character because you dislike an aspect of yourself?
3. Prioritize rest and self-care. Do you have enough time for yourself? Why or why not? Why is everyone else deserving of your time but you? You need to say no, but you say yes. Why? Why are you not important? Do others make you feel unimportant? When you take on the role of caregiver, the family "fixer," the person who jumps in to help before anyone even asks for help, your reality may reflect that you are not a priority. Being everyone's solution is an energetic leak. Is being in control more important than your wellness?
4. Practice active listening. Have you ever listened to a person talk, but you have no clue what they said? Why? What is distracting you? Is the conversation about gossip or another energy-lowering topic? Why are you involved with the conversation? Do you have a lack of respect for the person speaking? Do you lack empathy and compassion for the speaker or the topic? Do you feel unheard or invalidated when you speak? Are you belittling yourself because you do

not understand the topic? Do you feel like what you have to say is unimportant (or more important)?

5. Learn something new. Learning something forces you to think and act. Adults get set in their ways, which creates a sense of comfort. But it also fosters narrow-mindedness. Learning new things cultivates mental flexibility so you can adapt to different situations and remain relevant. When was the last time you took an interest in something new? Do you feel you are too old to learn new things?

☪

Raise Your Awareness

Elevating your awareness of your behavior in all situations allows you to evaluate if you are spending your energy efficiently and if the opportunity cost of your decision makes the use of your energy worthwhile. Every decision to do something means you are foregoing something else. Your energy is a scarce resource, so every action you take requires a decision about how to distribute your personal resources to satisfy your basic needs and wants. Awareness means you are purposefully distributing your energy to maintain a balance between self-care and the obligations that affect your level of satisfaction with life. For example, if you are on a diet and you choose to buy cookies when you know you will not eat just one, that is awareness. Ignoring your awareness (knowing what the cookies will do to your diet) lowers your energy before you even eat one. Having awareness in such a situation means you have evaluated your options and are cognizant of the cost (if you eat the cookies, you will not lose the weight you might have lost that week). Not only that, but in an energetic sense, eating low-vibrational food lowers your personal energy. Eating those cookies may lower your level of satisfaction with yourself because you know you are violating your intention contract. This creates regret because you may have thought you could manage your portion (or your alcohol or television consumption) this time.

Living with the intention of becoming healthier does not mean you don't buy cookies. It means you think about it, weigh the options, own the consequences, and go on with life. Money, time, sleep, your waistline, family time, alone time, and anything else you can imagine are things we sacrifice because we lack awareness. For example, when you purchase a magnificent pair of boots on a credit card, aware that you don't have the cash to pay off your card, you sacrifice your future financial situation. To get one thing, you must give up another. The give and take of awareness could look like this:

- Give up procrastination and become more productive.
- Give up blaming and hold yourself accountable.
- Give up envy and become grateful.

Awareness helps to get rid of the negative in your life. I have an eating disorder, and now that I have awareness of it and my triggers, it is easier to stop. My emotions trigger my eating disorder. Emotions can also blind our attentiveness toward inspired action. I have identified the false belief that created my eating disorder and the triggers that activate my impulsive eating. I'm mindful of the feelings that are stirred up when I am triggered. While I am not yet able to overcome my eating disorder, being aware is helping me internally heal my body and mind. As you raise your awareness, you will achieve extra levels of healing.

People are helping to raise awareness of many things by putting awareness and prevention together, because awareness can sometimes prevent terrible things, like suicide, domestic violence, or human trafficking. In this same manner, you need to create awareness to stop preventable things in your own life. In my case, I was prediabetic when I began working on my emotional binge eating. The message I received loud and clear was that type 2 diabetes can be prevented if I become aware of my eating habits. Because I gained awareness of my behavior, I am no longer prediabetic. I may not always be able to stop an episode of binge eating, but most of the time now, I eat mindfully. Through self-care, my health is improving, and my energetic frequency is increasing.

You are an energetic being, a soul, and a scarce resource, meaning there is only one of you. You do not have a limitless supply of energy, so prioritize living an intentional life. Living a life in which you matter and raising your awareness will help you gain an advantage. Otherwise, you are sacrificing yourself in all areas, including your health. Choose to nurture a healthy sense of awareness so you can experience:

- better relationships.
- calmer moods with less worry.
- a clear head with better cognitive function.
- increased productivity with less procrastination.
- optimal health and wellness.

Your heightened sense of awareness can help you appreciate your power to choose. By living intentionally in the present moment, you can reconnect with the characteristics of yourself that lie dormant in your shadows and reach your full potential, live your truth, and find your purpose. Finding your purpose takes commitment and self-exploration, and you can discover yourself in your everyday choices and actions.

Emotional Triggers

Through the waxing lunar phase, we can create contingency plans and build our sense of awareness, but still find our progress derailed. If we react to our environment and the people in our lives, it is because of an emotional trigger. An emotional trigger is a person, place, or thing that causes uncomfortable feelings inside you. These triggers exist because our experience is frustrating or unsatisfying. Just as I provide journaling prompts throughout this book to inspire you to express your feelings, triggers are outside prompts that provoke a reaction in you. Look back at the emotional journaling exercise in chapter 3. Have you gained awareness of what is triggering you? You can add value to your journaling by including an emotional component. Discomforting emotional triggers include negative feelings, like feeling unworthy, unloved, invalidated, unimportant, etc. If you can pinpoint the real emotional trigger, you are making progress.

Exercise – Emotional Trigger Incident Report

Making progress means being responsible and accountable for what you do, say, and think. Progress happens when you can identify what happened (as a list of facts), acknowledge the facts, then remove your feelings and opinionated commentary. The views of others (and even your own opinions) are unhelpful and do not facilitate understanding. Asking, "Why do you think that [fill in the thought that sparks your opinion]?" can help you understand your trigger. When triggered, evaluate the event and complete an "incident report" for yourself.

Take out your journal and list facts that helped or hindered your progress in achieving your goal. As you prepare your incident report, notice how you feel.

- Explain to yourself what occurred.
- List the damage you may have suffered.
- List the damage you may have caused.

- Identify the people present (do not blame; just list facts). Are there names on your list of people that curled your skin, broke your heart, or evoked negative feelings?
- Identify the weather and general atmosphere. Were you having fun before it rained? Did the start of a storm bring back a negative memory?
- Identify where you were, the exact location. Have you been there before? Was it a place you've never been? Did a poster or picture on the wall spark a memory?
- Identify how you got there and your purpose for being there. Were you looking for trouble? Did you go with a friend?
- Were you upset before you arrived at this location?
- Identify extra details using your senses. Did a specific smell or sound trigger an emotional response? Did someone receive a phone call?

Being aware of facts and holding yourself accountable for your actions can help you analyze your emotional triggers.

Since your reality grows from what you think of most, you must elevate your thinking mind to see and create goodness around you. Restorative, supportive activities heal you on a subconscious level, change your thoughts, influence your behavior, and encourage mindful, intentional actions that create positive change. Refer to chapter 7 and start incorporating restorative activities into your daily life to keep yourself present, mindful, and aware so you can prevent upsetting emotional reactions.

Lack of Motivation

What do you do if you feel unmotivated, unproductive, or directionless? First, know that you are not alone. Don't fight it by overcompensating with extra effort; you will only exhaust yourself. Relax. Consider your thoughts. You may be depressed, so talk about your situation with your doctor. Examine any energetic leaks in your life, such as:

- Are you getting enough rest?
- Do you doubt your abilities?
- Are you overextended?
- Are you avoiding discomfort?
- Does your strong belief keep you in an argumentative, unproductive frame of mind?
- How much time do you spend alone?
- When was the last time you spent quality time in nature?

The best thing you can do when you have a lack of motivation is cultivate self-compassion and be kind to yourself. Suffering comes from what we *perceive* as being inadequate or a personal failure. When we are sensitive to our suffering, we want to ease it.

One of the best ways to gain perspective on where your lack of motivation is coming from is to figure out what has your attention. As I stated before, thinking can help you make progress, but too much thinking causes anxiety. Anxiety tells us there isn't enough time to complete everything we must do. When your brain is yelling, "It's impossible to get everything done!", how can you feel motivated? Organizing your thoughts makes things seem achievable. You get motivated when you can "see the light at the end of the tunnel," and getting organized helps you create a plan of action.

Exercise – Where Is My Attention?

Lack of motivation can stem from overwhelm, so the goal is to figure out what's on your mind. There are two main reasons your life may feel overwhelming: emotional triggers and chaos. A chaotic life starts with an unorganized mind that's filled with verbal reminders of everything that is not going right, everything you must do, and everything you can't do. If you don't know up from down, how can you find motivation? Meditation is a fantastic way to quiet the mind, but a busy mind cannot jump into a successful meditation routine. So, write it all down. Writing things down provides visual reminders and clears your thought process. It gives you emotional stability and even a grateful heart. To organize your thoughts, all you need is pen and paper.

There are many benefits to writing things down:

- It serves as a visual reminder – Things like a grocery list, a calendar, and to-do lists help organize all the data in your head so you feel in control over everything you must complete in a day.
- It clears your thoughts – Writing down everything that has your attention clears your thoughts. It gives you a sense of relief, even though you have done nothing.
- It stabilizes your emotions – There is a reason journaling is a huge part of Wild Moon Healing. Writing things down helps you process your emotions. It also helps you make connections you would not have otherwise made.
- It inspires a grateful heart – Writing things down encourages progress. In a chaotic world, checking things off your to-do list can be gratifying.
- It increases focus and mental clarity – Our minds are amazing, designed to catalog the information

> we gather throughout our life experience. I'll bet that, like me, you can remember your childhood phone number and your favorite outfit from your teens! The super-computer that is your mind offers that information as soon as you think about it. But today, with technology, we don't have to keep as much information in our conscious minds. Writing thoughts down with the intention of processing and prioritizing what is in your mind can be helpful.

If we don't write down our activities and responsibilities to help us organize our thoughts, it's no wonder we sometimes lack motivation. Lack of motivation can also come from not having a clear sense of your life purpose. This also stifles your energy to the point that you can't find joy or happiness in anything you do.

So, create the habit of writing everything down. Carry your journal with you, or use voice settings on your electronic devices to record your thoughts (use a hands-free device when driving). When you have an experience that wakes you up or inspires you in some way, write it down!

☪

Fear of Consequences

Fear is mentioned countless times in this book because it is what kills dreams and derails progress. Fear helps us react to expected danger, and the fear hormones in our body's command center elevate blood pressure and increase our breath rate for this purpose. We are born with the ability to sense danger. Once the fight-or-flight response is over and we realize we are still alive, we can feel exhilarated. Another type of fear is paranoia. For Wild Moon Healing, I am not referring to life-or-death situations, nor am I referring to phobias or irrational fears, such as the fear of flying or public speaking. I'm referring to the fear of karma, or the consequences of your actions (or inaction). Fear is an instinctive, uncomplicated emotional response, yet it is so powerful that it can derail your progress (just as triggers and lack of motivation do). When you refuse to explore who you are at your core, are you revealing that you are afraid of looking at your unfulfilled life? Our minds are programmed to perceive karma as a negative consequence. Are you afraid of karma?

In the physical world, fear can be physical (the fight-or-flight response to danger), or it can be mental (as it is with the fear of consequence). It bears repeating: Karma is nothing to fear. It is neither good nor bad. Spiritually, the principle of karma is associated with the idea of rebirth. Karma in the present affects one's future in the current life, as well as the nature and quality of our future lives. In Western culture, karma is considered a natural consequence of one's actions. Karma is just the theory of action and reaction (or cause and effect). Fear plays a key role in society because rules and laws govern the consequences of certain actions. Looking at religion, the promise of utopia or heaven alone does not motivate people into action in the same manner that the fear of hell or a bad rebirth seems to influence certain actions.

The mind is a precarious place. Why do we give into our fears before we look at our strengths? Why does worry prevail? Wanting something for your future or worrying about it does not in and of itself bring about a karmic response. Whatever the consequences of your action, it does not mean you did something wrong or that you are a bad person (although you may judge yourself harshly). Every action has an equal or opposite reaction, an energetic ripple, a karmic consequence.

Think of consequences as a body of water. Your behaviors, thoughts, and actions are pebbles that interact with it. However you drop, throw, or place them affects the water's flow. And if you do nothing? Everything changes. As wind blows against the water, it creates ripples of its own. Everything you do has an energetic consequence and affects life within and around you. Even if you do everything "right" in life, a negative consequence could still be the result.

You can work hard and go after and achieve what you want, but some unwanted consequences could create a state of fear. Imagine that a woman named Tina is living an amazing and successful life with no wellness issues, like depression or disordered eating, but her sedentary lifestyle leads to weight gain. She worked a full-time job while going to school, and her hard work paid off; Tina earned that promotion she worked so hard for and deserves. The unanticipated, unwanted consequence of her sedentary actions was weight gain. This example blows the "bad action equals bad consequence, good action equals good consequence" theory out of the water, right? But the success of Tina's present moment is overshadowed by fear. She is afraid of her current appearance because of the weight gain and afraid of her future appearance because after she loses weight, she might have stretch marks or loose skin. This fear is not irrational or emotional. It is legitimate, but it's a mental trap at the same time. What should Tina do now?

- Acknowledge fear – We all experience fear. Don't avoid it. If you are having a hard time staying the course, ask yourself, "What am I afraid of?" Identify your fear and acknowledge it.
- Evaluate the impact – Whether you address your fear or not, it will impact your future. In five, ten, or twenty years, what will the impact of changing be? Of staying the same? In Tina's example, does she keep the weight or lose the weight? What are the pros and cons of each scenario?

- Focus on your strengths and the positive impact – Focusing on what you know you can do and what you are good at can minimize worry and fear. Tina could commit to her self-care with confidence and have the fortitude and drive to see her goal through, but she fears the consequences of becoming healthy. It doesn't seem to mesh, does it?
- Imagine no fear – If the fear were to go away, what would happen in your life? The karma of releasing fear is relief, freedom, and confidence. Go back to the *Visualize Your Intention* exercise in the last chapter. What does your future feel like when you reach your goal? In thinking about everything you dream of achieving in your future, there is no room for fear. Tina can lose her weight *and* look great.
- Thirst for knowledge – Karma is here to help you, not break you. As you keep exploring and discovering things about yourself, you'll find what does and does not work. Examine the action you take (cause) and the result (effect). Learn from everything you do or do not do. Now that Tina has completed her education, she replaces her study time with self-care time.

Now, move past your fear. Transform. I know that is difficult to do, and it will most likely take a lot more than one lunar cycle to accomplish. It takes hope and faith. Don't try to leave your comfort zone altogether or all at once. Just the thought of doing that could create paralyzing fear in some people. Think of it as expanding your comfort zone. If you commit to one minor change, and regardless of what happens, learn from it, that action makes your comfort zone a little bigger. It expands. An energetic ripple does not stop. It is not bound by time or space. Believe that your actions today are creating a better tomorrow for yourself, your family, your community… and the world. A little faith can take down a lot of fear. I have faith in you. Have faith in yourself.

10

FULL MOON PHASE

Inner Child vs. Shadow Self

Early in my research, I learned about the inner child and the shadow self. From what I've read, the inner child is the childlike aspect of each of us that's created from an emotional wound received in childhood. The shadow self is the archetype we repress in ourselves that expresses deviant behaviors. This dark aspect of ourselves hides undesirable ideas, instincts, impulses, weaknesses, desires, perversions, and embarrassing fears in our shadows.

We portray the inner child as our truth—an uncontaminated, innocent version of who we are—while we portray our shadows as the parts of us we disconnect from because of rejection or the fear of rejection. As I studied the shadow realm, I questioned the distinction between the inner child and the shadow self, because both concepts paint a picture of a fragile, dark place deep in our subconscious minds, except one is an innocent child and one is perceived as a perverted facet of the self. I reject aspects of these definitions and believe that in order to remove the stigma so many people suffer from, our society must abandon the parts of these philosophies that label parts of a person as degenerate, peculiar, or abnormal. For example, the stigma of mental disorders like depression can lead to a lack of support and empathy for the suffering person. The absence of help leaves sufferers feeling embarrassed and misunderstood; therefore, they do not seek help.

You don't have all these different people (or versions of yourself) living inside you. There is only you. *You* need healing and acceptance, not just the nine-year-old version of yourself, because right now, you are every age you've ever been and every experience you've ever had. Your entire life makes you who you are right now. The wounded person reading this book needs love.

We push our hurt into the dark recesses of our minds to protect our hearts. In this aspect, we have shadows that are good places to hide things because people, including us, cannot see or access what we reject about ourselves. Our shadows contain the parts of us we do not share because of fear from the ego that:

- believes our false, limiting beliefs.
- gets mad.
- cries when we do not get what we want.
- holds us back.

When we hide our unhealed traumatic wounds, we stifle our energetic flow and keep ourselves stuck in trauma. This means we cannot grow into our true selves, because we remain hurt and frozen in time. Uncomfortable experiences create wounds, too, and over time, unhealed wounds create emotional triggers. When something occurs that sparks the memory of a negative experience and unhealed emotional pain, it elicits a behavioral response. Your reaction—a protection mechanism to prevent further hurt or rejection—

may be displaced. The person on the receiving end of your reaction may not deserve it—especially when it's yourself. Emotional triggers gained that name because such a reaction is always based on sentiment. Examples of this include:

- Yelling at someone because you don't feel heard. You believe raising your voice will make people listen and hear your message.
- Bingeing on pounds of sweets because you don't feel important. You've established an eating disorder that allows you to engage in unhealthy behavior because the people you need validation from never give it to you.
- Drinking to the point of sickness and blackouts to "have fun" because you fear rejection. Your insecurities exist because you don't know (or don't like) who you are, so you drink to become someone—anyone—else.

When triggered, unhealed traumatic wounds surface from our shadows, and we experience the related emotions again. Over time, our protective mechanisms develop as negative behavioral and thought patterns. Our shadows bring a sense of isolation because we cannot share the shameful, guilty parts of ourselves we hide. To compensate, we behave negatively, numbing our shame and guilt. We come to believe that those feelings are absolute truths and that we deserve to feel this way because something is wrong with us. We are abnormal. These self-imposed feelings limit us, creating the message that "This is it. It doesn't get any better than this. I don't deserve better than this." When you believe you don't deserve better (or can't do better), you cannot level up, which weakens your self-esteem.

Low expectations for yourself and your future deteriorate your sense of worth. Experienced trauma is the root cause of low self-esteem; it gives the ego a reason to release fear in your outer world through different thoughts, emotions, and behaviors. The ego uses fear to tell you, "You will fail. It is impossible. You will look silly. You will lose. You will fall. You will hurt yourself." It limits you and stops you from taking inspired action that can create positive change in your life.

No one is immune to fear, as it is the reason our conscious ego mind chooses routes that appear easy, safe, or free from criticism, and if no one is critiquing the ego mind, it feels satisfied. But the shackles of false, limiting beliefs create an unfulfilled life because you are not free to achieve your boundless potential. As long as you hold on to unhealed pain, this scenario will keep replaying in your life.

This "Groundhog Day effect" enforces the protection mechanism you created to shield yourself from further pain. *Groundhog Day*,[27] a 1993 movie, is a story of personal transformation. It teaches us that when we keep living in a place of pain, we live in defense mode. The main character, Phil, relives the same day over and over, seeking attention and affection from another person. In the end, he chooses honesty, self-acceptance, and self-actualization. Through living his truth, Phil breaks the cycle of being stuck in life.

Pain does not have to derive from a traumatic experience, like the sudden death of a loved one, war, physical assault, or surviving a natural disaster. Even negative experiences that do not appear to cause physical injury or emotional wounding, like embarrassment, bullying, a turbulent relationship, or problems at work or home, can be traumatic. If a life event resulted in a negative emotion, your ego mind knows it does not want you to live through that again.

Our conscious mind is where we "live" because of the level of awareness associated with ego. When we live through a trauma, the ego assigns an emotion to the experience. The intensity of that emotion determines the power of our triggered reactions.

Reactions come in two forms: either you lash out at another person, or you take it out on yourself. Such behavior is what psychologists refer to when they talk about the inner child.

---

[27] *Groundhog Day*. Directed by Harold Ramis, 1993. Columbia Pictures.

When a child expresses themselves by having a tantrum, you cannot reason with them. In the same way, no one can reason with an adult who is in the midst of an emotional response. Adults who never learned to express themselves in healthy ways as children may engage in negative behaviors, such as day drinking, overspending, or overworking in adulthood.

But adults who exhibit childlike reactions to present-day trauma are not responding from their protective ego. Although rooted pain means it has been with us for quite some time, we can experience new trauma at any age, and that trauma can create an inner-child-like reaction. False belief systems about who we are arise from trauma and are secured in our shadows. In adulthood, our emotionally triggered reactions can create challenging experiences for us in the future, such as health and wellness issues.

Health problems that arise from the way we treat ourselves are preventable with self-love. Psychologists say that the inner child desires love and hugs and wants to play. Your inner child wants to be spontaneous and explore curiosities, but it cannot. Why? Because it is not free. Guess what? Adults want the same thing. Adults can play. It is not irresponsible to be spontaneous or explore curiosities.

So, why limit yourself to playing like a child to give your inner child what it needs? Remember, everything in your life is either giving you energy or draining it. Dreaming of going back to or reliving days gone by drains your energy. You are not a child anymore, and wanting to go back in time to play like you used to or wanting to have your sixteen-year-old body back are energetic leaks. A child can enjoy rock climbing at an indoor center with bouldering rooms, but adventure-loving adults have resources to pursue that interest by taking their hobby to new and more challenging levels. Although we can all benefit from keeping our pure, childlike wonder, don't limit yourself to playing like a child. One reason we adults can feel stuck is that we believe our inner child is an uncontaminated version of us, and that as adults, there is something dirty about us—the things we were told were polluted. We believe we are not normal, so we hide.

Our shadows are not our perversions or our abnormalities. The shadow is not an evil twin, alter ego, or personality disorder. It's a place where we hide parts of our true self because of the negative emotions created from our wounds. We cannot be authentic when our ego stores negative emotions, bad experiences, or wounds in our shadows. To live authentically is to be pure at heart and free; this is the true unadulterated version of ourselves, not your younger self. Hiding things about ourselves is one of the reasons undesirable behaviors manifest in our lives.

Life's struggles come from denying parts of yourself, striving to be something you are not. Your adverse actions are not indicative of a flaw or defect, just hurt. Negative behaviors can be a cry for help. You should want to learn how to become who you are, even if your conscious mind does not realize it needs help.

Perhaps there was a time when a person told you your behavior or some aspect of you was bad or wrong. When you believe that a part of you is abnormal, you'll likely want to hide it. But we can create a new narrative in our minds and can change our memories. (Refer to Losing Contact with the Present Moment in chapter 4). But we cannot change an emotion. While our memories may lie dormant, our emotions do not. The negative emotions and wounds we hide create a defense inside us to safeguard us from experiencing that negative feeling (emotional trigger) ever again. For example, as a child, I was a tomboy. Part of my true self needs to be outside, loves to get dirty, and hates the color pink. But for my family, "tomboy" had a negative connotation (or at least I was made to feel that way). The more effort my mom put into "making me ladylike," the more I dug my heels in and said, "Not going to happen." But it happened. Sometimes I wonder if my tomboy side hadn't been repressed, where would I be now? What remarkable things could I have accomplished if I hadn't adulted-up and stopped doing the things I enjoyed? I accept the tomboy in me now, and that makes life more enjoyable. I spend more time in nature, get dirty, and never wear pink.

You can heal from past traumas that keep you stuck, too. By doing the self-discovery activities in this book, you can understand yourself and your pain and break free from your emotional wounds. The energy of a full moon helps reconnect you with what you hide in your shadows and allows you to reprogram negative conditioning into positive thoughts and behaviors. As you cultivate self-love and self-acceptance, your self-esteem will increase, and safe boundaries will replace your defenses. Healthy boundaries negate the need to be on guard. You can live spontaneously, be curious, play, and have adventures.

Shadow Work

Healing and freeing the parts of ourselves we hide in our shadows is called "shadow work." The focus of shadow work (and the entirety of Moon work during a lunar cycle) is to heal internal wounds and unfreeze the stuck emotions. Shadows are our wounds. Our wounds are not just emotional hurts; they are characteristics of ourselves that we scold. We tell them, "Stay hidden," because someone somewhere said something about us not being normal. Maybe they made fun of us, belittled us, did not take us seriously, or took advantage of us (or we perceived their reactions as such). We tuck away these little pieces of us in our minds, in our shadows.

When you clear your shadows and release your internal wounds, dormant creative outlets awaken, causing your vibrational energy to rise. These processes work in tandem; as you heal, you'll change your creative center and tap into your magic. You'll gain a sense of clarity and begin to self-actualize. You'll notice connections and learn lessons from your experiences. Getting in tune with your energy and intuition brings about synchronicities, signs that you are on the right path. Keep moving forward!

Sometimes you need help recognizing whether you are on the correct path. Carl Jung, a twentieth-century Swiss psychologist, spent his life studying the human personality and mind. He coined the term "shadow self" and defined synchronicity as the "simultaneous occurrence of two meaningfully but not causally connected events."[28] Healing from trauma creates synchronicity, and when that happens, you'll feel you have a little magic in your life. Synchronicities (or magical events) come from forces stronger than any one person. These signs may seem to occur by chance, but meaningful coincidences are a thoughtful wink from heaven, the universe, angels, your ancestors, or any energetic force you believe in that is greater than you. Maybe the energy of "As above" uses our collective energy on earth to create synchronicities as encouragement to keep us pressing forward when we are going in the right direction!

Accepting the spiritual significance of synchronicities means you acknowledge you are not on this journey alone. There is divine guidance available to you. These thoughtful nudges from above are just God or angels reminding us they are here to help. Here are a few examples of synchronicities:

- Have you ever run into a friend who you were just thinking about and were going to call? Your paths crossed for a reason.
- Have you ever been running late for work because you couldn't find your car keys, and then come upon an accident you might have been in had you been on time? There was a reason your keys were not where they should have been.
- Have you ever experienced seeing things repeatedly, such as certain numbers? I call those "angel numbers," and they mean something, even if it's just your loved ones in spirit saying, "I'm here," or "You're doing great!"

---

[28] Graham Wallace, *The Art of Thought.*

I have experienced many synchronicities in my life. For example, when my son was young, I picked him up from daycare, knowing I had no food at home and no means to purchase any. I didn't know about food banks or church food pantries; that could have also been my pride. As I drove home looking at him sleeping in his car seat, I cried, wondering how I was going to feed him that night and the next night, as payday was not until the end of the week. When I pulled into the driveway, I saw grocery bags at the door with several bags full of formula. I am fairly sure I know who delivered them, but I don't believe I've ever said anything. So, Ms. Sharon, if you are reading this, thank you! That little wink from heaven helped restore my faith.

If you lack faith right now, pay attention to things that repeat themselves or that you feel may be a coincidence. Shadow work is difficult, and synchronicities are the inspiration and encouragement from the universe you need, so accept it.

Full Moon Energy

The full moon is about celebration. It's a time to rejoice about yourself and how wonderfully unique you are and to honor the gifts you have to offer. Use the energy of the full moon to express your true self. This energy heightens emotions, feelings, mental processes, and dreams. As these things speak to you, pay attention. Those little nudges from above can provide you with valuable information and encouragement. When you tap into the energy created when the sun illuminates the moon, you can use it to bring clarity to personal relationships and situations. Are you attempting to understand the truth of a situation? Do you need a reality check? Are the important people in your life treating you as you deserve? Why are you not stepping into your authenticity? As this energetic healing light illuminates your shadows, use it to help you identify triggers that cause you to react. This energetic healing light illuminates your shadows and reveals your truth. Revelations occur through reality checks, wherein you attempt to understand the truth of a situation.

Because you can gain so much insight during this part of the lunar cycle, it may seem that Wild Moon Healing should begin under the light of the full moon. There are two distinct reasons you do not want to create intentions under a full moon. The first has to do with the alignment of the sun and moon. At the full moon, they oppose each other. This opposition has the potential to create heightened emotions, tension, and uncomfortable friction. You never want to start a fresh story and start living your new, inspired life in a triggering energy. The second reason is that, spiritually, the full moon represents fulfillment or completion. While this time supplies greater amplification of vision and potential possibilities, allowing you to identify things in life that hold you back, you must first discover what the thinking mind wants under the new moon. Then you have to go after that dream under the waxing moon. If you discover that things are not working out as you had hoped, before you blame or make enormous changes in your life, use the energy of the full moon to analyze and see yourself in your situation. During this lunar phase, you want to see things within yourself as well as in your situation. While looking at your life at a micro level (yourself in a specific situation), the full moon can help you put that into context on the larger scale of your life as a whole.

Part of shadow work is accepting and acknowledging the way our life experiences unfold. Our life experience results from personal choices and actions. When we identify the choices we've made and the actions we've taken and accept responsibility for them, we aid in our personal evolution. As we evolve, discover the power of our true self, and actively participate in our lives, we learn that forward is the only way to go. Shadow work is the path forward. Illuminating our shadows and bringing them to our conscious minds can be painful, but we can wonder,

"Why did I deny that part of myself?" With the bright light of the moon shining on our entire self, we can give our shadows attention—one at a time. This is a powerful opportunity to process, acknowledge, and accept our true selves.

This type of self-exploration requires brutal honesty and self-transparency. Because we typically hide the things that hurt us, such memories can lie dormant. Full moon energy helps illuminate your metaphorical path, including your memories, and shed light on obstacles that hinder your forward progress. When you see your life as a path, you can visualize yourself turning back to view what has already come to pass and looking forward so you can make changes. The full moon lights up the past actions that led to your current situation. Maybe it is hard to see yourself in this light. Maybe it is easier to blame others than to be accountable. But don't let this deter you. Everyone is on a life path, and when the moon lights your way, you can see crossroads or a fork in the road. Which route will you take? Through shadow work under a full moon, you'll realize choices and see prospects you couldn't see before. But if you shut down, the shadows will fall over your path again, and you won't be able to see the way forward.

Facing uncomfortable truths is difficult, so suspend self-judgment, validate your feelings as they surface, and ground yourself with supportive activities. The way you feel is always OK, so rather than blaming yourself for being emotional or angry, acknowledge your feelings. The more truths you discover about who you are, the better you'll get to know yourself. It is logical that the better you know yourself, the safer you will feel. This work gets easier over time. The best way to give honest feedback is to know your listener, right?

By addressing the emotional baggage that's been long buried in the shadows, you can show up in your life and be present for commitments and relationships. Showing up for yourself is the ultimate act of self-love, self-worth, and self-respect. It takes hard work and practice to ask yourself, "What do I want?"

before thinking about others. Through shadow work, you'll gain the power and control necessary to show up for yourself, and you'll learn healthy ways of expressing your shadowed characteristics. You'll become more genuine.

Exercise – Shadow Journaling Under the Full Moon

When you practice learning about yourself, you'll uncover the foundations of your limiting beliefs and detach from a lifetime of difficult emotions and experiences. This is like emotional journaling, but the focus is on your shadows. Emotional journaling focuses on your response to a triggering situation, whereas shadow journaling focuses on how you are feeling to help you discover why you feel that way. To begin, do some stilling, restorative activities that help you become present. Start off by asking yourself questions to identify things about yourself. Your revelations should lead to more probing questions. For example:

Explore how you feel emotionally…

- Are you happy? Are you unhappy? Why? Is this how you want to feel?
- If you don't feel happy or unhappy, can you identify how you feel? Can you describe it with one word, like "sad," "crushed," "secure," or "peaceful"?
- Are you afraid of something? Can you identify it? Why does it scare you?
- Do you feel unaccepted or unworthy? Why? Does a specific person make you feel this way? Do you feel this way around anyone else?
- Do you feel you are letting yourself down? In what ways?
- How does drama make you feel? Why?

Explore how you feel physically…

- Are you experiencing any discomfort in your body?
- Have you done anything to cause yourself discomfort? If so, what caused your pain?
- Why do you think you do/did that to yourself?
- Do you treat your body well by eating healthy and moving daily? Why or why not?

Explore how you feel about yourself…

- What do you dislike about yourself? Why?
- How would you change yourself if you could? Why?
- Do you have regrets? About what?
- Are you indecisive? In what way?
- Do you have self-sabotaging habits? If so, what are they?

Explore your behaviors…

- Are you judgmental of yourself and others? If so, what are you judging?
- Do you numb your pain with anything outside of yourself, such as drinking alcohol, playing video games, bingeing on television, or working out relentlessly? Why?
- Do you avoid specific people, places, or things at all costs? Why do you do that?
- Do you refrain from activities you enjoy doing? Why?
- Who or what has the most influence over your actions? Are these influences healthy?

Explore aspects of your spiritual or religious life…

- Do you spend time with a Source from which you glean strength and inspiration? How do you feel when you don't?
- Do you spend time in nature? Do you notice feeling different the more time you spend in (or out) of nature?

- Do you engage in prayer or meditation? If not, do you feel you don't have the time? Why?

Explore specific situations…

- Has someone presented you with an opportunity to go after your dream job, but you didn't apply? Why?
- Did someone offer you the chance of a lifetime to take a dream vacation and you didn't go? Why?
- Are you having a challenging time sticking to a healthy eating program? Why?
- Are you unable to pay your bills with your current income? Why?
- Have you always wanted to skydive, learn to swim, or say the alphabet backward, but never looked into your interests? What holds you back?

☪

You can think of shadow work as a water well: you lower a bucket into the well and pull up only the water you need. If you pull up too much water, it may spill and create a mess, so you hoist up just enough water for that moment. When you are ready for more water, you lower another bucket down into the well. Our metaphorical well is the mind, and the buckets are discovery questions. Every time you seek more information, your brain will provide what it believes you can handle in the moment. So, asking yourself questions about how you feel and why you engage in certain behaviors will fill your bucket with experiences from your past and help unravel your protective layers. Let one discovery lead you to the next.

The process of shadow journaling with the full moon energy is not as easy as exploring and then discovering. For example, if you want to correct your overspending habit, you'll need more information. Can you identify a specific financial category in which you overspend? By questioning, you can see the reason. Perhaps you spend too much money shopping online for clothes, so you make an intention to stop buying clothing online. But while this inquiry into your behavior tells you what you are doing, it does not tell you *why* you do it. If you don't investigate the feelings behind the action, you may curb your online spending, but develop other habits that affect your finances and life in different ways, such as overeating, excessive drinking, or spending too much time in front of the television. By identifying the problem but not doing an in-depth analysis of your emotions, you cannot create a healthy behavior. To see progress in your shadow work, you must keep inquiring.

Shadow Work Journaling (Example)

Going back to the online shopping example, overspending is your energetic leak. It keeps you from achieving a positive financial experience, but it is a symptom of an emotional issue; overspending is not the principal issue. So, you need to ask yourself the questions from this and the previous exercise to get to the root of the problem. Your shadows formed because of emotions like fear, rejection, insecurity, and shame. Discovering, acknowledging, understanding, healing, and detaching from these feelings can be freeing. But before you can be free, you must identify what you need to heal.

- What or whom is holding you back or keeping you from your goal?
- What behavior or habit do you engage in that is keeping you from reaching your goal?
- Can you identify what is depleting your energy?

Delve deeper into your financial issues by asking yourself questions like:

Q: In what categories do you overspend? (Try a budgeting or money management app to determine your personal expenditure categories.)
Mary: It's unbudgeted clothing items that keep me from meeting my budget.

Q: Who is with you when you shop for clothes online?
Mary: Typically, I'm alone. Sometimes I'm waiting for someone.

Q: What are you feeling when you are alone and shop?
Mary: I don't know. I just don't want anyone to see me standing alone and feel sorry for me.

Q: Are you worried people would feel sorry for you, or were you frustrated about waiting?
Mary: That is frustrating. But I still feel like people are looking at me, like something is wrong with my outfit or something.

Q: Is something wrong with your outfit? Do you need new clothes? Do your old clothes not fit?
Mary: No, I don't need clothes. But I have to update my wardrobe.

Q: Everyone needs to update their wardrobe from time to time. What does your life look like with your new wardrobe?
Mary: I'm not trying to impress anyone or anything like that, but I need to look professional at work.

Q: You're not trying to impress anyone. How do you react to compliments?
Mary: Well. I don't know. It depends on who gives it. I like when my friends notice.

Q: How do you feel if no one notices a new outfit?
Mary: Lost in the crowd, just like everyone else. Nothing special.

Q: Lost in the crowd. Do you often feel unnoticed in other settings?
Mary: Unnoticed? Well, growing up, my brother, John, was the football god.
Q: So, he received more attention than you, and maybe you felt insignificant?
Mary: No. Yes. I don't know.

Are you going to get to the root of a problem in one Q & A session? Most likely not. When you keep questioning, you'll find out that going over your budget and buying clothes you don't really need are symptoms of a false, limiting belief, like "I am insignificant." Start with the obvious and see where it takes you.

☪

Answers and Memories

Only you have the answer to your current life challenges. In the previous example, Mary discovered some underlying feelings of loneliness and insignificance that could be factors in her shopping habits. That was Mary's "big discovery" about herself.

When you do this exercise, right before your big discovery, you may become frustrated because your ego doesn't want something to surface. In the example, Mary got frustrated as soon as she started thinking about the recognition her brother, John, received growing up. There is something to that. Perhaps her frustration relates to the accumulated recognition her brother received, or maybe Mary repressed a memory of a specific incident that is separate from John being a football god. Don't force answers. If that is as far as you get in one lunar cycle, that is considerable progress.

Memories are stories. We use our stories to share with others, learn from our past, and establish our identity. Our stories change. We can change the facts, leave facts out, or add false details. The extent to which we do this depends on our level of self-esteem and how much that past situation influences this present moment. With a repressed memory, our nervous system becomes overwhelmed from stress or trauma, so the ego hides it in the shadows and blocks it from our present thoughts and actions. Remember, while memories are dormant, we are still building a protection mechanism because of them. If a traumatic memory surfaces for you, reach out to your doctor. You may need professional guidance to navigate your thoughts and separate fact from fiction.

Shadow work is about exposing yourself under the light of the full moon. Revealing your truth is the only way to discover who you are. Being real with yourself or anyone else is about vulnerability. As you become vulnerable, false and limiting beliefs may make you feel exposed, creating fear. Since your belief system is not true, after the trigger or negative life event is over, fear turns to anxiety. If you are open, concern that something might happen may set in, and you might be susceptible to other negative life events. Most people find being vulnerable uncomfortable because they fear that if they are themselves, they will have to withstand judgments from the outside world. Vulnerability is courage. Courage is the source of innovation, creativity, and change. When you discover and accept your authentic self, you will choose to no longer hide behind things like overspending, addiction, fear, or shame.

You must go down the proverbial rabbit hole before you can detach from the actual issue that's causing your energetic leak. By integrating your shadows, you will develop a deeper sense of trust and confidence in yourself. But before you can integrate your shadow, you must find it. Use Moon work to find all those pieces of your true self that you've buried. As you are honest with yourself and love those aspects you've hidden, your greater self-awareness will lead to relief, growth, freedom, and authenticity. To develop this way requires surrender, as well as acceptance of your true self and the unique gifts only you can offer the world. The world needs you more than ever. People who have confidence, know who they are, and love themselves empower themselves and others. These people express compassion in the world.

Shadow work involves exploring deep inside to find answers that allow you to heal, awaken, and experience growth. It is about identifying where you spend your energy and discovering the root cause of your energetic depletion. If you are not sure where to start, identify your energy leaks by assessing your reactions in certain circumstances or around specific people. For example:

- Is there a specific person you always say yes to when you should say no?
- Do you get quiet and become withdrawn around a person in your life who belittles you?
- Do you have an energetic vampire in your life... perhaps a friend who gossips?
- Do you overreact?
- Do you ever act from a place of fear, engaging in behaviors or taking actions you do not like? If so, why do you do that? How does it make you feel when you do that? What are you afraid of if you do not do that?

Shadow work is hard, so please take quality time for yourself. In the "Supportive Activities" section of this chapter, you'll find activities that can support you as you explore your shadows.

Exercise – Challenge Your Assumptions

Are you sure your answers and memories are accurate? Sometimes we think we already have the answers, but our knowledge is false or a half-truth. Knowledge is a system of belief; it's true because you believe it to be true. Recall that strongly held beliefs can be energetic leaks. Beliefs can be opinions rather than facts. So, the question becomes, "How do I know that I know?" Therein lies the importance of challenging your assumptions.

Challenge yourself, your thinking, your knowledge, and your beliefs. Discover whether your true self believes your truth as you understand it. Question your judgments, prejudices, stereotypes, and gossip.

Challenge Questions:

- Where does this belief come from? When did I believe it?
- Is it really my belief?
- Is it true?
- Where did my expectation of how this story will unfold come from?
- Why do I make assumptions about a person's character?
- Why do I assume people have a specific agenda?
- What is at stake if I do/do not challenge my belief?
- Do I trust the source of my knowledge?
- What things do I say, "I have to," "I should," "I never," or "I ought to" about?
- Where do these demands ("have to," "should") come from?
- Do the demands arise from a place of wanting to fit in or people-please?

Supportive Activities

Like restorative activities, supporting activities are foundational in encouraging self-care while you explore your shadows. These activities build a positive infrastructure to encourage progress with your Moon work. By adding these activities into your shadow work, you'll provide yourself with ongoing support that will lead to positive breakthroughs and progress. Choose to no longer take a passive role in life. Choose to heal with the energy of a full moon.

Exercise – Shadow Work Journaling Prompts

Here are a few more examples of journaling prompts for shadow work:

- Identify a time when you were embarrassed. Why was the experience embarrassing?
- What promise did you make to yourself that you broke? Why was the promise hard to keep?
- Do you keep your promises to others?
- In what ways do you feel guilty? Why?
- Do you feel you need to forgive yourself? Why?
- Do you have issues with time? Are you always running late? Are you strict with yourself for being early so you are not late? What feelings do you experience if someone has to wait for you?
- Do you express your feelings constructively? Can you recall your last emotional outburst? Was it the topic, person, or place that sparked powerful emotions?
- Do/did your parents provide you with everything you needed? Why or why not? What do you consider "everything"? What about those things is important to you?

- What makes you angry or sad? When you are sad, do you know you have the option to be happy? If you believe you can choose an emotion, where else in your life might you be able to choose better for yourself?

☪

Meditation

Over time, a consistent meditation practice sets the stage for significant breakthroughs and emotional healing. Before you meditate, make the intention that the light from the full moon will reveal what you most need to know or work on right now. Trust that what comes up from your proverbial well is what you need right now.

Recall from the meditation you did at the new moon that being still is a healthy, effective way to tap into the moon's energy. Meditation creates the perfect calming conditions in your mind. It reveals real thoughts and feelings while inducing self-awareness.

Exercise – Full Moon Meditation

Sit where you can see the moon. If you cannot be outside, sit where you can see it through a window. If you cannot see it, know that it's there.

Pull your shoulders up toward your ears, then roll them down like you are putting them in your back pockets to help release any tension you're holding in your neck. Close your eyes. Take three deep, slow, smooth breaths to calm your mind. Breathe in through your nose for 3 to 5 counts. Hold for 1 to 2 counts. Breathe out for 3 to 5 counts. Hold for 1 to 2 counts. Repeat. Envision the moon's beams filling your physical space, illuminating everything in your room. The moon's light moves around your room to reveal its supportive energy. Now, breathe in, letting the healing light fill your body. Visualize the moonlight purifying your body, mind, and soul, leaving nothing hidden in darkness. See the light move slowly and smoothly throughout your body, livening your senses and accepting all that is coming up from your shadows. Acknowledge any thoughts, feelings, or physical sensations, then bring your attention back to your breath. Breathe in through your nose, and feel your body fill up with life from your breath. Notice your stomach and chest rise. Then slowly breathe out through your mouth. When you open your eyes, begin shadow journaling, or work your way through the shadow work journaling prompts.

Tarot Cards, Oracle Cards, and Pendulums

Tarot cards, oracle cards, and pendulums are divination tools that work off your energy to tap into your inner knowing. They provide insight into your shadows and help you make sense of you (and only you). You will not gain reliable knowledge if you seek information about the feelings or motives of another person. When seeking wisdom from the cards or pendulum, trust your intuition. Inquire whether your feelings and instincts about a given situation are accurate. Meditate with the intention of hearing your inner voice. Also, seeking information about your future gives answers based on your current energy. Since you are Wild Moon Healing, your energetic vibration will increase, and as it does, the cards will reveal different answers. What can the cards and pendulum do for you?

- Warn you about your behavior or motivation.
- Encourage you and let you know you are on the right path.
- Let you know you are right to question a situation.
- Help you make sense of your emotions.
- Decipher details that come up in your journaling.
- Encourage mindfulness.
- Provide insight into how your current behaviors are creating your future.

Pendulum work helps clarify the cards' meaning. To ascertain more in-depth information, hold the pendulum over the card and ask it to affirm that you have received the intended message from the cards, or if there is more you need to know about your reading (or a specific card). Ask clarifying questions, like:

- Is this card referring to a business or personal relationship?
- The ace in my reading tells me that I will be offered this job. Is it in my best interest to take it?
- The jumping dog on the Fool tarot card has my attention. Does this mean I should have my guard up concerning this relationship?

Clarifying helps direct you to the message the universe wants you to receive. You may need to revise your questions. This is also an intuitive exercise to listen to your inner knowing (such as noticing that the dog on the card has your focus). Let these tools guide you rather than letting them give you an answer.

Exercise – Working with a Pendulum

Some friends and I walked into a store that had pendulums displayed in the front window. All the pendulums connected to our collective energy and started swinging in every direction—every single one! The store owner had never experienced that; it was a crazy kind of cool. Pendulums are great tools if you know how to use them.

There is no wrong way to do pendulum work. If you have a new pendulum, see the *Program Your Pendulum* exercise in chapter 7. Sometimes, when you are learning to use the pendulum, it won't move very much. Don't worry about this. The best thing to do is to speak to your pendulum with certainty, knowing your answer is coming. You can even ask the pendulum if it is conversing with you. It will let you know it's there for you. Sometimes it's just a matter of speaking up or increasing the volume of your voice. If you are emotional or upset, the pendulum will interact with that energy. Once you raise your energy vibration, you will notice your pendulum gaining momentum. To complete my question, I always put my hand under it and say, "Thank you," then it stops swinging.

☪

Ground Yourself

A full moon ritual should involve anything that makes you feel free and connected to a source greater than yourself. You can achieve this through grounding activities that encourage an individual approach to healing. We all have our preferred ways of being open with ourselves to experience personal growth.

Grounding is mindful and active. Examples of grounding activities include:

- Going for a hike in the woods, or spending time in nature or anywhere you can clear your mind and reflect
- Lying on a beach and allowing the ocean waves to put you in a hypnotic state
- Finding a comfortable spot to read a book and forget your worries from the day
- Walking barefoot on the grass
- Taking a hot yoga class to ground and relax your body
- Playing with and invoking the healing energy of laughter

Examples of activities that are not grounding:

- Working or playing on an electronic, blue-light-emitting device
- Mindless, passive activities, such as watching a movie

Grounding activities will remind you of things that make you feel alive and happy. They can also deter stressful thoughts. Regardless of what type of grounding activity you choose, make sure it works for you. If rolling around in the grass with your dog makes you feel introspective, go for it. Have fun!

11

WANING MOON PHASE

Let It Go

The phrase "Let it go" is vague and creates frustration—at least, it seems this way to me. There was a time when my mind was cynical about the "letting go" process. I know now that this process was hard for me because of my delicate ego, and the need to laterally think from multiple random perspectives since everything is connected. Lateral thinking is creative, a function of the right brain. If someone is looking for an out-of-the-box idea, they'll need to engage their right brain. My brain functioned in a linear, left-brain, analytical way, seeing processes and steps to accomplish things (you must first do *this* before you can do *that*). I was living life that way. But when I started my spiritual journey and began engaging in both right- and left-brain activities, my life improved. Only then could I grasp the concept of "letting it go."

Linear thinking is logical and follows a sequence or natural progression. It is efficient and organized (e.g., solving a mathematical equation). There is no room for creativity, originality, or a personal spark. There is one way to do something, and you do it that way because that is the proven way it works. On the other hand, lateral thinking is divergent, visionary, flexible, and creative. There is no logic in "letting it go." Emotions are nonsensical and unique to every person. There are no rules or patterns to follow; therefore, "letting it go" can be hard to grasp.

There are multiple ways to let things go, and everyone grieves in their own way. With so many ways to accomplish this necessary part of life, why is it so difficult? To let something go, you must engage in lateral thinking. When you reflect your inner, creative self to your outer, logical mind, uncomfortable emotions can surface. You need to let negative feelings go, but because emotions are not logical or sequential, the ego wants you to push them back down into your shadows. This creates the illusion that the emotions are gone, but really, they never leave. They grow, and their existence causes the surrender of other positive emotions. Later in life, an emotional trigger can cause these negative emotions to resurface. When that happens, it can hit you like a ton of bricks, so the ego pushes them back down. In my experience, I did not want bad feelings or behaviors (my grief, my emotionally triggered binge eating, or my depression), but I could not banish them. My ego mind couldn't deal with them. Some of my experiences hurt too much, so I kept pushing them back down every time they surfaced. It became mechanical. Every time I pushed them back down, my life drew further away from where I wanted to be. To move forward and experience the positive, I had to surrender the bad. But surrender eluded me.

To understand surrender, you must make the connection between what you have versus what you want. You can be content, but a disparity exists because the two things cannot exist at the same time. For example:

- If your current experience is pain and disappointment, you are surrendering the experience of joy.
- If you live from a place of grief, you are surrendering the happiness you want.
- If you live from a place of addiction, you are surrendering your well-being.

Grief and disappointment are a part of life, but you do not have to stay there. The deep-seated emotions that define addiction, grief, or fear are just words that describe the place someone is living in right now; they do not define who that person is. Are you living in fear or addiction? You can choose to leave that place. It is hard. It takes love and responsibility. But you have the right and the power to choose differently and create a new story. You need to know the difference between a *place* and an *emotion*. All emotions are valid, but without experiencing them, you push bad feelings down inside your shadows, which creates a place within you for them to grow. To achieve wellness and a balanced life, you must let go. You can let go by:

- experiencing and honoring your feelings
- surrendering your struggle and pain
- practicing self-care
- loving yourself
- acknowledging and living your truth
- accepting yourself and your past
- experiencing personal growth

Experience Your Feelings

It is *always* OK to feel what you feel. When you push feelings down, you are not validating your emotion; you are resisting it because it hurts. Hiding emotions creates struggle. Letting go of emotions means you allow them to exist. With trauma, your reality can change in an instant, and your new reality can be incomprehensible. It is difficult to bring emotions into a new life story that was forced upon you. Under the new moon, you dreamt new life into your story, and pain wasn't in the plan. I'm not talking about denying your circumstances; it's just that pain is difficult to experience, so we tend to block it. To cope with emotional pain instead of experiencing it, people often develop coping behaviors, like watering their shame with alcohol, dulling their grief with pills, hiding their insecurities with gossip, or nourishing their pain with food. If you feed your emotion, it grows. To rid yourself of a negative emotion, you surrender it.

Surrender Your Struggle and Pain

To surrender your grief, disappointment, shame, and insecurities, you must be present, mindful, and intentional with your actions. Surrender is impossible when you are in a low-vibrational state. With extreme emotions like grief, you can surrender by screaming and crying it out. In a breathwork class, there is a time when you can hold a pillow up and scream into it. It is because you have to surrender. The first time I experienced this, I tried to scream, but I couldn't. I sobbed. You cannot raise your vibration by keeping it in. Restorative and supportive activities are the key to raising your vibration, shifting your energy, unlocking your ability to surrender, and facilitating healing.

Practice Self-Care

You must let go of more than just your emotions and struggles. For example, you can love someone, but if the relationship with them is not healthy for you, you'll still need to let them go. If your current group of friends is holding you back, you'll need to let them go and find a new tribe. The difficulty with letting people go, especially when you care about them, is the fear of loneliness. But you must let go of all the challenges you create for yourself.

If you establish a coping mechanism for your pain, you create challenge, drama, or chaos in your life, and you need to let it all go. You may need to release old perspectives that keep you stuck in negative thought patterns. Challenges arise when you support a coping mechanism. So, instead of nurturing the coping mechanisms, make a different choice: choose self-care. The calming energy of the waning moon can help you choose to care for yourself and heal your pain.

Love Yourself

Chances are that if you need to let go of something in your life, it has existed long enough to have negatively affected you. At this point in the book, you've identified the changes you need to make in your life. But you can know *what* you need to do and still not know *how* to accomplish it. Because of the ego, you get caught up in drama and chaos, which do not help you stay present and mindful and can derail your progress. The present moment is the only place in time you can see your truth and love yourself through it. You can show love for yourself by:

- Asking for help
- Resting your body and mind
- Remembering that healing does not happen in a straight line (it's not linear)
- Being kind to your pain and the parts of you that hurt
- Enjoying moments when you can, even though your pain is still there
- Knowing that pain is not a punishment

Acknowledge and Live Your Truth

When you do not feel worthy, negative life experiences can rob you of your power, causing you to give it away to things outside of yourself to feel worthy or accepted. In doing so, you lose yourself. You do not have to experience trauma again to let it go. In fact, living your pain again is impossible. The experience happened, it ended, and it left behind a fragile ego and negative emotions. To let go, you must accept all aspects of your life, including whatever you gave your power to. You must accept your whole story up to the present moment. This is part of letting go.

Another part of letting go is identifying the protection mechanisms you created to support you through your trauma. The energy of the waning moon helps you let go and accept how all your experiences, choices, and behaviors are a part of who you are.

Accept Yourself and Your Past

A Stoic philosopher once said, "The obstacle is the way," meaning (in the context of our topic) that the only way to heal from your trauma is to go through it, acknowledge it, feel it, be accountable for it, and learn the lesson. Being passive-aggressive or using similar evasion tactics might help you avoid dealing with challenges, but you cannot practice avoidance forever. Delaying your self-acceptance comes from the fear that your past trauma might cause more pain. The pain still exists, but the experience itself has concluded. It is over. To accept yourself, you must move the stuck emotions and stagnant energy the experience created. Letting go is about learning how the emotion you have carried around for so long has affected you.

Do you have difficulty acknowledging your truth because you deny parts of yourself? For example, a person who overcame a drug addiction (a concluded experience) is often referred to as a "recovering addict" because that is part of their story. They are no longer an "addict," but the phrase describes an authentic part of them. It is one of their titles because they are susceptible to those circumstances, and it reminds them of a place they don't want to return to. Accept all of yourself so you do not return to a place you do not wish to be.

Return to Your Body

Much of our struggle begins in the mind. We push emotions down inside and structure our thoughts in a way that minimizes the negative emotion or experience, or makes us forget it altogether. As you now know, when we push things out of our mind as a protection mechanism, it affects our physical body. We leave the experience or emotion we don't wish to think about in our body. Instead, we need to create space to allow our body to release what it's holding on to.

To keep my emotions pushed down, I kept putting things in my body. I binged on food, drank too much, and smoked cigarettes. These bad habits and behaviors were physical expressions of me pushing my pain down. Because I did not digest my emotions and thoughts, I manifested physical digestive health issues. Do you see ways the emotions, struggle, and pain you are holding on to are manifesting as physical illness in your life? Return to your body—change what you hold onto to create space for healing.

You can return to your body through breathwork meditation. This practice includes various breathing techniques to consciously control the body and influence your mental, emotional, and physical state. This practice brings air into the body, which is the element that moves us; it is a catalyst for change. Air represents the power of the mind; it is the force that directs (moves) the intellect, imagination, and inspiration that propel us toward our dreams, new life, and new possibilities. The masculine energy of the air element allows us to use breathwork to move stuck emotions and release them.

Return to and take care of your body as a form of surrender. In what ways do you think you can honor your body for holding all your struggle and pain?

Experience Personal Growth

Just as letting go is not a linear process, personal growth is also not straightforward or logical. There are so many ways to achieve personal growth. By thinking laterally, your creative center opens, helping you explore and discover the synchronicities of "random events" in your life. The journaling process throughout the lunar cycle helps you connect your experiences, behaviors, and thoughts, which can create "ah-ha" moments. That moment of clarity is personal growth.

Wild Moon Healing is multifaceted, and to experience healing, you must go through all its phases, using right- and left-brain activities. There will be times in which growth occurs from a linear process of doing things on your inspired action list, but at other times, you must think outside the box, get creative, and grow into your truth in a cosmic-sized way.

Letting things go is about releasing what no longer serves you, so you can grow into your authentic self. You cannot become your authentic self:

- without experiencing your feelings
- without self-love
- by struggling against your current situation and pain
- by neglecting yourself
- by rejecting your truth
- by denying your past choices and behaviors
- by remaining stagnant

If you cannot be truthful with yourself, you will not find the strength or courage necessary to accept yourself, experience your emotions, or let go of everything that no longer serves you.

Exercise – Your Life Box

Now you see how ambiguous letting go is. Whether you deliberately create change or it is out of your control, change is inevitable. It is scary. It may sound like the process of "releasing, detaching, and surrendering" creates new traumatic experiences, like detaching from a person you care about or releasing grief for someone you lost, but these aren't new negative experiences; this is how you free yourself.

Close your eyes. Take a few deep breaths in through your nose and out through your mouth. When you feel settled, imagine a large glass box in the distance. Fill it with everything a person could need: food, water, love, and affection. You can eat, play, and rest as you choose in this box. Walk toward the box. As you approach the box, you notice there is a person inside it. They seem to struggle. As you reach the box, you realize it's you. This is your life box.

Notice your body language and facial expression. How does it make you feel to see yourself in your current struggle? Observe how your life has affected you. See your scars. Watch yourself bite your nails or overeat. See how you mistreat yourself. Do you have compassion for yourself? Do you feel the need to hug yourself? Do you want to yell some sense into yourself? How does it make you feel when you yell but you don't listen, or you need a hug, but you cannot hug the box? The only way you can communicate through the box is with your eyes.

The eyes are the windows to the soul, so stare into your eyes. Rotate your box if you have to. Negative thoughts about yourself and the ways you neglect yourself are all you can see. You see your pain, your failed relationships, an empty wallet, or perhaps a hollow heart. You see your struggles all weighing you down.

At first, you did not see a way into the box, but your compassion for yourself has created one. Look around. Find a door. Knock, and ask if you can come in.

Talk to yourself. Get to know yourself. If you notice yourself talking about an experience or a person who made you feel a certain way, remind yourself that experience is over. It's not happening right now. It's just you talking to you. Refocus the conversation. What do you need? If you need a hug, first ask if it's OK. Do you need ice cream? Go get it. Now that you are inside the box, you can do anything and have anything you want.

With this outside perspective, you also notice what you need to do. Maybe you need to eat healthier foods or leave a toxic relationship. Maybe you need to move more. Maybe there is a friend you need to energetically cut yourself off from, so their burdens can stop affecting your health. You know what is correct for you at this moment. Trust yourself to do the right thing. Now, help yourself do it—whatever "it" is.

Now that you've created change, you realize you are looking relieved, unburdened, healthy, and vibrant. You notice another person walking toward you. It's your future self. You look amazing and are incredibly happy. Your future self is so grateful you made these changes and tells you about the amazing things that are to come because you did whatever your "it" is. That decision led you on a path of healing and happiness. Your career is satisfying. You achieve financial stability, go on an annual vacation, and have wonderful experiences you never thought possible. You are grateful you started taking care of yourself and looking out for yourself. Sit and listen to all the stories of your dreams that have come true.

It is time to come back now, so say your goodbyes. Bring your attention back to your breath, and when you are ready, open your eyes.

Now, go create that life—the life your future self raved about. You can do it.

☾⋆

Live in the Present Moment

When you are present in the moment, there is no time. Nothing distracts you. Become immersed in the present moment. Savor a meal. Enjoy the flavors. Walk through the park. Appreciate everything around you. Being present is healing. The healing process changes your neural pathways, allows your energy to flow, and helps break down your protection mechanisms. Healing progressively shifts your thoughts and feelings toward positive beliefs, so your actions and behavioral patterns change. You can only adjust your energy in the present moment.

An energetic shift is a release. Your brain makes a connection between events, emotions, or cycles in your life that seem to repeat. You experience a moment of clarity. You acknowledge that you do not need protection from trauma anymore because you have changed. Your life is different today. You believe you are worthy of feeling better. Experiences, feelings, and emotions can happen only in the present moment. You can mindfully choose your state of mind or the mood you want to experience.

Mindfulness is a present state of mind that can provide a higher level of satisfaction with your life. Do not look for connections so you can choose differently; in seeking it, you will attract more of what you don't want in your life. Let it occur naturally. Just recognize feelings when they come up. When trauma turns on your ego's autopilot and you avoid your feelings, become introspective. The more you engage in Moon work, the more you will recognize when the ego takes over. This higher level of awareness can help you choose behaviors, thoughts, and actions that enhance (rather than detract from) your life.

Negative emotions make it impossible to choose to be mindful or aware in the present moment. Anything that detracts from your present moment is a distraction. Adverse feelings that stay (feelings you can't let go of) distract you from experiencing faith and hope in the present moment. In this way, anger (an adverse feeling) can lead to anxiety (a lack of faith in your future). Energetic leaks also create distractions that rob you of enjoyment in the present moment. For example:

- Taking on excess responsibilities – You become so busy planning for and helping others that you do not recognize how run-down you've become. You need to rest for your mental health.
- Having an electronics addiction – You play video games for hours or days without stopping. You become so involved with your avatar that you neglect your basic needs.
- Being bored – Your mental procrastination distracts you. There is always something to do to create a better life for your tomorrow.
- Being in an unclear relationship – You focus on what you want in a relationship rather than on your reality. Your worry and fear of loneliness distracts you from finding the type of relationship you want.

If you are distracted, you are not taking inspired action. If you are not creating a life you love, you are living in a place and time other than the present. As author Myrko Thum says, the present moment is all there is:

> *The present moment is the only thing where there is no time… the point between past and future… it is the only point we can access… Everything that ever happened and will…*

can only happen in the present moment. It is impossible for anything to exist outside of it.[29]

☪

Being in the present moment helps you realize you are safe, stable, happy, and healthy. If you are not these things, manifest with the moon to create the life you want. Seek help if you need it. Receiving help should encourage, validate, and empower you. When you are present, your past cannot hurt you. You can only be free in the present moment. You can refresh your perspective and become present under the waning moon by resting, eating healthy meals, moving your body, or meditating. Being present helps you wash fear from your shadows and release the false beliefs your shadow created. Trust that everything will be OK.

Grief

It is a false, limiting belief to think that releasing grief means you release your loved one. You can let go of the emotion of grief while holding on to the cherished memories of those you have lost. Grief is not you, and it is not your loved one. It is an emotion, and it has its purpose. The experience of letting go of grief is lateral because there is not a straightforward approach to accomplish this task. You must surrender in all the ways discussed in the last section, in any order that best serves you. When you surrender to grief (or any emotion), you experience the pain of your loss. To acknowledge your truth, accept who you are right now. Love yourself. Practice self-care. The caveat is that you must do so in the present moment, not in the moment of your loss. If your brain is stuck in the moment

---

[29] Myrko Thum. "What Is the Present Moment?" https://www.myrkothum.com/what-is-the-present-moment/.

when you found out your loved one was gone, your energy will be stuck in that moment as well. Being present helps you move through grief with intention. When thinking about those who have gone before you creates anxiety or overwhelming feelings in your body, honor those feelings. Calm yourself. Try:

- focusing on your breath and slowing it down. Don't breathe deeply, just slowly.
- grabbing your wrist, squeezing your fingers, or tapping parts of your body that bring you back to the now.
- saying, out loud, five things that you see in your environment to bring awareness to where you are.
- repeating, out loud, "I am safe to experience this emotion."

There is nothing easy about this. It is OK for you to continue living and learning to be happy again in the life you still have, despite the trauma you have experienced. It is not selfish to do so. Honor yourself. Don't repress your emotions. Anything can trigger a memory that brings your grief back. When that happens, intentionally go through all the phases of letting go. You will see that, over time, the cycles of releasing grief occur less frequently.

The most traumatic event of my life was losing my brother. I did not know how to experience, honor, or release the feelings. He was older than me, a Marine, a son, a brother, a friend. He was my everything; the sun and moon rose and set around him. Not being able to (or not knowing how to) release my grief led to many negative things. The message I received was "Suck it up. Life goes on. You need to get past this." I understand people don't know what to do with the uncomfortable feelings of others, but the subconscious message was "My feelings are not valid. They are irrational, so I shouldn't feel this way." So, my life went on, only I was an empty shell holding on to so much anger. I hated God. It is OK to let your higher power know your feelings. God, the universe, spirit, etc. can take it. It is part of honoring your feelings.

Unbeknownst to me, the false and limiting beliefs my mind created from that experience affected my entire life (and still do). For example, I have never had a long-term relationship—nothing past superficial. I've never been able to put my whole heart into a relationship, because I couldn't risk experiencing the pain of losing someone I loved again. Sometimes I think of all the amazing experiences I've missed out on because of the emotional wall I've built around myself. The physical things related (not exclusively) to this experience include loneliness, depression, and physical dis-ease from neglect and self-abuse. Letting go never made sense. When I finally made sense of it all after living in grief for over thirty years, the healing I experienced became one of the driving forces behind this book.

Forgiveness of Self

What is forgiveness? In the Bible, God's mercy is, at its core, forgiveness. He is the essence of true love and absolution. Christians are supposed to live like Christ, but I believe we would be hard-pressed to find anyone with much God-like mercy in their heart. I suppose one purpose of religion is to show us how hard it is to forgive. Because of the ego, it takes tapping into the collective energy of God, the universe, angels, nature, etc. to cultivate a forgiving heart. Forgiveness is a path to healing, a state of mind that can lead to feelings of compassion, acceptance, and understanding. You can find personal freedom in the power of forgiveness.

We make forgiving ourselves difficult in relation to life's traumas because our focus is on the trauma that occurred, who was responsible, and how that trauma affected us. It's difficult to trust that everything will be OK and forgive ourselves if we compare our pain and experience to that of others. But this process is about you, not the pain you see others going through. Your trauma is your business. You can relate to others with similar experiences, but your emotions, opinions, and beliefs are personal and affect only you.

Forgiveness of self requires action. You have the right (and the obligation) to leave any experience in which you do not love yourself or cannot be your true self. The only way to shine is through an energetic goodbye, detaching from a person and releasing any emotion that dimmed your light. Leaving a person or situation is a big step in letting go. Surrendering your emotions to move forward in life is another necessary step. But forgiveness of self is the decisive action on this energetic journey to achieve love and acceptance of self, and it can be very emotional. The energetic goodbye is vital to living a life free of anxiety and shame. It is liberating to say goodbye because it takes personal power to choose not to carry that burden any longer.

Unlike political leadership or corporate power (all of which can be corrupt), personal power is magical. Only our internal magic can spark encouragement and uplift us. But this energetic spark also affects those around us. We can rewrite our script as many times as we need to until we find where we belong and what makes us happy. The most courageous thing we can do in life is what's best for us. But before we can do that, we must practice forgiveness.

Forgiving others is difficult because we tend to hold on to negative emotions. We lose trust and become fearful. Forgiveness does not mean excusing the harm someone caused you. You are never obligated to forgive a perpetrator who caused you harm; you are not responsible for releasing them from their guilt or shame. But forgiveness is surrender. In choosing to forgive your offender, you take your power back. You energetically hand the shame or anger back to them and release it from yourself. Forgiveness cuts the tie that energetically bound you to that experience. It breaks through your protection mechanism so you are no longer "stuck." The healing energy of forgiveness frees you to move forward in your life. Forgiveness is a gift you give yourself, so forgive yourself for the heavy feelings you carry around.

Forgive yourself for creating whatever protection mechanism was born out of your trauma. Forgive yourself for living in fear. If everyone strives to forgive themselves, we would have that much more love to spread around. By forgiving yourself, you open your heart to receive love, which creates more love. Surrender reverses the wheel of self-destruction, struggle, lack, and pain into that of love. Before you can shine your love into the world, though, you must first love, trust, and accept yourself, which is why forgiveness of self is harder to achieve.

Forgiveness accomplishes so much healing in your life. Forgiveness:

- shatters our mental prison
- releases us from the captivity of our limiting belief system
- breaks the bonds of our energetic leaks
- dissipates chaos
- frees us from fear
- heals our suffering
- returns our personal power and confidence
- renews our focus and outlook on life
- reconstructs our self-respect and self-esteem
- forges our fresh path
- validates our feelings
- acknowledges that our suffering matters to us
- whispers to our heart that we matter
- allows courage to grow
- allows peace and clarity to rule our minds so we trust ourselves to create a life we want and deserve

---

Exercise – Forgive Yourself

To forgive, you must identify what you need to forgive. This exercise helps guide you in identifying everything you need to forgive yourself for, from how you have treated your body to all your poor life decisions.

Pull out your journal. Read your entries from your shadow journaling, including all those "whys" you listed, the negative thoughts you have about yourself, and the disappointments you hold about yourself. This is how you release them. Remember, there is responsibility in Wild Moon Healing, so acknowledge how you have mistreated and neglected yourself. Use forgiveness, surrender, and release to love your body. Love yourself, accept yourself, trust yourself, and uncover your worth. Write down all the things you have done that need your forgiveness. For example, forgive yourself for:

Your Physical Self

- failing to prioritize your well-being and becoming obese
- thinking and feeling negatively about your body
- being infatuated with an idealized body image and doing everything possible to achieve an unattainable, perfect body at the expense of your health and relationships
- buying into the mainstream vision of beauty or conforming to a certain standard of beauty
- breaking the promises you made to yourself and not respecting your boundaries
- spreading yourself thin

- being susceptible to addiction and having addictions

Your Thoughts

- giving away your power to things such as food, alcohol, or the opinions of others
- spending time on mindless activities or being lazy
- allowing your shadows to deteriorate your level of confidence in following your dreams
- suppressing your weaknesses, because without them, you would not know your strengths
- engaging in self-criticism and not knowing who you are
- lacking self-respect
- avoiding alone time that could help you discover all the amazing things you have to offer
- setting unreasonable goals
- failing in school

Your Emotions

- being angry
- living in grief for so long that your loved ones here miss you, too
- hiding your emotions
- not learning from your mistakes
- feeling disappointed because you did not meet your high expectations
- feeling alone in your struggle
- forgoing your hopes and dreams
- having regrets and not following your passion
- longing for a person, an ideal, perfection, etc. that was not yours to have, that you no longer have, or that never existed
- fearing judgment and rejection from others

- losing time you cannot get back and not exploring the things you enjoy

Your Choices

- making poor choices and being indecisive
- creating financial troubles
- causing more distractions [or chaos] in your life
- quitting instead of seeing a failed attempt as a learning opportunity
- taking on too much responsibility
- giving your time to everyone else while neglecting yourself
- making mistakes or using poor judgment
- wasting time before getting to this moment of healing

Your Relationships with Others

- avoiding the people you care about while hurting yourself
- hiding and not talking about an illness, depression, boundaries, feelings, etc.
- being unable to show up in a relationship
- being unable to move past your past mistakes and failed relationships
- staying in judgmental, toxic, or unhealthy relationships
- judging others or burning bridges
- giving so much weight to the opinions of others that you compromised your values
- acting like a certain kind of person or being untrue to your authentic self in order to be accepted socially

Earlier, I stated that when your heart whispers, "Go ahead, you can do it," and a spark ignites, your heart needs courage first. When you surrender and forgive, you'll feel release on a physical level. People will notice a change in you when you walk into a room. They'll feel your magnetic energy before they even see you. Your friends will make assumptions about your love life, and your doctor will tell you to keep doing whatever you are doing. When you fall in love with yourself and life, people notice.

Human beings are emotional creatures, and we feel deeply. During the waning moon phase, the only journaling prompt you need is this:

I forgive myself for…

or

I forgive my trauma, struggles, depressions, binge eating for…

Then, let your thoughts flow from your hand onto the page. This will allow you to cease resisting the negative thoughts and emotions you have been attempting to control. You cannot control having emotions, but you can break the behavioral pattern of ignoring them or thinking that your emotions do not matter. Through Moon work, you will find that you do not have to allow your emotions to control you. Just let them be what they are.

Alternatively, write a letter to yourself. Acknowledge everyone and every situation that has contributed to your negative body image. Apologize for all the harmful behaviors and thoughts you experienced. Forgive your body for all the pain it has caused you, but also express gratitude to your body for still functioning after all you have done to cause it harm. Express your appreciation of your mind and the false, limiting beliefs that protected you from harm. Forgive yourself for the regrets, frustrations, and setbacks you won't let yourself move past. Let go of the guilt and shame you held while not accepting yourself. Tell all your thoughts, behaviors, and habits that do not serve you anymore that they are no longer required. Let them go.

You are not your weight. You are not your emotions. You are not your addiction. You are not your relationships. You are you. Surrender to that.

Dear Me,…

☪

Choose Love

Fear is a powerful emotion driven by the ego. Love is a powerful emotion driven by the heart. You cannot feel fear and love at the same time. Living in fear means you are surrendering love. To experience love, you must surrender fear. The love and the feelings I am referring to are personal. This is about love of self. For you to choose love, your actions, thoughts, and words must be about you and no one else. For anyone who has overcome an addiction (i.e., living in fear), you know that you do not just choose sobriety (i.e., love of self) once. You choose that every second of every day, being mindful, present, and aware of your triggers. In any situation in which you choose to love yourself, you will experience freedom, an energetic shift. This shift allows you to feel the amazing emotions that come from loving yourself. Use the energy of the waning moon to become more self-aware and less fearful.

Fear comes in many forms, including grief, anger, anxiety, and other negative emotions. Choosing love over fear is hard because the ego believes fear helps keep you safe, but you have the right and the power to choose differently. Choosing differently is the key to opening new doors so you can succeed. Succeeding at giving love is easy for most, but receiving love can be much harder. When you choose to receive love from yourself, you open your heart to receive love from others. That is when:

- you find your healthy relationship.

- it becomes easier to incorporate healthy daily habits into your life that result in weight loss.
- you find it easy to stop gossiping, blaming, and complaining and disconnect from social media.
- you can stick with your budget to improve your financial situation.

Fear closes off your heart, leaving you susceptible to toxic relationships, bad habits, and poor financial situations. Fear makes life difficult, while love makes life easier. Love opens creative outlets that help you engage in personal interests, get your dream job, earn more money, engage in healthy relationships, and stay active in ways you enjoy.

Choosing love over fear happens not only in times of crisis (such as leaving an unhealthy relationship) or when you do something scary (like starting a new business or planning to hike the entire Appalachian Trail). You can choose love over fear in every moment every day. It is not life or death at stake. What is at stake is the survival of your authentic self, regardless of whether that is who you are now or who you want to become. You react from a place of fear when you feel threatened, but you can change that. Responding from a place of love happens when you know and love yourself. When you live authentically, it is harder to feel threatened by the actions or opinions of others. But, for example, choosing to complain about being lonely (instead of putting yourself out there), binge on Netflix (instead of doing something physically active), spend your money at the casino (instead of paying your mortgage), or take part in gossip (instead of engaging in a conversation that expands your consciousness or compassion) is choosing fear. Choosing fear means it is creating your reality or current experience. When we feel attacked, blamed, or criticized, we experience a state of fear. If our ego, identity, or the narrative we hold about our self is threatened, we jump into survival mode. Conflict threatens the survival of the ego, creating a reaction. By living in a perpetual state of fear, we avoid conflict, crisis, or failure. We never take action. Fear blames others and eliminates accountability and responsibility. Fear pushes love away.

Fear gives permission to someone else to create your life. Have they planned to create a wonderful life for you? The only person who can figure out what is best for you is *you*. Even in a relationship, you are an individual first. You need to determine your needs, values, dreams, and ambitions, then love yourself enough to do what you need to do to go after the life you want. Love puts you back in the driver's seat of your life so you can create change. Love is dynamic and requires action. By loving and believing in yourself, you raise your energetic vibration so you can create change and experience personal growth.

Our thoughts become our reality. So, in the words of Henry Ford, "Whether you believe you can do a thing or not, you are right."[30] Your ego uses fear to tell you, "you cannot," but your heart uses love to tell you that "anything is possible." After you let go of what you need to right now and practice forgiveness of self, the energy from the waning crescent moon will help you choose love. In doing so, you'll choose yourself.

As the waning moon turns to a dark sky to start another cycle of Wild Moon Healing, keep the following affirmation in mind. It will help you focus on you, what you want, what you need, and what you will soon discover you are capable of.

I choose love. I walk through a new door, leaving the old behind to start my next adventure now. I accept the responsibility to do and create anything I want in my life. I am attracting fun and fulfilling experiences. I am attracting nourishing and loving relationships into my life. I commit myself to a self-care practice to achieve and maintain good health. I trust my intuition. I believe in myself and know that I am worthy of wellness. I trust that a higher power supports and guides me. I know I can change.

---

[30] Flow Lab. "A Psychology Geek's Take on Self-Efficacy and How It Relates to Flow States," https://www.linkedin.com/pulse/psychology-geeks-take-self-efficacy-how-relates-flow-states

12

CONCLUSION

As you continue Wild Moon Healing, you will create your own personal monthly practice. The monthly routine you create, whether or not you follow the lunar cycles, will affirm your commitment to personal transformation and help you reach your full potential. We are all spiritual beings, and the answers we seek lie within each of us. Therefore, your personal practice will nurture your physical, mental, and emotional well-being. Do what is best for you.

A practice that focuses on your well-being is exploratory, meaning self-exploration and discovering all that you can about yourself is the beginning. You start to create change in your life. All the journaling exercises you engage in throughout each moon phase will teach you more and more about yourself, and you will develop a level of awareness that's necessary for a healthy and fulfilling life. Each month, you'll want to engage in activities that support your wellness, such as meditation, which allows you to hear the messages your body sends you. You'll also want to take part in restorative activities, like practicing gratitude. Such mindful actions create positive change, which in turn increases your energetic frequency. The practice you develop is about you and you alone.

You can learn about yourself, heal yourself, and go after your goals at the same time. All we really have in life is time—time to do meaningful things. At the end of life, most people regret the time they wasted thinking about and doing unimportant, mindless things. Stop thinking about the things you did not do and most likely cannot change. Discover what is holding you back from doing meaningful things today, so you can do things that add value to your life tomorrow.

Slow down. Enjoy this moment. Enjoy the stillness and simplicity of it all. Life is short, so do not rush. And remember, happiness is not a destination; it is a way of being, a way of traveling through life, of choosing what's best for you every step of the way.

Travel authentically.

Phase 3

SUPPORTING INFORMATION

EPILOGUE

The book has ended, but your journey has just begun.
The pain comes.
The pain goes.
Then it comes again.
You become angry with yourself; everything must be perfect.
You loathe yourself. Everything is chaos.
Today is amazing. Tomorrow not so much.
One lunar cycle—you can commit to that.
Use her energy.
You go after your goal, then hit a barrier in your progress.
Life is a dance; recognize the steps.
She illuminates what you need to see.
Find your inspiration in her; become excited and have fun.
Moon work is effective, its energy real.
Discover your true self, restore, and heal.
You will create your amazing life.
Persevere through *Wild Moon Healing*; prioritize self-care.
Discover, grow, and become the person you were meant to be.
Because that is a beautiful thing.

CONTINUED HEALING SUPPORT

To continue with your healing journey, manifest your goals and dreams, and achieve your best life in a supportive and safe environment, sign up for my FREE members' content page on my website, https://wildmoonhealers.com. There, you will have access to content, like a new moon intention worksheet and an intention contract form. You can also learn about my personalized and group life coaching services.

On my website, you can also:

- sign up to receive newsletters that contain encouraging and action-oriented information.
- follow my blog to receive an email every time I make a new post.
- follow Wild Moon Healers on social media: Facebook, Pinterest, Instagram, and Twitter.
- listen to my blogs and other content on my podcast.
- purchase the Wild Moon Healing oracle deck to support your Moon work.

I sincerely appreciate you and the time you have spent reading *Wild Moon Healing*. May I ask you for a favor? I would love it if you could leave your honest review on the retail site of your preference. And because I wrote this book in service to all who read it, I would love to know your opinion on how I can improve my message, or how my message has supported positive change in your life. Please visit my website and leave your comments there. Thank you!

After reading my book, I hope you desire to become a Wild Moon Healer and your best self!

I look forward to interacting with you online.

Authentically me,
Donna S. Conley

AFTERWORD

I'm not sure when I started calling my personal healing practice "Wild Moon Healing," but I remember how it all started. I was a sick, sad mess, seeking ways to be happy. After researching many modalities to achieve mental health, my self-care practice took its own form: I found comfort in the moon.

With Wild Moon Healing, I've experienced two major "ah-ha" moments that had a powerful influence on shifting my energy. The first was realizing that I was confusing artistic ability with creativity. I come from a family of artists, but I can't draw a straight line with a ruler. After making this mental connection, my creativity skyrocketed. I painted a couple pieces of furniture—and if I do say so myself, they are amazing. That mental connection led me to a hobby that is calming and rewarding and opens my creative center on many levels.

During the harvest moon that year, I hit another turning point in my healing by connecting the experiences of my past and my triggers to my emotional binge eating. I spoke of this earlier in the book. I returned from a trip that included a lot of waiting on my sister (again). She made excuses to justify the behavior, but never said sorry. I binged and binged because of it. I knew I was doing it, but I could not stop. That age-old message of "I am unimportant, so I must wait" hit me hard. When I am angry but can't talk about my feelings (because it always becomes about the person who hurt me), I take my anger out on myself. I say nothing. All my feelings turn in on me. I posted about my situation in a social media support group. Someone responded with something like, "I don't know if this will help you, but I discovered, for me, that wait = weight." I mentioned this in chapter 6, and I'm saying it again now because that statement has been the cornerstone of my healing journey. That statement alone raised my awareness about why I binge and what my triggers are. It allowed me to level up and make changes in my life. My friends noticed.

My amazing group of friends started commenting on the positive changes they saw in me and asking me what I was doing. I tried to explain as best I could, and they responded with interest. That's when I began putting the concept of Wild Moon Healing into writing. I wrote my first lunar cycle report in May. I created a blog (https://wildmoonhealers.com) in September that year and sent my first-draft manuscript for editing in December. It was a busy year. When your creative center is open, things happen!

Sometimes, my creativity moves too fast for me. As this book moves through the publishing process, I am drafting a Wild Moon Healing oracle deck and a children's book. I am also preparing to start a health and well-being program at Duke to prime me for my future! I'm claiming right now that I will create a full-service self-care and healing program that encompasses healthy eating, movement, and mental well-being. I will influence our youth to create a better tomorrow, and I will help integrate self-care into mainstream medical practices. Dream big or don't dream at all, right?

One big dream I had for this book was a customized artistic cover. Below is the original description I messaged to the artist as she began working on a visual concept for this project. This is my picture of *Wild Moon Healing.*

> *I'm writing a book called* Wild Moon Healing, *and I have a vision for the cover. I want the cover to tell the story of Wild Moon Healing visually.*
>
> *I want a b/w sketch (maybe color… idk) that incorporates a beautiful woman representing our personal development, uniqueness, and individuality.*
>
> *It also represents the tree of life and how we all have the answers inside us and incorporates a version of the Star and Temperance tarot cards.*
>
> *A quick summary of the picture is to manifest with the moon to heal, develop a renewed sense of hope, learn to trust your intuition, and create balance in the present moment.*
>
> The picture angle is from the water looking toward land. A beautiful lady is walking onto the land, with one foot still in the water and one on land. Her arms are out to her sides, slightly bent, holding scales. One scale holds the celestial sun and the other the celestial moon to express how we each carry our personal strength and the beauty that makes us unique.
>
> We see her from behind. The angle of her body is such that you can see the silhouette of her left breast and the left side of her face. Her hair is long, flowing, and dark, and it's blowing in the breeze. The picture should make you wonder if she's turning back to her past, to what's comfortable. Perhaps she is reminiscing. Maybe she's hesitant to move forward—or she is turning forward toward her truth.
>
> *The water should show movement… maybe just ripples from her feet. The water represents so many things. It represents life in constant motion. If you're feeling stuck in life, it could be missed blessings and opportunities flowing by that you never even notice. It could represent chaos or trauma in*

your life, because even still water has a strong current. It looks one way to represent all the facades people put up, but that is not the truth. Or, it could mean cleansing/renewal…

I don't have a clear picture of the land in my head, because the purpose of moving forward in life is that you don't know what's out there. In my head, it kind of looks like a desert rose stone. Maybe there are paths… one might look rocky or bumpy, but the reward could be greater than the path that looks smooth…

Then the sky… It's the night of the full moon. The star of Bethlehem is visible to represent faith in something bigger than yourself. In tarot, the Star is about faith. I have a tapestry on my wall and below it, I have decals that say, "Have faith, I will light your way."

The full moon has a waterfall of stardust flowing from it into the water below. The moon sheds light on what is unseen, our personal shadows, or provides clarity in situations. I'm not sure whether there should be some clouds.

Maybe reflect some stardust in the lady's hair to represent her own personal magic!

In all, we make wishes on stars, which represent the intentions or goals we make, and the moon shines light to help us navigate making our dreams come true. The universe hears us, and the response is illuminated by the moon in all her beauty.

Use *Wild Moon Healing* to help you step out of your turmoil, chaos, and pain. Trust you will choose the correct path for you. Walk into your future embracing your personal magic. Always dream big, admire the moon, embrace your personal power, and remain authentic.

APPENDIX A — MOON NOTES

Moon Notes:

APPENDIX B — LIFELINES

A LIFELINE IS ALWAYS AVAILABLE

Performing Moon work is an inner-truth-seeking journey that's necessary to heal from trauma in your life. This work will bring up buried emotions and help identify what created your limiting belief system. If you are experiencing intense emotions or if Moon work becomes too intense, these resources may help.

If depression or addiction plague you, Moon work will help, but you must also seek help from medical professionals. Being able to ask for and accept help is empowering. Reach out to your primary care physician as a first line in seeking medical help.

UNITED STATES

If you experience intense emotions or have suicidal thoughts or tendencies,
call the **National Suicide Prevention Lifeline** anytime, day or night, twenty-four seven at
1-800-273-TALK (8255).

If you are with someone who is in danger of committing suicide, call or text 988.

Eating disorders can be life-threatening, but are they treatable. If you need help or if you have an unhealthy relationship with food, here are two resources you can use:
https://www.bulimia.com/topics/eating-disorder-hotline/
https://www.nationaleatingdisorders.org/help-support/contact-helpline

---

If you use alcohol to deal with emotional distress, Moon work can absolutely help, but seeking help from a medical professional can help get you to a safer place.

Alcoholics Anonymous – https://www.aa.org/

The Substance Abuse and Mental Health Services Administration (SAMHSA) provides information and referrals to local treatment facilities, support groups, and community-based organizations.

SAMHSA's National Helpline – 1-800-662-HELP (4357)

UNITED KINGDOM

Samaritans – Whatever you're going through, a Samaritan will face it with you.
They're available twenty-four hours a day, 365 days a year at
116 123.

Childline – For children and young people under the age of nineteen, call
(this number will not show up on your phone bill)
0800 111.
https://www.samaritans.org/

https://www.getselfhelp.co.uk/helplines.htm
https://www.mind.org.uk/information-support/guides-to-support-and-services/crisis-services/helplines-listening-services/

APPENDIX C — UNALOME

If you can't find the words for Moon work, then cook it, paint it, sew it, knit it, or draw it!
Use your creativity!
This is what I see when I think of Moon work.

The unalome is a symbol for the journey to enlightenment, a visual metaphor for your path. Moon work is difficult because you have to see and accept what is in your reflection. The path is rarely straight, perfect, or in the direction you intended. Let go and trust.

Notice the top of the unalome. It's a straight line with two dots that point to the sky, the universe, heaven, Source, your higher self, etc. This is a state of awareness that only faith can bring, a place where Moon work can take you.

The semicolon at the bottom is to remind you to never give up, because you are not alone. Life is always worth living. There is calm both before and after the storm, and you can even find calm within the storm.

Learn to love yourself to the moon and back.

Find happiness. Be wild. Stay authentic.

APPENDIX D — MOON PHASES

NEW MOON – The dark sky makes it natural to want to rest, reflect, plan, and create a steady foundation from which you can achieve your goals. Use this creative energy to ponder all your aspirations and ambitions—even what you think is just fantasy—and let the excitement of possibilities take over. Create your intentions.

WAXING CRESCENT – It first appears as a tiny glimmer of hope in the sky. It shines light on your intention and helps your intention grow through your inspired action. The crescent moon is both gentle and insistent, both grounded and visionary.

This is the time to anchor your intentions and think about what you want to manifest.

FIRST QUARTER MOON – The halfway point between the new and full moons brings an energy boost. This is a time for learning, so find workarounds to address challenges proactively and productively. You may also notice triggers that steer you away from your goal. Don't give up.

WAXING GIBBOUS – This is the time for massive action. Go after your intention with your whole heart. You may feel tension, stress, or worry that your efforts are not working. Evaluate to see what you need to change. If you change nothing, nothing will change. You may also see truths, or the universe may offer you new perspectives on situations.

FULL MOON – The spiritual and energetic pinnacle, a metaphor for fulfillment and completion. Now you can analyze what might hinder your progress by investigating your shadows. Explore deep inside yourself so you can heal, awaken, and experience growth. Identify the things that are depleting your energy and create awareness right now.

WANING GIBBOUS – This phase signifies a time for gratitude, forgiveness, and surrender. Reflect on how you feel. Practice stillness. Now is the time to discard the things that do not work. Recharge, make room, and prepare yourself for the positive things that are coming your way.

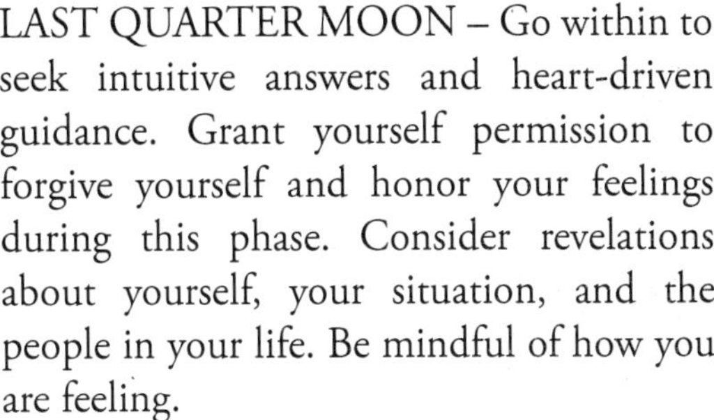

LAST QUARTER MOON – Go within to seek intuitive answers and heart-driven guidance. Grant yourself permission to forgive yourself and honor your feelings during this phase. Consider revelations about yourself, your situation, and the people in your life. Be mindful of how you are feeling.

WANING CRESCENT – Exert no effort to control anything. Go with the flow. This is an opportunity to reflect on the entire lunar cycle. Review your journaling to evaluate how you've changed since you wrote it. Let what you discover guide you on what you should work on in the upcoming lunar cycle.

GLOSSARY OF TERMS

- Ego – The conscious mind. Its purpose is to keep us safe and satisfy our desires in a realistic and socially acceptable way.
- Emotional Freedom Technique (EFT) – A healing technique that involves tapping key meridian points on the body to clear old, limiting beliefs and program new ones.
- Energetic Deficit – A depleted energy reserve that makes us feel fearful, heavy, anxious, insulted, frustrated, overwhelmed, self-doubtful, lonely, stuck, disrespected, devalued, unloved, or unappreciated.
- Energetic Leak – The action of expending energy in ways that cause an energy deficit.
- Energetic Vibration – A vibrational frequency that transmits messages in the universe's language.
- Energy – The foundation of all matter. Energy is always flowing and changing. Wild Moon Healers' use of energy is spiritual. It is about the inner "me" as a force in all of us.

- False, Limiting Beliefs – False opinions you hold for yourself on a subconscious level that you believe to be absolute truths.
- Full Moon – The moon has no light of its own, so when the moon looks most full, it is reflecting maximum light and vitality from the sun's rays. The full moon is the best time for shadow work.
- Inner Child – The part of each of us that needs healing.
- Inspired Action – Creating an intention that inspires you to act. Physical "doing" that helps you accomplish your goals.
- Intention – A mental state where you commit to an action or goal and create a plan to carry out that action mindfully.
- Journaling – A platform for self-exploration and self-discovery that allows you to uncover, process, and understand your thoughts and feelings in ways that thought alone cannot achieve.
- Life Box – The "Pandora's box" we create for ourselves through our limiting beliefs and energetic leaks.
- Limiting Beliefs – Opinions you hold on a subconscious level that you believe to be absolute truths, which limit your behavior and actions and stunt personal growth.
- Living Intentionally – Being present in the moment, so you can make better choices for yourself (because you matter).
- Lunar Eclipse – Occurs when the moon moves into Earth's shadow, blocking sunlight from reflecting off the moon. A lunar eclipse ushers in (often abrupt) change.
- Mindfulness – A conscious state of awareness in the present moment.
- Moon Ritual – A physical expression that's symbolic of your intention to purposefully create positive change in your life.

- Moon Work – It is whatever you need it to be—a wellness practice, a healing therapy, a self-discovery journey, a spiritual pursuit, a psychological process, a religious awakening, a time-management tool, or a habit-breaking model. No one's journey is the same, so whatever Moon work is for you is correct.
- New Moon – The beginning of a twenty-nine-and-a-half-day lunar cycle that occurs when the sun, moon, and earth are in perfect alignment. It is a time to reflect, plan, and create.
- Personal Power – One's ability to choose their thoughts, actions, and behaviors with intention.
- Preventive Care – Inner work that allows you to identify energetic leaks and false, limiting beliefs before their negative influences can create lack or struggle.
- Restorative Activity – Health and well-being activities that affect your mental and physical health positively.
- Restorative Theory – You are working with this model when you are experiencing lack or struggle and you do the inner work to identify your energetic leaks and false, limiting beliefs.
- Ritual – A physical act that expresses or symbolizes your intention to create positive change in your life.
- Self-esteem – A person's overall subjective sense of self; how much you appreciate and value yourself and your abilities; self-respect.
- Shadows – A place in the subconscious mind where we hide our hurt and pain and create our protective mechanisms.
- Shadow Work – Healing and freeing the parts of ourselves we hide in our shadows.
- Subtle Energy – An invisible force that drives your potential and affects your actions and reactions.
- Surrender – Allowing emotions to exist; feeling and experiencing those emotions, so you can let them go.

- Thought Journaling – Journaling that concentrates on what you were thinking of before or after something triggers a negative reaction in you (rather than focusing on the event or your reaction to it).
- Thought Stopping – The action of proactively looking out for negative thoughts or behaviors so you can correct them. Thought stopping has the opposite effect of being mindful and is therefore unproductive.
- Trauma – An experience that affects your ability to cope, diminishes your self-worth, or cripples your ability to feel a full range of emotions and enjoy new experiences.
- Trigger – A person, place, or thing that prompts a negative emotional response.
- Waning Moon – The waning phase of the moon is approximately fourteen days long. It follows the full moon phase and completes its cycle before the next new moon. It is a time of reflection.
- Waxing Moon – The waxing moon phase is approximately fourteen days long and follows the new/dark moon phase. It completes its cycle before the full moon. It is a time for inspired action.
- Wild Moon Healing – A personal journey of self-exploration and self-discovery through which you create your best life intentionally based on how you want to feel.

INDEX

BIBLIOGRAPHY

Books/Films

Allen, James. *As a Man Thinketh*. England: Solis Press, 2014.

Bewitched. Directed by Harry Ackerman. Created by Sol Saks. American Broadcasting Company. September 17, 1964–March 25, 1972.

Eden, Donna and David Feinstein. *Energy Medicine*. New York: Penguin Group, 2008.

Groundhog Day. Directed by Harold Ramis. Screenplay by Danny Rubin and Harold Remis. Produced by Trevor Albert and Harold Ramis. United States: Columbia Pictures, 1993.

Hermes Trismegistus. *The Emerald Tablet of Hermes*. Digitized by Watchmaker Publishing. Merchant Books, 2013.

Ortner, Nick. *The Tapping Solution*. California: Hay House, 2013.

Tuttle, Carol. *Mastering Affluence*. Utah: Live Your Truth Press, 2018.

Wallace, Graham. *The Art of Thought*. England: Solis Press, 2014.

Electronic

Blickheuser, Katharina, Donna Back, Dawson Church, et al. "Clinical EFT (Emotional Freedom Techniques) Improves Multiples Physiological Markers of Health," *Journal of Evidence-Based Integrative Medicine.* (February 2019), https://www.ncbi.nlm.nih.gov/pmc/articles/PMC6381429/.

Brown, Joshua and Joel Wong. "How Gratitude Changes You and Your Brain," *Greater Good* Magazine, June 6, 2017. https://greatergood.berkeley.edu/article/item/how_gratitude_changes_you_and_your_brain.

Cross, Michelle. "The Four Gates of Speech," April 3, 2014. https://www.michellecross.co.uk/four-gates-of-speech/.

Flow Lab. "A Psychology Geek's Take on Self-Efficacy and How It Relates to Flow States," LinkedIn, November 8, 2021. https://www.linkedin.com/pulse/psychology-geeks-take-self-efficacy-how-relates-flow-states-#:~:text=Henry%20Ford%20was%20right%20when%20he%20claimed%3A%20%E2%80%9CWhether,but%20our%20belief%20whether%20we%E2%80%99re%20able%20to%20succeed.

Hall, Jeffrey C., Michael Rosbash, and Michael W. Young. "Press Release," Accessed March 2, 2022. https://www.nobelprize.org/prizes/medicine/2017/press-release/.

Harvard Health Publishing. "Sleep Deprivation Can Affect Your Mental Health," Last updated August 17, 2021. https://www.health.harvard.edu/newsletter_article/sleep-and-mental-health#:~:text=Sleep%20and%20mental%20health%20are%20closely%20connected.%20Sleep,likely%20to%20have%20insomnia%20or%20other%20sleep%20disorders.

Mental Health America. "Depression," Accessed February 12, 2022. https://www.mhanational.org/conditions/depression.

Military Veteran Project. Accessed March 10, 2022. https://www.militaryveteranproject.org/.

Mind. "Crisis Services and Planning for a Crisis," Last updated October 2018. https://www.mind.org.uk/information-support/guides-to-support-and-services/crisis-services/helplines-listening-services/.

National Institute of Mental Health. "Depression," Last updated February 2018. https://www.nimh.nih.gov/health/topics/depression#:~:text=Depression%20is%20one%20of%20the%20most%20common%20mental,at%20any%20age%2C%20but%20often%20begins%20in%20adulthood.

Samaritans. "We're Waiting for Your Call," Accessed March 26, 2022. https://www.samaritans.org/.

Stuart, H. "Reducing the Stigma of Mental Illness," *Global Mental Health*, May 10, 2016. https://www.ncbi.nlm.nih.gov/pmc/articles/PMC5314742/.

Thum, Myrko. "What Is the Present Moment?" August 31, 2008. https://www.myrkothum.com/what-is-the-present-moment/.

The Carol Tuttle Healing Center. Accessed April 2021. https://course.liveyourtruth.com/hc/.

Well, Tara. "What the Mirror Can Teach You About Yourself: Advice from a Mirror Gazing Expert." January 2, 2020. https://www.mindful.org/what-the-mirror-can-teach-you-about-yourself-advice-from-a-mirror-gazing-expert/.

SUGGESTED READING LIST

Carol Tuttle. *Mastering Affluence: 6 Lessons to Create a Life You Love*. Utah: Live Your Truth Press, 2018.

Deepak Chopra. *Reinventing the Body, Resurrecting the Soul: How to Create a New You*. New York: Three Rivers Press, 2009.

Don Miguel Ruiz. *The Four Agreements: A Practical Guide to Personal Freedom (A Toltec Wisdom Book)*. San Rafael, CA: Amber-Allen Publishing, 1997.

Shakti Gawain. *Creative Visualization: Use the Power of Your Imagination to Create What You Want in Your Life*. Novato, CA: Nataraj Publishing, 2002.

Simone Butler. *Moon Power: Lunar Rituals for Connecting with Your Inner Goddess*. Beverly, MA: Quarto Publishing Group, 2017.

Yasmin Boland. *Astrology Made Easy: A Guide to Understanding Your Birth Chart*. California: Hay House, 2016.

Yasmin Boland. *Moonology: Working with the Magic of Lunar Cycles*. London: Hay House, 2016.

ABOUT THE AUTHOR

Donna S. Conley began her career as a life coach, blogger, podcaster, and author of *Wild Moon Healing* while working full-time in corporate America. Donna is currently working toward her goal of transitioning to a full-time career to help remove the stigma of mental health and normalize loving, believing in, and respecting yourself. She dreams of a world without addiction, depression, suicide, type 2 diabetes, and other preventable illnesses. Donna writes about wellness and self-care with spiritual and metaphysical influences. From a total wellness perspective and addressing people as a whole, she believes strongly in the spiritual aspects of health in addition to physical and mental health. She deeply believes that everyone has their own inner magic and can use it to create their best life and inspire others. *Wild Moon Healing* is Donna's first published work.